Zen Love

The True Journey of a Blended Family

teZa Lord

Zen Love
The True Journey of a Blended Family

Copyright © 2019 teZa Lord

All rights reserved.
No part of this publication may be reproduced, distributed, or transmitted in any form or by any means, including photocopying, recording, or other electronic or mechanical methods, without the prior written permission of the publisher, except in the case of brief quotations embodied in critical reviews and certain other noncommercial uses permitted by copyright law.

Ocean Entertainment
OceanEntertainmentBooks@gmail.com
www.tezalord.com
218 Harvard Rd. St. Augustine, FL. 32086

First Edition 2019 Transcendent Publishing
Second Edition 2024 Ocean Entertainment

Cover art by teZa Lord
Illustrations by teZa Lord

Paperback ISBN: 978-1-7365501-3-7
eBook ISBN: 978-1-7365501-4-4

Printed in the United States of America

for Big Cat

contents

Before Casting Off i
Part One: Heart's Desire vii
   calling Love in 1
   from the fog of the night 17
   at the river 37
   together we plot the course 51
   the building of our boat 61
   setting out at last 93
   batten down the hatches 101
   strange and distant shores 115
   learning the ropes 123
   the See-er 133
   green scaly monster 141
   old salts 157
Part Two: Lightkeepers 175
   the sun and the stars are our compass 177
   darkness in the light 197
   prepare for the unexpected 207
   snafu 227
   journey within the Journey 231
   stormy seas 249
   devil mom 255
   the main blows out 261
   rite of passage 275
   lightkeeper 287
   shipwreck 303

Part Three: Nearing Port 305
  steady at the helm 307
  oh, starry night 315
  boy overboard! 327
  the waterfall 337
  ready the anchor 345
  port compassion 357
About the Author 367

before casting off

This true story of mine was written purely as an analogy of what is taking place on a much grander scale in the world today. We humans are, with each new day, becoming a universally-blended family. My own family is but a microcosm of the macrocosm. That's why our story is, in effect, all of ours story as well. Each group of us, no matter how small or large, represents how this blendedness is happening worldwide. Today's world is comprised of a blending that's never been so evident as current times. Homo sapiens is now quickly becoming a hybrid vigor mix of different races, different cultures and often-incompatible religions, different worldviews, all of which demonstrates that as a combined human race, we truly are all One. One big blended family.

Einstein said, "The most beautiful experience we can have is the mysterious. It is the fundamental emotion that stands at the cradle of true art and true science."

Exploring the mysterious beckoned me. Following this call, my life quest became to explore great and small mysteries, as deep and diverse as I could find. My first fascination was with Nature, then God, then Art, and finally Myth became my passion, or something along that order. All aided my search for my own Truth, what works for me, pathways that have enabled me to eventually discover—and trust—*The Mystery*. When I found it, I realized that Truth, my own *Truth* (not to be confused with anyone else's) was right in front of me all along.

Love—in its innumerable forms—the wildest of risky adventures as well as the quietest, most deeply felt soul-journey, is right here inside us all. Love is the ultimate Mystery.

But I continued to ask myself: Is discovering this Truth of mine a good enough life mission? And, wanting to share that with others, a righteous enough reason to indulge my passion of creating ways to do just that, wanting so much to help my fellow humans lessen the burden of fear, anxiety, and oppression so many suffer, more and more in modern times?

Today, unequivocally, I can answer both with a resounding Yes. Because today, I know the mysterious power of Love, and anyone's efforts to share these discoveries with others does justice to their existence.

As an artist who writes, my work compels me to reach out to help others heal: male or female or a "them," a single person or in a family setting, with or without children, having the comfort of a loving pet, or having no living companionship at all. For everyone, Love is the way we humans, and many other species, heal. First, by learning to love our self, and then by loving others. Our entire world can heal this way, one person at a time. Heal yourself first, then your family or tribe benefits from this Self-love you have within you. Then, organically, the sphere of Love grows wider around your healed essence, one intertwined circle at a time in your immediate relationships.

Love is contagious.

Today I know that Love is the weapon of mass illumination. A person's awakened awareness is synonymous to the healing properties of Love.

This story is about the love of my life, who by chance was a family man, a single-parent with two young children to raise on his own.

In many ways, I believe this love story of ours reflects what the world is going through, in general. The challenges of today's world can be distilled down to the same that any two people face, in whatever human relationship one has. Any two persons (or cultures, for instance) who wish to have a healthy, mutually rewarding relationship, must cultivate respect and love among themselves first and foremost. Otherwise, none of their subsequent efforts will come to mutually beneficial fruition.

Our world grows smaller every day. The same complications every individual faces in trying to get along with others, are the same challenges that face our modern, worldwide family:

—how to communicate

—how to focus on positives and not negatives

—how to heal from our wounding, from the most ancient to the most current.

A twosome of any sort that comes together, must find new ways of exploring *The Mystery of Love*. We humans forge every kind of group, from aloof partnerships to a close blended family. Today we're beginning to see ourselves as the blended human family we are, learning to live in cooperation on Earth. Each human-unit, whether comprised of two, twenty, or twenty thousand, is a microcosm of the world's blended, global population. Every single individual, her/his/them-self is a microcosm of the whole, reflecting the same variables as the entire macrocosm of human existence. Truly, what goes on within us, as human beings, reflects the interaction of all of known creation.

How do I know this? Ahhh, this is the story before you: *Zen Love*.

This book documents the pinnacle of my lifelong quest to know, work with, and spread to others The Great Mystery of Love.

Love, the greatest kind of consciousness that supersedes emotion, is a universal bonding, a feeling, or a *sense* that I here call *Om* (pronounced as it's spelled, rhyming with *home*)—or, as yogis like myself more Sanskrit-correctly spell it—*Aum* (pronounced *AHh'-oum*).

These days, when speaking of expanded awareness, I prefer to use the sacred word Aum because of its gender-neutrality, and also because of its ageless scriptural significance. Aum is the unseen force we all know, have, and can partake of at will. Love, or Aum—*is* God;

the same divine Life Force that tongues translate variously as Dios, Dieu, Allah, Great Spirit, Qi, Prana, and myriad other ways, as Joseph Campbell points out in "The Hero with a Thousand Faces." Love is consciousness, the energy force that not only unites us, but heals us, making us become better people through Aum's unlimited power within us, and within All that is.

From the moment I experienced Aum's spiritual force in my soul's deepest core, I wanted to know the heights and depths of Love's possibilities. I became a meditator at an early age when, not yet twenty, learning how to tap Spirit's innate power within healed me of a debilitating physical ailment brought about by my skewed emotions (my parents had just disowned me for being non-compliant with their worldview). The moment I met Aum within, through being formally initiated into meditation by a trained instructor—I began to heal. Exploring Spirit, inside myself, ignited me wanting to know Spirit, Aum, as much as I could out in the world, with or without teachers. Spirit became my life's passion. My pursuit of Love—which I am equally comfortable calling Aum, or God, or the One—took me to far-away places as well as deep within my own inner psychic realms, when my desire to be One with Spirit led me to explore expanded, heightened, intensified states of consciousness.

At first, I thought I had to forego being an ordinary person to know Aum-God intimately. The thought of having a family and doing all that a domestic life entails seemed too distracting, too demanding for my fly-high desire to truly know Love. But I was wrong. For me, becoming part of a family, when I finally met my match, was key to fully knowing and trusting the power of Love.

△

And now, the beautiful and mysterious experience that Einstein himself recognized as the most fundamental, the multifariously called, most important force of all—has been given another name by quantum physicists: the Higgs boson. With its prescient nickname, the discovery of the *God Particle*, the only so-far *proven* energy force ubiquitously found in all known matter (after having been speculated upon for ages) has been acknowledged and accepted. Thanks to its

2013 scientific verification, quantum physicists at CERN, in Europe, have proven beyond a doubt that We Are One—in a physical manner, rather than just metaphysically speaking.

The reason I looked for Love—God-energy, Aum, Oneness—in so many places must be the same reason why many of us do: to connect to The Mystery, to feel *truly alive*. The reason I'm writing this book is to instill in you, the reader, a similar thrill about the power of Love, and to deepen your already intimately knowing that.

△

Life brings us many roles. One of mine that I enjoyed for so many years, was that of an ex-pat sailor living in the steady winds of the West Indies. Because of my past association with relying on charts with its latitudes and longitudes, I'm forever remarking on the uncanny similarities between a sailor navigating a boat on the big wide ocean and me wanting to find The Mystery of Love. Both entail choosing a destination for what can often turn out to be a long and arduous voyage. Both benefit from plotting a course and sticking to it. Both, then, need to find a boat that doesn't leak, responds well, and has a crew that won't mutiny (if we're not a solo navigator).

This is why I've chosen to use the analogy of a boat's allegorical voyage down an imaginary waterway for this, my otherwise true, completely real adventure story I'm sharing here.

For this quest of mine—to fully embrace both the highs and lows involved in pursuing Love in the intimate relationship realm—I used a crew aboard a safe and ruggedly outfitted vessel as a metaphor for the family unit itself, as we travel along the mythical river I dare to call *Rio Blisso*.

Many of the names in this logbook of real events have been changed either per request, or respect for others' privacy.

If any liberties have been taken in my recounting, it's to have omitted many of the innumerable peaceful and quiet moments of family life in order to illustrate our journey's most pivotal, extraordinary experiences.

All Love,
teZa Lord

PART ONE

heart's desire

CHAPTER 1

calling Love in

The phone rang on a quiet spring equinox morning in East Hampton, New York, where I was working as a garden designer. Answering without a care, I didn't know my life was about to spin in another direction. Exchanging a few words of greeting, the stranger's strong vibrato leapt straight into my guts, like how a strong shot of rum used to feel shooting hot flames all the way to the tips of my toes. Everything around me suddenly swirled and became electrifyingly alive. My toes tingled at the sound of his deep voice.

Weird, he and I never met before, I thought.

But he laughed when I said that aloud. Then claimed he'd met me before. But I had no memory of ever having met him. *How could he possibly be right?* This stranger was calling, he said, because Elsbeth, a close friend of his, who also happened to be one of mine, had insisted.

"Go on, call teZa," the caller perfectly intoned our friend's sing-song southern cadence. "You won't regret it. She's a good person, an old friend, like you are, Will," he mimed Elsbeth's distinctively soft whisper.

Sure, I'd heard snippets about Will during the many years Elsbeth and I had known each other. I remembered her telling me he'd lived and worked with them on their ocean-going tug that she co-captained with her husband, plowing their way around this watery world as she raised their five kids. I knew Will had to be an interesting person, merely from our unique mutual connection.

"Will's like a brother to me. He's the most spiritual man I've ever met," Elsbeth once told me many years before. "I'd trust him with my life, and my kids' lives … and I can't say that about anybody else except for my husband."

The last time I spoke to her, a few weeks earlier, she'd mentioned that Will had called her to say he wanted to give up alcohol and pot, as I had done years before, after decades of doing my share of weed, wine and other mind-numbing substances. That's why, he said now, she'd been urging him to call me—

"To find out how you gave up partying for the healthier, smarter choices I've decided to make," Will exuberantly explained.

As he talked, the scant insights I'd had about him blossomed to outright shock when I discovered he knew more about me than most did in my current circle of friends. He knew, for instance, how in the early 70s I'd lost a lover I was wild about when he finally came out, preferring men, and how I ran from the country instead of running stark raving mad over my heartache. Will shared how he'd heard from Elsbeth how I'd transformed myself from a Vietnam protestor to a sailor, by fleeing continental America. As he spoke of such details, I knew he couldn't have known how, in that act of fleeing, I then ran straight into entanglements with what turned out to be my dark shadowy side, not my country's anymore, by hanging out with equally hard-drinking outcasts and misfit druggy roughnecks as I was, back then. I knew Will couldn't know any of my other deep secrets, no matter how much Elsbeth had told him. Like how in my earlier college years I'd always felt drawn to the homeless drunkards I noticed hanging out in Boston Commons, close to where I was studying, until, after escaping such dull classes for clandestine partying like I did, I was eventually expelled from that uppity eastern university. Then I was free to finally become one of those sad and blurry-eyed lost souls of the Commons instead of observing them from afar.

Miserable, and nearly always non-stop drunk or stoned twenty-something, all for losing my man for another man, of all things! I stayed in my cups as I roved for years all over the Caribbean like a hell-bent she-pirate. From Elsbeth, Will had heard about my ill-fated, three-month jailing in the islands, for a crime I never committed. That escapade ended pathetically because, of course, I'd been shit-faced. It happened when I was on a work-trip that I got ambushed and framed as a political scapegoat while working with farmers in the netherworld, in the back country of the Dominican Republic.

Crazy, eh? That was me, all right. Sitting in that DR jail, a nervous and physical wreck by then, past thirty, and worse, abandoned by the U.S. Consulate for prickly political reasons. That was the first time I was sober since my teenage years.

"That one time, at least, I was innocent," I reaffirmed to Will, my caller now.

"Sure, Sure," Will said with a jolly laugh as if I'd told him I'd just won an Oscar.

Will continued recounting my wayward ways to me with such bawdy irreverence I stopped being shocked. I breathed in relief. Somehow, I instantaneously could relate to this stranger, this brazenly laughing fellow. *Was he laughing at me, or with me?* Along with other tidbits, he somehow knew of my rowdy past that honestly, I preferred keeping under wraps.

I was, after all, a sober woman now. I'd earned the right to not let everyone know about my past exploits. Years in recovery had taught me a lot.

Will chatted away on the phone, entertaining me with antics of several other friends we had in common. I can't deny how annoying it was when Will related a rumor he'd heard from one of them.

"You're infamous, teZ," Will reported. "Another friend, not Elsbeth, told me that you eat men for breakfast."

"Not me!" I vehemently disclaimed. "Anyone who said that doesn't know me, not one iota. I pursue Love to see where it leads me, not for a stupid conquest," I defended myself.

After claiming he'd never tell his source, a "forever-to-be-unnamed, mutual friend of ours," we both agreed to let it go. As we spoke, I tried to conjure a mental picture of what Will looked like, after he again claimed that we'd met. My curiosity was piqued. And okay, I found his voice to be an undeniable turn-on, I couldn't stop myself from asking when and where, exactly, we'd met before.

"You don't remember?" He seemed genuinely incredulous, almost hurt.

"No, sorry." I was grateful he couldn't see my face turning color.

He claimed we'd met in Boston nearly twenty years earlier. At another mutual friend's, whose place was below mine in our three-story, nineteenth-century sea captain's mansion-turned-into-apartments, set atop the highest hill in the then-ghetto of Roxbury. Back then, I was just as passionate about mingling with people of color as I was about making art and growing plants and learning how humanity benefits from all of that, and how our obligation is to protect Nature, the same as I do now. Back then, I was a botanical illustrator for a renowned university, involved with taxonomists, ethnobotanists, as well as other earth scientists. We were researching Native and South American divination plants that have supported ancient as well as today's indigenous people's efforts not only to survive, but to guide them to their source of strength, to the unseen world of Great Spirit. Back when I was drawing these plants humankind has used to gain insights, I was imbibing them as well as learning from them, and the scientists I worked with, how the gifts of Nature always have and always will aid us on our journey of discovery—if we can just get stupid humans to stop destroying our bountiful natural world.

After getting expelled from my pre-law university studies, I jumped into making art knowing this was my true calling. When I got a job illustrating plants, I considered it my duty, as their formal portraitist, to immerse myself in any shape, way or form in whatever brew of jungle potions the botanists happened to be researching. I felt it my duty to study and draw these sacred plants for all posterity, not just for my job. My goal was for humans to understand them more intrinsically, and therefore get to know other facets of Nature Herself. I focused on sketching in pencil, then taking my steel-tipped pen and pot of India ink and making tiny pen strokes or dots, illustrating my subjects' minutest details—of the Solanaeae and Erythroxylums, datura, coca, and other drug plants used alone or along with ayahuasca—with the deepest care and artistic illumination I could muster. Ah yes, I remembered all this now, as I spoke to this guy I was supposed to have met once, as I listened to Will talk about our meeting for the first time.

Those times, tripping on psychotropic plants—suddenly I understood—*that's why* I can't remember meeting Will! Meeting this man who was now telling me details about *us meeting*, was lost to me. I hadn't a shred of recall about the encounter he just described. *Drug-induced amnesia*, I reckoned. *Must have been all those weird jungle brews I did to better know my subjects.*

Will's disembodied voice on the phone drawled on: "You were friendly like all get-out. Perhaps a little too much that day. Carl and I walked unannounced into that sunny, plant-filled Roxbury digs of yours, so alive, so fragrant, I remember it like it happened yesterday.

"There you were," Will's reverberating voice suddenly dropped to a soft dreamy tone. "Sitting at the kitchen table with another chick your age, both of you having a cup of tea, but … you were both … ahh …" He was stumbling over his words.

"Both of us, what, Will?" I asked, hoping to rescue him

"Well … you were … both stone-cold buck-naked," he choked out.

I couldn't help it, I laughed out loud.

"I was? We were?" I acted dumbfounded but continued chuckling silently, not surprised at all.

Listening, now in my early forties, I could admit I wasn't embarrassed in the slightest to hear of this youthful folly of mine—relayed on the phone from an embarrassed, perfect stranger. I couldn't deny it. That was pretty much how I lived my Nature-loving life back then, even when I called the ghetto of Boston my home. In those days, I experimented with every shamanic tropical specimen I was passionately drawing, not just for my living, but for the sake of the destiny of all humankind, I actually thought. Sure, my crazy friends and I spent a lot of time au naturel, but I also frequented the hallowed academic halls of properly uptight, decidedly non-tropical

Cambridge, where I had a tucked-away office at Harvard's Botanical Museum. Speaking quickly, I now explained to Will that the experimentation I was doing back then, when he met me, he says, in the buff, was of Brazilian, Ecuadorian, Peruvian and other Amazonian Indians' divination jungle potions—and I, I was merely ritually sampling my drawing-subjects by doing what every primitive tribe member did, well, only men I was told, because women in Amazonian indigenous societies are forbidden to, but I could because I was American, right? Besides, in order to draw the best portrait of every plant I was assigned, I had to make contact with their Nature deities, now didn't I?

"So," I offered in explanation, "like the mythical Amazonians, my girlfriend and I, when you and that fellow, Carl you say? walked in on us, we were no doubt shedding our ego's exterior, our hardened shells. And that included taking off all our clothes."

I took a sustained breath, hoping to detract, jog, maybe begin again with something new after this long boring rattle of explanation.

"No wonder I can't remember meeting you," I added. "I was either high or coming down from some shaman's brew."

But Will wasn't interested in my theories right then.

On a roll, he continued in a jesting tone, "Both you and your girlfriend were bare as newborn babes. And with those fully ripe, grown-up bodies of yours—man, I was floored!"

I muffled a snort and let Will ramble on. This guy with the sonorous voice was obviously excited. I liked listening to him, he was so amusing. And if there's one thing more than Love that I'm gaga about, it's enthusiasm.

"On our way up to your apartment, Carl had stopped to warn me. 'Will,' he said, turning to face me just before knocking on the door, 'promise me you're gonna act normal. Because teZa will probably be naked.' But, c'mon! how could I act normal? You were, you were ... *arrgh* ... not so normal yourself, so tall and thin, with endless legs and those mahogany eyes like bayonets stabbing into me. And that long hair. You looked like some statue come alive, made of sculpted butter and honey."

I flushed hearing this but kept quiet. No one had ever spoken like this to me, ever.

"When you stood up, naked, and came over to where I was standing," Will continued in a measured beat, "I felt like a fool. My mouth must have been stuck wide open—you blew me away. Then you ... you fucking reached out to me for a *handshake,* and I—I lost it. Stood there shaking your hand like an idiot. Like I was there to interview you for a job. Man, it was the weirdest thing that'd ever happened to me, I'm not kidding."

"Sorry I freaked you out, man," my small voice said, but I don't think he heard.

"I just had to get the hell out of there. I couldn't stand it," Will said really low.

On the other end of the line I worked hard to stifle the guffaws welling up, thinking, *Is this guy for real?*

"I'm sorry I made you feel so uncomfortable," I said softly. "I really don't remember a thing about that day. Back then, admit it, practically all of us our age were getting high. My boyfriend the botanist and I were. Carl, the filmmaker, for sure was. Weren't you?"

"No ma'am," Will said, as if I'd just accused him of sticking up a bank.

I couldn't believe he'd just called me *ma'am*! Who *was* this freak, anyway? Good thing Will couldn't hear the silent alarm bells blaring in my head.

"I was an athlete so I missed the drug-crazed sixties," he said. "I didn't jump on the free love bandwagon until the late seventies, when I started smoking weed during that tugboat stint with Elsbeth and her old man, hauling barges between Florida and Puerto Rico. Back when I met you in Roxbury, I'd just returned to Boston from months of working my ass off in the Amazon."

"Doing what?"

"Chasing jaguars, canoeing the Amazon, exploring South America. Learning Portuguese and Spanish."

I explained to Will how back then, I was drawing for several botanists who'd hired me to research different families of drug plants.

One thesis was on the family of Erythroxylum, of which E. coca is the only species from which cocaine is derived. Another group of illustrations was on the genus of tree daturas, called Brugmansia. I'd do a whole family at a time, so I got to know all the cousins intimately, even the extinct ones, whose portraits I'd then be able to draw from dried up and pressed specimens sometimes a hundred years old or more. There were other shamanic plants we studied, like San Pedro and peyote cacti. And of course, the most powerful divination plant of all, the vine called ayahuasca—all these plants had been used by native peoples since before recorded history, by the indigenous of Latin America for the sole purpose of attaining heightened, altered states of being. Humanity has always wanted to commune with the Sacred, the Divine, through whatever means they could. In those days I'd been deeply involved with scientific studies about every aspect of how ancient peoples have sought Nature's gateway to the unseen world—that's all around us.

△

The first edition of the book that documents the indigenous use of psychotropic plants as one of the most sacred portals used to connect to The Mystery, *Plants of the Gods,* featured some of my botanical studies. When taken internally, divination plants alter human consciousness in such a way that the Sacred remains knowable when the imbiber returns to a so-called normal state. At that time, in my young twenties, I was just developing my art form. What interested me most, besides botanical precision, was learning how ancient humans received sacred teachings from plants, and all of Nature, long before receiving guidance from other humans, prophets, or those enlightened individuals whom various world religions deem as the Divine Incarnate. Before drawing for botanists, I'd become fascinated how art's beginnings started as depicting and honoring the Divine. Drawn on natural rock walls inside deep caves, and in rough carvings on caverns, rocks, and cliffs, iconic shapes the primitive people worshipped or recorded are millennial-old epiphanies demonstrating the quests of early humankind, of the spiritual as well as every day, mundane discoveries.

"I've always loved Spirit, the Great Mystery of life," I told Will, who spoke to me that day from his central Florida home a thousand miles away from mine in Long Island. "Nature has been my greatest teacher throughout my entire life."

Feeling more amused than anything, not caring whether my old Boston persona appeared foolish or disarmingly naive to Will, I thought this man a most unusual and intriguing person, he who had reached out to call me on this beautiful first day of spring.

△

Our conversation continued, going right to the heart of things, my favorite way to commune. Quickly we found we were both romantically free. He'd been divorced for more than a year, and had full custody of his two small children.

My heart fluttered at that. Kids? It'd only been a few months since I'd escaped from yet another in the uninterrupted chain of inappropriate relationships that kept pointing, again, to the next lesson being dished out to learn about Self-love, and not much else. Full Custody. Will, me? *Hmmm*. A chilly challenge entered from stage right.

Yet a next hour of yapping flew by. We discovered we both loved to journey on the deep blue sea (he, on boats with engines; me, preferably those with sails) and we both did our share of checking out exotic cultures, near and far away. Surprised by how many different kinds of friends, disparate tribes we had in common—a noted scientist, an author-physician, a good-hearted entertainment lawyer, a TV set-builder, a documentary filmmaker, several random seamen and a few other no-good-niks—we finally had to get off the phone. My one good ear was ready to fall off from being pressed to the receiver; I didn't want to miss a single word. As soon as I said goodbye I rushed to my journal and wrote:

Who is this man named Will?! What's this new vibration within me? A kind of energy I can't identify, making me tremble inside. Chest thumping, toes buzzing, my mind's on fire. I can't stop grinning.

And Will? Before he hung up maybe he heard the disappointment in my voice when I commented, "Oh—you're a smoker?" after hearing him take an obvious, long drag in. He'd tell me later, "After your comment, I put it out. That's the last butt I smoked. That was, my dear, *that*. I knew I wanted you in my life."

I called him back the next day, and after that, he or I called every day. Each time we spoke I was all a-quiver just from the sound of his voice. The way he sibilated his Ss thrilled me no end; I felt I'd died and gone to bad-boy heaven. But wait—*he wasn't one of them*. He made it perfectly clear from the start he was "a hard-core practicing Christian."

△

In my journal I asked myself what I was doing with someone like him. I, who since a rebellious teen had been anti-religion *for myself*, anti-organized anything, for that matter, and now considered myself a resentful, recovering Catholic along with being a gratefully recovering addict. In our phone conversations over the next few days I mentioned to Will several times that I had no idea what he looked like. His only response to my asking about himself seemed to be more details about the after-effects of our initial encounter, back in Boston.

"I carried you around in a little box I built specially for you in my head, Miss Not-Give-a-Damn Naked Lady," Will chortled. "In my mind I labeled that box I put you in, the *Femi-Nazis*. Sure, I put other women-libbers like you, who conquered and discarded men, right in there with you. You were the very first, though. That's who I thought you were: a stuck-up feminist man-hater. Ever since meeting you naked like that. I got pissed every time I thought of you, how foolish you made me feel; your gorgeous girlfriend sipping from a teacup while you stood and greeted me, so self-effacing, flaunting your Amazon-sized self, right at me. In my mind, at that moment, and every other time I thought of you—you'd become my nemesis."

"Ouch! That's harsh. Really?" I squeaked. "That's pretty strong, isn't it, Will, after just having met someone?"

"Maybe," he said. "But after that one slam-dunk meeting, the painful memory of you shaking my hand while you stood there, big and nude, as if you did it every day to every guy—got shelved in a part of my mind where I put all citified broads who refuse to meet a real man like me halfway. There were plenty of them back in New York when I was living there. Extreme women-libbers, the man-loathers. Your not giving a damn about being bare-assed in front of me pissed the hell out of me."

I hoped I didn't sound mocking of his seriousness when I said, "I'm no city slicker, Will." Such an easy target, I thought, if I were in the mood, for a volley of wits with this conceited yet comical guy.

But I was more intent on masking my shock. Me, someone's nemesis? I was stunned. Yet I was also glad he was upfront enough to tell me. Almost embarrassingly honest, this one. Most guys never admit that they despise the man-haters. Even I hated the man-haters. Will's words felt more like my kind of wild-child tribe's credo than recrimination. He wanted a real woman because he thought himself—let me guess—a real man, as he said? I laughed to myself. Neither his tone nor his words held any accusation. This guy had no filters, just like me. I quickly recognized our similarity and smiled in relief. His words were brutally honest, yes. How could I not appreciate a guy like him, with such rare openness and vulnerability? I began to imagine Will as some kind of Siegfried, from Wagner's *The Ring*, whose search for truth and love heralded his fearlessness, his bravado daring.

"Will, I'm just the opposite of a women's libber. I've never once called myself a feminist, ever. I've always believed men need to be liberated as much as women. I feel sorry for any male or female stuck in a material, heartlessly competitive world, with no clue how to access their sensitive, so-called spiritual side. That's why I prefer to honor the feminine aspect of the Divine. I interchange God with Goddess, but the sacred word, Aum makes me most comfortable. We all get so defensive using that much-maligned word, *God*. Either God or Goddess works, but Aum is best for me when referring to the ineffable, The Mystery."

"Well, not me," Will said. "I was raised by spiritual Christians."
I was glad to hear this.

"I use Jesus—God as man—to mean the sacred and that's pretty much it," he plainly stated.

Although I love Christ, who represents to me all of humankind's having Christ Consciousness, the ability to tap our divinity while in our human flesh, and Jesus certainly was and is a shining light-symbol of the Divine, I sincerely appreciate Jesus' incalculable impact on the spread of unconditional, universal Love. Yet I don't single out any historic enlightened figure, neither Christ nor Krishna, Lao Tsu, Confucius, Buddha, Muhammad—as a solitary, one-and-only Divine human in the flesh. To my mind, all in existence makes up the intricate parts of the whole, the One about what I know to be, and experience as God, within me and everywhere else. Whether we're *His/Her/Its* children, each of us is a human cell within the whole of the Divine, no person being an "only" son or daughter (or progeny, for those sensitive about gender identity). Every creature and every-*thing* is part of God's creation. To my thinking, God is the energy of Love, the Oneness we all are part of, remember? There is nothing that is *not God*, in other words. All the more reason why I stick with the all-purpose, all-inclusive name of Aum for The Mystery, to convey this sense of the One. It's impossible to describe using meager words. But I try, along with paint this ineffable connection that I *feel*. The concept of *words* is important to me, though. "In the beginning was the word, and the word was God." Indeed, I find creating visual images a lot easier for me to express what the idea of "the Divine" means to me.

Words are magical and often just plain freaky-weird, how their evolution came to be. The similarity of the sounds of certain sacred names, for instance. Especially Krishna and Christ. Jesus was the name Mary and Joseph bestowed upon their child, his "common Aramaic name" while Christ, or Kristos (also, spelled Christos) was an ancient Greek word meaning "messiah or anointed one" and was often referred to, by that word Christos, in the original language of the Bible, Greek. Other kinds of sacred word-puzzles tickle my fancy, such as how many names besides AHh-oum that conjure the Divine have the *AHhh*, the same breathy-sounding syllable in them: such as AHh-men, AHh-min, YAH-weh, Jeho-vAH, Krish-nHA, Dur-gHAa, At-mAHn, BrAH-man, Bud-dHAa, AHh-lah, Shi-vay-AH, and I'm sure, many others. I have always been under the spell that words as well as images can weave. Since childhood, words have been visual and audial portals through which I can dive through, growing ever closer to the Source of Wonder *It*-self.

So as Will's and my conversations went deeper, became more intense, our use of words surprised me, signaling to me that we'd left the gravity of having to be *right*. Both of us spoke without fear, without needing to impress. Our zany laughter seemed to be our audience, clapping, urging us on to reveal more and more. I felt all the ideas I expressed in our talks were welcomed, so I released more, free-roaming, as if he and I were swimming in the endlessness of possibilities, together; both of us able to perceive the clarity of a bottomless clear spring, each of us weightlessly leapfrogging, pulling, pushing, dancing, flirting with each other long-distance. Was I drunk or was this real, unknown-before happiness? We agreed on most every point, something both of us knew was a rarity, even spooky, in this rough world of conflict and alienation. Most important, we concurred that every person, at the stage of life we were at, especially, needs to be absolutely free to believe what they want, without judgment or anybody's warped perspectives about our birthright to be unique individuals.

△

Right after the God discussion, we established that making art— he as a filmmaker and I as a visual artist and wordsmith—was of central importance to both our lives. He shared something with me I'd never considered. And that was, to him, raising his children—it being the most important job of all, guiding the next generation—was his life's highest accomplishment to date, worthy of anything, including extreme personal sacrifice. I complimented Will on being a full-custodial parent, when he explained that his ex was basically out of the picture.

"She's got mental issues," he blithely stated.

Our talk bounced from subject to subject. We became downright giddy sharing how we both happened to be completely, madly intoxicated with Spirit, no matter what name we or anyone used to call It. Our biggest difference seemed to be that he was a Christ follower and football aficionado while I was passionate about art and yogic meditation. Okay, so he called his Divine source *Jesus* (whom I fondly call JC) and I called my Source a strange name he laughed over. Explaining how Aum was "to avoid discussions just like we're having right now about names for God. I prefer *no name*, no particular *one*," I offered. "No name explains the God-thing well enough for me. Because for me, the Sacred, the Divine is masculine, feminine, *and* Nature *It*self."

We shared that earlier in our search for the Sacred, we'd both held more cynical views than we did now. I told him how for me, the conventions of religion had long-ago stopped working. He just laughed, saying he used to be like that, too. We agreed that in our wild, experimental youth, we both believed spirituality to be a big woo-woo, a hiding place for softheaded folks who needed to escape from the harshness of life. But now, again, we were utterly delighted, realizing that both of us placed God, or Spirit, or any of Its countless names, at the center of our lives. Embracing the sacred Mystery of Life was our real source of power and joy. We laughed at how ironic it was that we both believed so strongly that *everything* was God, good or bad. We spoke nearly on top of each other when we both asserted: "Choosing well … is part of … making life itself … sacred."

We laughed like two drunken monkeys over our secret joy of seeing God everywhere, agreeing this perception was our life's highest aim—and Truth. Both of us were oddly, weirdly, wonderfully in synch with the *God-thing*. Honestly, we couldn't help ourselves, we were high on each other, feeling exhilarated over our great good fortune to be meeting each other again. He had been a passing ship in the dead of night, I'd once bumped into, he whom I might never have known about. Yet here he was, back in my life, so I could meet him again, and know who he really was, this time—this man whose ease and tenderness surprised me so much, even though he was just a voice coming over the phone.

calling love in

CHAPTER 2

from the fog of the night

After that unremembered first meeting in Roxbury, Will and I had our separate destinies to explore that took us to far different worlds. Mine included an early stint as an owner of run-down, multi-storied Victorian houses I rebuilt in Roxbury during the gentrification of Boston, during which time I became a gallery-exhibiting jeweler of body art and had a months-long Bahamian cruise after first learning to sail in Gloucester. As soon as I got hooked on sailing, I flew south and caught a berth on a cruise from the Pacific side of Costa Rica through the Panama Canal to the Caribbean Sea. That spectacular experience—including how a curious whale courting our little sailboat like a dance, back and forth under us, as we bobbed listlessly out of sight of land during many days of doldrums—began my wanting to explore every place I could in tropical waters. I fell captivated with the land too, coming ashore to meet the wet fertile jungles wherever whatever boat I was on happened to anchor.

Soon I was swaying to the rhythm of balmy breezes, exploring exotic flora and fauna that called me to explore their steamy verdant habitats. Between the tropic's crystalline waters, the beautiful soulful folks I met on every island I landed, and the richness of each new spot's beckoning jungle—I became a total addict for anything West Indian, on land or sea.

Soon after that first meeting with Will—which I never recalled and often wonder if a hypnotist might someday help me to—I landed in the Leeward Islands of the Caribbean, which I would call my home turf for the next decade. When I first arrived I used Saint Thomas as homeport, and began to sail the chain of volcanic islands south and west, until I discovered the place where I really belonged.

Dominica (pronounced Do-ME-nee-ka), located between the French islands of Martinique and Guadeloupe, a veritable dreamy paradise, was where I discovered my heart sang and laughed best of all. It was there I met Will's and my mutual friend, Elsbeth. She'd come to the most enchantingly primitive island in that part of the world after many years of living and working aboard her family's international tugboat. Elsbeth was a spontaneous and spunky woman of the sea. She was one of the few other white ex-pats, besides myself, who came to live with the potpourri-mix of islanders: the original Carib Indians and descendants of former colonialists and slaves that make up the population of Dominica. As soon as I met her I knew this painfully shy woman, who played the piano like a female Van Cliburn, was a kindred soul.

In Dominica, another ex-pat American and I created an inter-island tropical food-shipping business. Every day we'd either get our hands dirty alongside native islanders, harvesting gigantic yellow tropical yams, digging up the purple-fleshed vegetable called dasheen, pulling out heavenly aromatic ginger roots from velvety-green hillside gardens; or cutting soon-to-ripen banana and plantain hands from their juicy, way above man's-height stalks. From taller trees we'd harvest citrus, avocado, tamarind or mangoes, depending on the season.

Some days, I'd join the assembly line with our island workers to prepare bananas for packaging. I'd dip the pre-cut hands in an anti-fungal and place them in wax-lined banana boxes, all necessary for the tonnage of produce we harvested and immediately shipped north to the barren Virgin Islands. Such hard work not only made my yoga-flexible body stronger, but allowed me to earn a living, plus helped the locals earn good incomes too. I was thrilled to be able to stay as far from the materialistic world of the States as I could. Working with bi-weekly shipments of seasonal foodstuffs and kind-hearted agriculturists gave me plenty of down time to pursue my obsessive need to make Nature-infused art.

During my art studies, I swore to forever be untainted by fine art's fickle cousin, commercialism. After preparing and shipping our two-ton shipments of provisions (naturally grown food in island-speak), I painted in my panoramic hilltop studio. Metamorphic visions called out for me to depict intra-species adventures, conjured by simply looking outside my window (with an added pinch of imagination). Fantastic scenes unfolded before me as unbounded as my compulsion for adventure and living far from my birth family. My painted juxtapositions, oddly quirky, energetic and colorful, were just as real, as attainable, as flavorful and surprising, yet just as common to my mind as the buttered and jammed homemade toast I ate for breakfast every day.

For me, good art has always been about expressing new ideas, never about duplicating reality. Important art makes reality more precise, interpreted through lenses of personal perception. And my favorite kind is when the invisible dimensions of space and time simultaneously converge in everyday scenarios. In Dominica, surrounded by the splendor of Nature Herself, I concentrated on painting the merging of all life-forms' uniqueness, their energies—a winged man and a serpent-woman, wrapped around each other as they fly high above a buoyant planet Earth; a passionflower-headed, tangerine pointy-titted lady in the act of being pollinated by a man-sized honeybee; a jellyfish-shaped creature with a feminine face and happily, no body; a lion-maned roaring man; a sphinx woman sprawled in the desert sand; a human woman dancing arms akimbo, with a chartreuse-skinned long-tailed lizard. Dream-like visions—my art. Some call it visionary. I just call it my work. The aim of these surreal but totally believable compositions—sometimes in elaborate murals, sometimes on canvas, wood or paper—was to show how we humans can become *the other*. We are all various creatures in action, living out our drama, fulfilling the theme of my art: identification with all beings, all forms of life.

My business partner, Solstice and I leased an unrefrigerated sixty-foot cargo vessel. We organized local farmers, who up till our arrival on that backward island had no consistent way of marketing their vegetables and fruits. The government at that time, the mid-seventies, purposefully kept its citizens uneducated, and sadly, unexposed to better possibilities. So along came we two Americans, wanting to live in paradise and also wanting to help organize the local farmers. We helped the farming co-ops we organized to plant, cultivate, harvest and transport their provisions for sale to places up-island from our down-island base of Dominica. I called Dominica home for years, this unique place of abundant rainfall, with its hundreds of rivers, waterfalls and streams, a volcanic-crater's boiling lake (one of only two found on Earth): this magical heart-space I'd found, with hardly a flat spot anywhere on its vertiginous green slopes covered by abundantly rich soil. Life was very full, and very satisfying on this third-world island paradise of mine.

We filled our ship's hold with boxed or bagged orange yams and purple dasheen; green plantains, bananas, and avocados; fragrant ginger roots and every variety of citrus large and small; and any other kind of edible food when it was in season. Our bi-monthly shipments were among the biggest commercial enterprise on the island back then, along with products from the rum and bitters factories. Our cargo ship plowed the rough channels between the chain of islands—picking up fresh peanuts from St. Kitts; tomatoes from Montserrat; water-nuts, the immature green coconuts, in Nevis—until we arrived at our destination, the drier American and British Virgin Islands. Everywhere we stopped, we supplied waterfront retail markets on these drier, flatter, less agriculturally blessed islands.

Upon arriving in the West Indies, I first explored St. Thomas and then farther down-island, finally settling in Dominica, to live simply, to get away from the materialism of the U.S. I wanted nothing to do with mainland America's disco-driven madness, a dance beat that sounded more like a deadbeat dirge to my reggae-preferring senses. I called myself an island woman, proudly baptized that by my native friends. When I wasn't working the produce busi-ness, I soaked up the strong Earth-vibes of the land's rainforest greenery while all around surrounded me the pristine turquoise expanse of the Caribbean Sea. My un-shuttered studio, its windows screen- and glass-less, was situated high on a hillside above Roseau, the island's capital and one good harbor. From my studio I looked out onto the domed horizon of the Caribbean, the silvery sea's stillness reaching as far as my eyesight could roam, its constant movement frozen by sunshine and distance.

I loved my islander friends! Such strong, healthy, non-materialistic people, who cared mostly about Nature, growing living things, and enjoying the moment. Feeding their children, chickens, goats and pigs was what mattered most to them. Making lots of money or having a career wasn't worth their time or even a thought, because having more than they needed was beyond their scope of everyday reality. Grateful to live among such unblemished, pure people, no longer a stranger among them, not a single person ever asked me, "So Miss, what you be doing for a living?" I rejoiced in their company, the pleasant breeze, the fragrance of each show-stopping flower, the head-reeling whiff of a blossoming plant, the knee-weakening taste of a tree-ripe peach-colored mango, or the outrageously sweet assault of a white-fleshed soursop, a guanabana, all of which kept my mouth exploding in sensory ecstasy day after day. The magic of each moment—Nature unencumbered, right then, right there—was my world. I felt complete at last.

Years passed. And then ... one summer Hurricanes David and Frederick struck our island a deadly blow, piggy-back striking our exact spot, our puny island paradise, in the span of two weeks' time. The damage in Dominica was overwhelming. Not a plant was left—no fruits, roots, not even a bud remained on any well-established tree. Everything was uprooted and demolished after those two deadly storms I call *him-micanes*. This happened in 1979, the first year hurricanes received masculine names from NOAA, America's government weather bureau. After David struck his deadly blow, there would be no electricity in Dominica for a solid year other than by private generator. No clean water except bottled. No imported supplies, no wood or nails, nothing, arrived on the island immediately after David. And then—Frederick freakily followed David's same track—adding hallucinatory strife to every human in this second storm's carbon copy path.

Two weeks, two back-to-back himmicanes: in one swoop our uninsured inter-island business, *The Better Roots and Fruits Company,* was over. Ruined. Killed by David, then Frederick's devastation. Everything from our storehouse and office to my rented hillside house on the passion fruit and guava estate where I'd lived peacefully for years—everything, blown away. Everything my partner and I had worked long and hard for—was gone or irreparably destroyed. Such destruction kicks the very breath out of people. Two-foot-wide steel I-beams from the rum factory littered the landscape with what looked like sixty-foot lengths of twisted ribbons—but they were jagged clumps of heavy metal. The storms' destruction took my breath away. It took my livelihood, too.

With my peaceful life and work in Dominica abruptly terminated, I traveled to Europe to visit my art mentor and friend, Hundertwasser (whom I'll call here *H*), whom I'd met when he was sailing the Windward islands. I began to drink heavily again, after losing my heart's place, just as earlier I had after losing my man to another man. Life became a daze, a drunken, drugged haze. Somehow, I wound up living in the Middle East after visiting H in Vienna, living outside Tel Aviv to make art and drink cheap Israeli wine for an entire year. More fogged-in, numbed-out time passed. I met my perfect mismatch: a man who was as addicted to the self-sabotaging effects of chemical highs as I was then: a jock, a famous basketball player of all things! A man who offered to take care of me when I didn't know how to anymore, who consumed, snorted and drank as much as I could. We left Israel together and settled in New York City where, thanks to cocaine, the preferred drug of all pro athletes at the time, I bottomed out, got sober, and simultaneously, fortuitously, magically—met my long-sought-for spiritual teacher, right there in midtown Manhattan.

Thus—thanks to life's continuous stream of ironic, idiotic, *so-called* coincidences—I began my sober, sane, and spiritual life.

Five completely clean-and-dry sober years passed quickly, in which I learned to live naturally, imbibing pure, non-material Spirit alone. There I was, sitting in my rental home in Springs, a wooded area in the Hamptons of New York, taking a break from my job of creating gardens, when the man with the mysteriously beguiling voice, the infectious laugh, and inimitable love for Jesus Christ—a force of Nature in his own right—called that spring day from Florida, following the sweetly persistent advice to do so, from our friend Elsbeth.

▲

Meanwhile, Will's life had moved just as fiercely, just as intensely in the direction he had aimed it toward after we'd bumped into each other, two passing strangers in the night, back at that forgotten-by-me meeting of ours in Boston.

After having met me, his so-called naked nemesis, sipping tea, zonked-out with my girlfriend in my Roxbury apartment, Will set off for his next adventure after that stint of his as an Amazonian explorer-hunter. He signed on as crew for our mutual friend's (unknown to us till later), Elsbeth's family tug, on which he worked as a deckman for a year. With his fancy college degree burning his conscience, Will then traveled Central and South America as a businessman selling organic fertilizer, even eating it to prove to his shocked customers, knowledgeable agronomists, just how pure it'd be for the vast acreages they farmed.

Returning to the States he settled in New York City, years before I did, to learn the film business. He spent the next decade involved in all aspects of filmmaking—writing, lighting, directing, editing—before producing his first feature film, back in the swamplandia of Florida where he'd grown up. After his film tanked, losing most of his self-invested money, Will decided, in rebound-mode, to stay and marry Debby, a no-frills, country-loving gal whom he'd met while on location, deep in the scrubby pancake-flat cattle country of the Sunshine State. After this huge financial loss, Will decided to create a new life for himself as a responsible family and business man. He would build a secluded ranch from scratch. So he bought a patch of wooded acres, found a sizable house in the nearby cowboy town and, why not? split it in half and had it moved many miles away to his hidden spot, figuring that the three-story wooden old hotel would function as the secluded headquarters for making the movies he felt needed to be born from his vision and skill.

Soon after the children arrived, his hasty marriage—to a simple country gal with a penchant for getting high, a woman who couldn't begin to understand Will's complexities—fell apart. In a nasty, drawn-out court case, Will was granted full custody of both kids while Debby, whom the judge deemed not eligible for even joint custody (due to the drug-specific reports he'd gotten of her), awarded her the humongous house on the isolated twenty-acre spread. Dead broke and heavily in debt after his failed film and bitterly contested, custody extravaganza—but overjoyed to have full guardianship of his kids at its end—Will moved from the isolated retreat in the woods into a tacky suburban house his dad luckily got to purchase for him, right next door to his parents' place in a town I have dubbed here, *Lackland*.

▲

As soon as I managed to hop off the runaway train of my addiction-to-misadventure, my new sobriety mentor, Jane, taught me how to visualize. "Ask the Universe," is how she put it, what I wanted in my new, Spirit-fueled life. It was then that I made the conscious choice, the same choice Will would make, one day in the future, when Elsbeth would convince him it'd be beneficial for him to call me. I envisioned a future that was focused on the positive, productive inner journey of knowing Spirit up close and personal. Being sober meant that everything was, from now on, one day at a time, an *inside* job. Exterior, outside things would never mean as much to me—not any exotic adventure, no far-away fascinating place, or beguiling romantic partner—as how my connection with my Higher Power, my spiritual side, felt to me from then on.

One evening, several months before Will called on that spring equinox, I sat down to do my next round of visualizing. I wrote in my journal the wish list that Jane had recommended I make. She suggested this because, "It's time to send out to the Universe your simple, clearly written, now years-sober, clear-headed requests." She urged me to seal this ritual by having a *private talk* with the invisible realm. Meaning, communing with my HP, which I had not yet chosen to call Aum, having not quite surrendered to my Teacher's guidance in matters of the Spirit.

"I'm asking for any assistance I can get," I spoke aloud after I'd written out my deepest wishes, "to fulfill three major wants I've thought long and hard about, and know these I hold dear to my heart.

"First, I want to be able to see you, my Higher Power, The Mystery, everywhere: in every person, and everything. I'm fortunate to be sober and to have found, besides Jane, a spiritual teacher who's already shown me how. She calls HP by the name Aum and that's cool with me. She's taught me to go deeper in meditation than I've ever done, making a deeper connection to the Divine within. With practice, one day I'll make my teacher's expanded perspective my own. Just as she did her teacher's, and the other teachers did before, back through countless centuries.

"Second, I want a loving-kind, spiritual-sexy, playful, intelligent, open-minded mate. Is that asking too much? I don't think so. But please, make it a straight man, dear Universe.

"Third, I feel two kids coming. I know I've never even thought about kids before, but I've been sensing, and dreaming about kids arriving in my life, I don't know why. I just feel two kids coming closer, so I guess I'm ready. I never was before. I figure the great guy *who's waiting for me*, whoever he is, he and I will adopt—as soon as we find each other, since it seems I can't bear children myself."

After writing and speaking aloud these three deep yearnings that pressed upon me like a comforting weight needing to be relieved, I had a consultation with Jane's longtime trusted psychic, Louise, who'd helped my friend, and now me, get our lives back on track after years of self-destructive addiction. When I asked Louise for advice, she contacted her source and said, "It's clear to me. True love is coming for you in the spring." Sure enough, a few months later, on the very day of the spring equinox—Will rang me from his home in Lackland.

△

How could I not believe in Aum's benevolent potential? Life was indisputably bringing me what I so clearly needed. The three things I'd so humbly, so pointedly asked for, all in one! Will was everything, all I could want and then some, which I'd requested in my petition. The fact that he lived so far away didn't mean beans to me. For an experienced traveler like me, that was do-able.

I knew Florida. My parents had moved there when I was in college. I enjoyed its searing heat, its long, white sandy beaches, its pungent swamps and humid marshes filled with slinky, dangerous alligators, its saw grass and palmetto scrub foot-paths harboring deadly diamondback rattlers and recluse spiders whose bites rotted skin. Now that Will had arrived (thanks to my precise wish list), I was jazzed to know more about this strange place, my folks' and now this man's, the home state of plastic pink flamingos, the opposite of both the laid-back mystical jungle of tropical Dominica, war-torn Israel, and culture-chaotic New York City, with its ostentatious Hamptons where I'd been hanging out designing gardens for the last couple years.

△

But Florida's charms didn't intrigue me nearly as much as Will's. As we chatted daily on the phone, I still didn't have a clue about what he looked like. His allure was his voice, since that was all I had of him. The memory of our previously having physically met, nonexistent. For all I knew he could be short, bald, ugly, and fat. Blindly, I already had feelings for him and this was weird because swarthy good looks and strong physicality has always been the strongest aphrodisiacs for me. Yet with no clue other than his sexy voice, I was crazy for him.

After a week of our hour-long phone calls, I felt he was getting to know the real me, and in many ways, I felt like I already knew him, but of course, how could I? Perchance my still-*mocus* (New Yorker-*ese* for being newly sober, confused) mind kept arguing about whether to pursue getting to know him or not. He must have thought me pretty lame when I too-soon and too-boldly blurted out my heart's truth. "I think I love you," I muttered for no reason other than to voice what I was feeling. I felt foolish, but without a hitch he replied, "I love you too … like a friend."

"No, Will," I whispered to the faceless man on the line, "I mean, my gut tells me, I *really* love you."

"Oh," he said.

Rather hastily I murmured, covering my foolhardy tracks best I could, "Can you please send me a photo? It'd be nice to know what you look like."

He agreed I was being goofy, but said he'd send one anyway. We both laughed in relief, knowing how stupid it was to talk of love so blindly, so blithely, so soon. When the envelope postmarked from Florida arrived several days later, I tore it open while driving to the next garden in my trusty red Toyota mini-pickup loaded with rakes and shovels.

There the photo was: Proof. Strong. Swarthy. Square-jawed, short-haired, dark-eyed Will standing tall and proud, holding his pair of bright-eyed sprites, aged two and five, golden-haired tots held in their father's mountain-peak muscular arms. I secured the snapshot behind my Yo-truck's steering wheel and whenever traffic allowed, stared at the trio's image, transfixed.

"Three beautiful souls," I murmured, hypnotizing myself, conning myself, daring myself to plunge in. I drove from one garden to the next as if mesmerized.

The timing of his arrival stunned me. Exactly the first day of spring, just as Louise had predicted. Now I felt as if I'd manifested Will, pulled him out of a cosmic top hat, materializing him as easily as writing down three wishes and shouting aloud, the three big needs my heart ached for. I laughed at how magical it all seemed. You get a cosmic itch—speak it aloud—it gets scratched. It was as if Will had seen a personal ad in a passing cloud sent directly from my soul to his. And he came with—oh my Goddess, HP, and dear Jesus too!—the two kids I'd been feeling my dream-bones wanted to meet, maybe help raise. What had I asked for? Yipes! I wouldn't have to wait to go through any hassle of adoption. Stepkids were perfect. Will was perfect. I was perfect, in all my imperfections, just as I'd been hearing from the Teacher all these past years.

△

At the Teacher's very first dharma talk I'd attended in her secluded Vermont ashram, I clearly heard her say: "The life-force energy, this universal power, attracts or draws in what each of us needs to be spiritually fulfilled. Our job is to recognize this energy force that is within us all. We yogis call it Aum, the Divine Power in all beings."

She instructed us to "Hold constantly in your thoughts what's most important to you. Create your own reality."

But honestly, I didn't believe her until I'd proven it to myself, many times over. For years already I'd been listening to and emulating the Teacher's wise counsel. As one in her legions of spiritual students who are spread throughout the world, we are like seedlings of higher consciousness fertilizing the entire human race. Testing this Inner Power within us all is what she suggests her students focus on. "Work with Aum," she urges us, "it's within your power to create what you need, what your soul needs."

"You create your own life with your thoughts alone," she says. "So be careful what thought-seeds you plant. When you know what you want, then you're ready to ask. You're also then ready to receive."

I'll say. With Will's calling me that spring day, all three of my wishes looked as if they were about to come true in one swoop of fate's hand. I'd won my life's giant jackpot.

Will and his two kids came bursting from the fertile dream I'd planted with three clearly stated requests, sent out months before. Can life get any crazier, or more beautiful?

From the Fog of the Night

Lucky me, I got to meet again the *ship* called *Relation* that had passed me once so long-ago. In the fog of night Will's ship had sailed so closely to mine. This time though, I heard his call, I felt his spirit; I recognized who and what he was from his words. And his photo! Well, that got my juices going. This time though, as his ship was drawing close to mine on the Ocean of Life, I was paying attention. On this second chance, I was awake and aware (sober, that is), having already worked so diligently with my spiritual teacher to transform from misery-fueled she-pirate to a seriously, serenity-desiring seeker.

Lucky for me, I was able to recognize that Will was unique among all others.

At first, the idea of joining my spiritual life with his decidedly more religious one seemed *insane*. But I wasn't about to write off so daunting a call from Love without checking it out first. It's not as though I hadn't done anything so crazy before, right? Long-ago I'd been the only woman in a scurvy crew of Caribbean misfits making regular cargo runs, some legal, some not. Once, I'd had an island rogue drop me off on the deserted isle of Culebrita so I could draw and paint and lose myself in the magnificence of the tropics, documenting my inner and outer visions, sleeping on a straw bed in an abandoned lighthouse, cooking on a dung-fueled fire—until I ran out of the dried food I'd brought to last me. Then I had to hail a passing fisherman to take me to the nearby bigger island, Culebra. Still, the idea of becoming part of Will's complicated family scene challenged me in a deeper, more visceral way than any vagabonding I'd ever done.

At the time of Will's call, I had other options: several romantic possibilities, a lucrative and rewarding garden-design business, and many close and supportive friends in the Hamptons. Yet I couldn't help myself; I had to meet this man with the photo's disarming grin and the ultra-honest gusto in his phone-distant voice. Especially, I chuckled, after noting how much he resembled Apollo in the snapshot, rather than Quasimodo. I flew to Florida as soon as I could get a weekend free from Lyme ticks, prevalent everywhere as I worked my garden-tending business in the deer-populated Hamptons.

▲

As anxious as a schoolgirl on a first date, my body shivering, I immediately singled out Will at the Sarasota airport. He was the tall, movie-star handsome, incandescent-teeth grinning guy standing in the back line of awaiting arrivals. Feeling faint from the firecrackers exploding inside, I could barely stand. My face felt ready to peel off from the stretch of my jaw-splitting glee.

I gave him a polite peck on the cheek but wanted to throw him on the floor and ravage him right then and there among the crowd of airport gawkers.

Later, at the hotel, he insisted on paying for my room with, "The last hundred dollars I have to my name." I thought it chivalrous but odd, wondering at a forty-year-old's lack of credit cards, even in this pre-bitcoin, pre-social media era, the early '90s.

Will arrived at my room the next morning with fresh wholesome bread that he slaughtered with an oversized, serrated hunting knife, and then spread with peanut butter, which I dipped in the strong coffee he brought. He knew my preference because as he left me the night before he'd asked, "What's your favorite breakfast?"

The night before I'd been bitterly disappointed. Eager to jump his bones, I'd hinted about my readiness to snuggle, but Will astounded me by calmly stating, "I've given a promise of celibacy to Jesus. No more premarital sex for me. With kids now, I've got to stop making dumb choices. No offense." Then he left. I was shocked and disappointed beyond words.

His pronouncement, never mentioned during the intimate subjects we'd touched on in our phone calls, made me nervous beyond my initial disappointment. I couldn't help being suspicious. Memories of my heartbreak over another man who'd turned away from me, poked my heart. Too bad Will's gay, I thought, and not the first time I mistook a guy for straight. So why the big macho act, if he's celibate? I wondered. Bluntly dismissing him didn't set right with me either. He hadn't been dishonest, not exactly; the subject of sex just never came up. So at breakfast I asked a slew of questions about Will's motive for abstinence. My fears of being ripped-off and feeling more than a little horny were soon assuaged.

"Jumping into bed with women hasn't worked out so well for me," he clarified.

He better not be tricking me, I thought. Okay, sure, I knew he was a committed Christian. We'd talked *about that* many times during our lengthy phone conversations. But I never thought his religion would be *that* much of a big deal until, here in the flesh, Will was saying no to my sultry advances. Nothing budged him. I started to tease him, saying he was afraid. He kept saying he'd promised Jesus. I kept nagging him with, C'mon, furgettabout it. Ol' JC would approve. But Will didn't buy it.

How could this be happening? Didn't he claim to be a red-blooded American male? I could not stop wondering—because I'd been tricked like this before—if he was playing me the fool. I cringed at the thought of another sexual ambush by one more closeted, untrue-to-himself homosexual. The last time had been too painful. Oh God, please don't make him gay or bi, I prayed. Been there, done that.

Sure, there'd been plenty of mixed signals before in my serial-relationship past. But Will didn't seem like the kind of guy who'd lead me on, so I decided I'd go along with whatever this was. Let the God-energy, as the Teacher defined Aum—flow. And then watch, observe, and witness where Aum was taking me. The Teacher constantly reminded her students, "Let your own Better-me, the Aum-within, be your inner guide." Okay, I figured I'd wait to see how the flow of no-sex went with this hunk, who didn't want to make love even though I was more than ready. Abstinence: was it a bad omen, or common sense?

This time, with this man, everything was different. I tried consoling myself, reasoning, why rush? Too-early sex does complicate things. Will might be smarter than I in this regard. Nonetheless, be wary, I reminded my inner teacher, fondly called by the Teacher, "your Better-me."

"I'll be mad if you're playing with me, Will," I half-jokingly warned him, intending to be honest and real as he appeared to be. "You say Jesus wants you not to make love to me, but I don't hear anybody saying that. I respect you, though. I'm curious to see what's up with you."

"I swear, teZ, I've never done this before," he said. "I just don't want to mess it up between us. Please understand why I have to go slow. I have to make sure my kids aren't going to get hurt again. Make sure I don't get hurt."

"And me too," I said.

"Yeah, of course."

▲

Will had already told me that when "Jesus came" for him, he had to put away his beer-swilling, pot-smoking, self-sabotaging ways. After getting dunked in a backwoods gator pond by a man he fondly called Preacher Joe, Will was instantly saved, by gum, and became a devout born-again believer. My eyes rolled when I heard that fundamental crap, always a hard pill for me to swallow. But to each their own, right? Will said he'd started off as I had, a church-going kid. But unlike me, whose father was agnostic and mother, a by-the-book Catholic, he was raised by all-embracing, open-minded parents known in the parlance as mystical Christians.

After life kicked Will around a bit, he "got touched by the Holy Spirit," as he described it. "That's how I got saved and decided to stop turning my back on God. I decided it was time to change from my dark meandering ways and return to God's light, like my folks had shown me how, as a kid."

After getting an education, Will did his share of adventuring before marrying gun-totin', gum-chewin' wannabe-cowgirl Debby. Two years later his first baby, a daughter, Kara was born. Unlike Will, Debby never stopped using booze and drugs at that point. Maybe it was timely, since he was forced to solely care for the kids, but that's when Will said he "got struck by Spirit." Being born-again was just as drastic a change as all the other metamorphoses Will had undergone: from college football hero to crew on a tug, from filmmaker to—what he was when we met—a stay-at-home, working-dad who was also a *full-time mom*, long before that gender-switch became commonplace for manly men such as Will.

Working as a well-paid freelance broker of airplane parts from his home deep in the woods, Will exchanged making movies and guzzling beer by the case and puffing weed every day for studying *The Word*, which Debby, he said, was allergic to. Soon after the kids came along Will got dunked in the gator pond and saved by JC. That's when he donned the mandatory blue jeans and crisp polyester western dress-up shirt to sing mellow harmonies with the Horsecreek Nightingales, a peripatetic gospel quartet. Ex-rebel Will, with hair once as long as mine, had the deepest voice of the four-part harmonizing group whose Vietnam-vet leader left his concealed weapon in the parked truck whenever the Levi's-clad men walked into the next isolated country church to praise the Lord. While Will's passion was singing gospel, the divine preference of his no-God spouse escalated to the uncontrolled use of dangerous illegal substances, in addition to the uninterrupted, ever-present can of Pabst Blue Ribbon clenched in her hand. But it was Debby who filed for divorce, Will said, figuring her now returned-to-the-flock, Bible-quoting husband never would. And she was probably right. However it happened, divorce was inevitable from day one with this unlikely pair. But not before Jonny, their second offspring, joined us as an addicted-to-crank infant when he was born into this crazy mixed-up world.

▲

A few weekends after my trip to Sarasota, Will visited me in East Hampton. He flew into Long Island's MacArthur Airport looking like Indiana Jones' cousin, more ruggedly handsome that ever in well-worn butt-tight fatigues and nearly-rotten running shoes, more pumped-athletic than any limp-wrist metrosexual ever spied in Sag Harbor or Amagansett. He had another of those rare hundred-dollar bills in his pocket, amassed for mad money since we'd last seen each other, he said, laughing at his current, and not unfamiliar state of miserable poverty. I gathered his budget was as tight as mine and this made me even more glad that we'd found each other, being on equal ground like we were, financially, that is.

The energy between us sparked and sizzled inside my body as heady, fragrantly sweet smells from Will's sturdy, healthy body made me swoon. My knees went weak again. Listening to his sexy Ss slide from his mouth every time he spoke, resonated a mellow gong in my gut. Whenever he mentioned his love for Jesus, I determined to receive his declarations without judgment, because his sentiments were the same as I felt about Aum, my HP, so I rationalized we shared the same level of beliefs, we just used different names. To me, the essence of Aum is the same as Jesus—the *Oneness* that's God, the Divine, the Sacred, or, as the Teacher told us, "God is spiritual energy, the *Shakti* of life." I had to keep reminding myself: universal consciousness has many names, this one-and-same power, this *One* that has no second. The Great Spirit of the Universe.

From the moment Will and I first spoke that spring day on the phone, we shared what mattered most to both of us: this however-named, sacred side of ordinary life. Neither of us ever felt weird about stating our rousing, mutual anthem: "I love Aum, a.k.a. God," I'd say; "I love Jesus," he'd agree.

"To be clear," I further explained, "and for the record, Will, besides Spirit I also love art, good strong art, as much as other kinds of fanatics I know who love politics, say, or sports." I didn't mention religious fanatics because obviously I didn't want to offend Will.

"Me too," Will chuckled. "I was raised on the most far-out spiritual art by my religious mother, who makes kick-ass big metal sculpture. You'll see for yourself."

Even more so, I was hooked. Intrigued would be a modest word for how I felt.

Whether it was a shared fascination for all things spiritual and artistic, or how we both appreciated learning about other cultures, whenever we talked it always ended with Will and me agreeing that being content with one's chosen path is the highest indicator of a peaceful, God-trusting life. We both enjoyed our simple lives. We ate our plain meals with chopsticks, both of us tickled to have found at least one other person on the planet with whom we could feel utterly compatible, even comfortable.

That night he stayed with me in my rental house in Springs. Feeling like lovers, we held each other tightly in my tiny bed. But no sex, not yet. Will wasn't ready. And I was practicing patience. And hoping—God, I was praying—that he wasn't gay.

CHAPTER 3

at the river

Next visit, it was my turn to travel. Back to Sarasota where Will had rented a motel suite and brought his kids to play on the sublimely white sandy beach. "I'll introduce you to them as my friend," he winked. I was cool with that.

We'd been talking on the phone every day for more than two months. I'd shared most of my secrets and thought he was doing the same. No inordinate mention of swishy men friends. I admired him in so many ways. What modern guy, hip from all appearances, could so easily admit to a prudish promise like he'd made to Jesus? Whenever we spoke of what life meant to us, we had the same inner feelings, even though we used different words to express them.

Here was a man who intimately knew and loved Great Spirit, as I did. Calling that power by the name Jesus of Nazareth, just as I had when I grew up in my non-traditional Christian home, was familiar to me. Mom had been excommunicated by the Catholic Church for marrying Dad, an agnostic former Protestant. But by the time alcoholism ruled him, my father was suspicious of all organized religion, period. Having seen my parents accept each other despite their differences regarding the God-thing, I certainly could live with Will's and my not-nearly-so-wide preferences. I certainly wasn't going to let our other disparities—in family backgrounds, embracing politics or having none in particular, being a former sex-addict or presently having no sex, being the black sheep of a respectable wealthy family or the broke artist bum of my bourgeois and peasantry lineage, in addition to the dubious chasm between self-proclaiming to be a spiritual or a born-again person—no, I couldn't let the purely circumstantial differences we had, stop me from getting to know this man, unlike anyone I'd ever met.

When I arrived by taxi from the Sarasota airport, I let myself into where Will had told me to go. I found the Siesta Key palm-fanned motel suite, changed into a bathing suit, and headed to where he said he and his kids would be on the beach. Agile and built like the ballplayer he'd always been, from far away I saw tall lean Will playing catch with two sunny-headed shrimps, the three of them a unit, laughing and chasing a beach ball.

"Hi," I casually said, joining them as if this happened every day of the week. I gave Will a quick hug hello, knowing his kids were eyeing me, sussing me out as kids do. Kara, the oldest, a slender and confident five-year-old as pretty as she was extroverted, burst into a radiant smile at the sight of me, her eyes widening with wonder. She had the distinct, tight little form of an athlete-to-be. Every move she made was filled with determination. Kara came right up to me and firmly, happily shook my hand. When I leaned over to look into her sea-clear hazel eyes, she asked if I wanted to go in the water with her. "Sure," I said, "soon as I meet your brother."

Jonny peered from behind Will's wide calves, an elf hiding behind his tall fortress. A two-year-old, with a head as big as a bowling ball, his deep brown eyes were as wide as the unobstructed azure sky. Slim like his feisty sister, Jonny was very much a mini-man already, his barrel body proclaiming double-muscles that would one day arrive. He looked down at the sand instead of up at me, sneaking peeks when he thought I wasn't looking. I sensed his need for closeness to his dad, with no one else interfering.

"Hi Jonny," I said, getting down on my knees, "I'm your dad's friend from up north. Isn't this a nice beach?"

Will urged his son out from behind him. Jonny sort-of nodded his head in response and took another unwilling peek my way. Wanting to relieve his uneasiness, I laughed and jumped up from the sand and ran off to catch up with Kara, who was shouting for me at the water's edge. She and I splashed in the waves, made a larger-than-life sand sculpture of a lady's face with loose long curls, then threw a blow-up ball around. I looked over and saw Jonny watching, sticking close to Will, unsure about me, tossing a midget football with his giant dad.

After we returned to the motel, the kids were covered with the powdered-sugar textured sand. At bath-time I asked, Can I help? Have at 'er, Will said. Without planning it, I ended up doing the most intimate act a person can do when just meeting youngsters. I knelt beside the tub watching Kara and Jonny roll and tumble around the sudsy water with their slippery eel-like bodies, sliding right out of my soapy grasp when I tried to join the playing around; me outside the tub, them inside, all three of us wriggly-slick and giggling. We did way more playing than washing, but who cared? Soon, I was nearly as wet as they and even Jonny was laughing and enjoying himself as much as his sister and I were.

Naked Kara climbed into my lap as I sat on the bathroom floor. I toweled off her squirming body. Her soft arms around my neck hugged me hard. She had become a warm loving doll come to life in my embrace, so receptive to my offer of care. Wordlessly she expressed her need to be held, looking deeply, so deeply into my eyes, checking to see if I was the real deal. But as soon as Jonny got out of the tub, he ran gleefully damp and nude to find his dad, who was whipping up good old spaghetti, the kids' favorite fare.

Back in the bedroom as Kara briskly dressed, I watched Jonny hop-and-wiggle pour himself into the tiniest pair of blue jeans I'd ever seen. Alone, I joined Will in the kitchenette where he put down the tasting spoon and grabbed me, bringing me close in his strong, open-hearted embrace. Warmed by a day in the sun, his kiss tasted sea-salty, a wee tomato-y, too. He hadn't bathed yet, either. "Maybe we'll grow on you, huh?"

"Maybe," I said.

Kara rushed into the room then and eyed us without suspicion. Will and I immediately let go of each other, having agreed ahead of time to not give the kids any indication of our true feelings. Kara sat her sassy self on one of the chairs around the Formica-topped table, and looked up at me, smiling brightly.

"I saw you in my dream last night, teZa," she matter-of-factly proclaimed.

That made me skip a breath. "Hope it was a good dream," I said.

Not entirely surprised to find the shining aura I sensed around Kara to be her clairvoyance, I remembered meeting another indigo child once before. I found younger kids to be way more open to the bizarre, the amazing, the unseen, and the irrational.

"Yes, you were with some lady wearing a long white dress, who had a red dot on her forehead, right here," Kara said, pointing between her eyebrows.

My legs suddenly went weak. So I sat down. Kara got off her chair and came to sit on my lap again, as if this was the most ordinary thing and she'd been doing it all her life.

"You and this nice lady were just standing there, smiling at me, telling me a funny story. She was real pretty."

From her description, this person was no mystery to me. "That's my meditation teacher, Kara. She's helping me understand how we're all connected to one another by God's energy."

"Does she have short black hair, like this?" Kara indicated close-fitting hair ending above her ears.

"Yes, she does."

"Does her smile and her eyes and her skin sparkle an awful lot?"

"Yes, they do."

"I bet that was her."

Kara then gave her full attention to the plate of steaming noodles Will had placed before her. Cowboy-costumed Jonny roared into the room just then, wearing the world's smallest ten-gallon hat. He hopped onto his chair as if it were a bronco. I smiled at him but the savory meal outbid my attention. Well trained, both kids waited for Will to offer a short "praise and thanks to Jesus" prayer.

My family had blessed our food at mealtime too, my soulful dad always loving to pray. The way Will addressed JC was not much different from the way I thank Great Spirit and bless each meal I eat, something my recovery-friend Jane had reintroduced to me. As long as he doesn't force his beliefs onto me, I'm cool, I thought. He'd tried that once already, in an earlier conversation, before we'd met face to face.

"When you're ready," he'd casually said to me on the phone weeks earlier. "Jesus will come for you."

"Whoa, hold on there!" I protested. "You'd best keep those opinions to yourself, Will, if we're going to have any chance of getting to know each other. Fair enough?"

"Sure, fair enough," he laughed, brushing off my concern.

I sat at the crowded dinette inside that economy beachside motel in Sarasota, and couldn't help but think how strange this was for me—a committed bachelorette, adventurer, and spiritual warrior—being with a real family again. Even more shocking, as I tasted the tangy tomato sauce, was my idea—maybe—of joining it. Perhaps.

Not that long before, I was obsessed with exploring islands in the Caribbean. That decade of going everywhere I pleased, sometimes invited, other times just showing up, running as far from materialism as I could, had been my chosen career path. Sometimes I journeyed cheaply on native cargo vessels or on a mail boat, other times I hitchhiked between islands on someone's private boat or plane. There were never any hassles with crossing borders back then, as long as I had my passport. Having little or no money never stopped me, that's for sure. I carried art supplies with me so whenever I needed to make some cash. I'd set up shop in a hotel lobby and whip out fifteen-minute, twenty-dollar lifelike portraits for the tourists. Or find a boat yard where I could layer some fancy varnish on a yacht's fine wooden spars, or paint its name on the stern. I always managed to make enough to get by, always had enough to eat. I never worried about money. I owned one nice dress, a few changes of work clothes, and one good sturdy bikini. What else did a vagabond like me need anyway?

Yet here was off-the-grid me—back in nothing-special middle America, sitting in a starkly no-frills, neon-lit motel, surrounded by pitted ugly linoleum floors and threadbare furnishings. Was I insane? Thinking of signing on for this next life-cruise—joining Will's family? Yet here I was, seriously contemplating it.

Getting an affordable two-bedroom kitchenette for the weekend, located right on Siesta Key's million-dollar beach, was a minor miracle as far as Will, still heavily in debt, was concerned. Slurping my plate of spaghetti, I looked at his two ToysЯus towheads. How can I seriously consider joining this tight-knit unit, this family of a smart-sexy-spiritual man I'd not even made love to yet? How insane am I? I thought. How can I possibly think any kind of family life could fit well with me, after my earlier life's catastrophic history, when I was a confirmed runaway, a bona fide wild-child, unfit to be included in any family anywhere, or so I had felt.

In sobriety, everything was different. Now I only wished to follow HP's advice, the voice of my years-trained Better-me. I've always wished for my mind to be as expanded as possible, yet admittedly, I knew I wasn't exactly ground-zero normal. A family? Me? How many other family-type humans are obsessed about becoming enlightened? Still, five years sober was a major achievement, I proudly remembered. Not that I ever wanted to be ordinary in any way, never! Because losing my edge—as either artist or plain old sad-faced clown—I considered deadly for rational thinking. Avoiding normalcy, I always considered mandatory for the caliber of shock art I strove to make.

I looked around me, at Will and the kids eating their dinner, and smiled. The truth was—I couldn't think of any other place I'd rather be just then. Right here, sitting next to this man who titillated and intrigued me to no end.

Will was attentive to his kids in a way I'd never seen any man be before. I hadn't a clue where things were going with him, with us, but already knew I'd kick myself forever if I didn't follow my heart and check him out.

△

Enjoy the moment, I coaxed my reluctant self. Include yourself in this warm, loving family. My own family never felt this real, this welcoming. My father's decline into alcoholism inflicted fear and pain on me in childhood, leaving scant memories to cherish other than the day he embraced sobriety, as I did myself, just days before meeting the Teacher. Sobriety and spiritual disciplines had been the main focus in my life for years since then.

I didn't know if Will was *The One* for me or not. All I knew was my gut said: "Stick around to see where this adventure takes you." I certainly didn't believe of him, not for a second, that he *only believed in Jesus*, like he appeared wanting others to believe. Whenever it came up he assured me he agreed with me, that "We're all sons and daughters of God, not just JC." What I did know, as sure as I felt the satisfaction of his simple pasta meal before me, was how great a real desire to know Spirit this man had, and how creative and smart he was. Weeks before, I'd admired his artistry when some friends and I viewed the feature film he'd made, which he sent me right after his photo arrived. From his surreal yet down-to-earth imaginative film, I recognized how sensitive his soul was.

△

The surrealistic feature he'd made just before marrying Debby was a major accomplishment, even if "The Enchanted" did empty his bank account. He'd made shorts before this full-length movie. One of them, a documentary about an Egyptian expedition looking for proof of the prophecy that famed psychic, Edgar Cayce, in a trance had declared the so-called *Hall of Records* lay hidden beneath the Sphinx—pretty bizarre stuff, if not downright metaphysically mystical. The Egyptian government actually gave permission, Will ascertained, for this radical investigation by the Cayce group. Another of Will's film projects was photographing a trip to Bimini for the same group of esoteric explorers as the Egyptian pyramid film, this time though, they were searching for proof, some kind of underwater remnants of the lost city of Atlantis. From his eccentric art projects alone, I knew this man Will was anything but straight-laced despite his current suburban role of responsible single parent and hard-working salesman.

Before his mid-life return to religion, Will had been a bearded, longhaired, pot smoking, out-there alternative type. Although his current appearance was clean-cut, his chameleon-like, middle-America lifestyle was only of the moment, I knew deep down. Plus, he'd assured me of this fact from our very first phone chat. But still, calling himself born-again and all that goes along with that fervent label, was incongruent to his previously unconventional, quasi-barbaric character, the edgy mystic one that majorly appealed to rough-and-tough, edgy-arty me. The Will I sensed in my gut, who I was sure he really was, was not the *now-saved* goody-two-shoes, joyously saying "God Bless you!" to everyone he casually met, from gals in the 7-Eleven to other businessmen after a first-time handshake.

I sensed this outspoken display of God's blessings originated in Will from the same source as mine every time I bowed and said "Namaste": wanting to proclaim an affiliation to our respective tribes. His choice was now, to me at least, the ultra-religious types who wanted assurance they'd be going to heaven after death. My circle was mostly recovering addicts, Higher Power/spiritual types who'd already been to hell, so they knew "Getting sober's as good as heaven gets here on earth."

But heck, I thought, anyone who has kids has to get it together! I decided to cut him some slack. What did I know about straight except having run from my own folks' version of square as fast, as far as I could? And up till now, I'd never had to care for anything else alive but a few cats and dogs here and there, some chickens, a few boats; a lover or two, not too simultaneously. That's about it.

I decided I wasn't going to bail out on Will just because I didn't know the first thing about staying-put, kid-rearing, or home-making. Other than what my own folks had been, which I'd revolted against since day two of my own upbringing. I decided to sit back, enjoy the ride and see where my heart wanted to take me. Go with the flow, as the Teacher always reminded us, her students. I'd relax and stop analyzing, allow myself to get to know this man better, and see if Will and I were as good a fit as my gut kept urging. This required an enormous leap of faith for me. After a lifetime spent running from *domestic bliss* whenever it loomed too close to my orb, a concept as foreign to me as a trip to Mars, I caught myself wondering and smiling every time I thought, *Will's complex, broken family could be my life's next great adventure.*

Right then I started picturing how it'd be. I imagined joining Will's blended *circus troupe* as if I were taking a journey down *Rio Blisso*, an unknown mythical river (purposefully invented by me to be gently winding and always breezy tropical-warm in temperature) that would carry us, me with my new family—leading me trustingly, blindly—to a higher state, one I've always wanted to sustain, not just experience now and then.

Life was sending me a message. The image of this journey beckoning me became my next obsession. With each breath, I felt being there, with him, with his kids, was right where I ought to be. Thanks to the intense inner work I'd been doing in the past years with the Teacher—my mind was open to what before had insistently been shut out. With my rational mind, I may not have understood my attraction to Will, his unconventional quirkiness so pleasing to me who's always craved weird. But I couldn't deny how I felt so drawn to him. Not only did I find Will devastatingly attractive, his voice hypnotically sensual but his intellect excited me, and his clown antics made me roar with wild abandon. I've always been a sucker for a good belly laugh.

By the end of this first meal with his sweet offspring, I'd decided to stick around. Being stepmom to two endearing love monkeys such as Jonny and Kara just might be fun, I thought.

While Will got the kids snug in their beds, I tidied up the kitchen. Through the open window of the motel I felt a warm wave of beach salt-air caress my face. Silently, I promised to stop being resistant about joining this family.

From here on, I vowed to myself, I'd think of our story as an allegory, with our future family of four playing the role of crew aboard a sailboat traveling down this Rio Blisso I'd invented that I felt so strongly calling out for me to explore. Suddenly the thought of living in, instead of speaking and wishing for, love—being willing to sacrifice my own desires to nurture a family and still continue to nurture myself—felt like my best shot at real happiness. Such a novel and unexpected concept instantly brought me ... a profound sense of peace.

For now, knowing Will had had an equally adventuresome past—look how he'd willingly given up being a moviemaker, a traveling explorer, a gadabout, a womanizer, to live a more ordinary, simple kid-raising life—made me want to join his love-boat crew immediately, as co-captain. This man had forfeited the risky, financial insecurity of filmmaking for earning a steady income selling airplane parts, just so he could care for his *young'uns*, as he called Kara and Jonny. Now maybe it was my turn to be a responsible adult. I was curious to see if I was capable of the same kind of outrageous sacrifice and transformation as this barbarian-turned-papa, whose delicious kisses were promises of something deeper to come.

△

As soon as I returned to East Hampton, I wrote the Teacher and asked if she thought it wise for a student of Eastern mysticism, like I was, to even consider marrying a self-described "hard-core Baptist-redneck, former-communist knucklehead," as Will sarcastically spoke of his current leanings. Could two people sustain love, I asked her, coming from such opposing worldviews—he, now ultra-religious and politically conservative after an anti-establishment youth; and me, a lover of Aum, devotee of Nature, a former novice shaman, whose personal beliefs had evolved to steadfastly being anti-politics, anti-religion, anti-artificial high, anti-fanatic anything, especially anti-separation of any sorts? Could we two, in other words, so different yet both of us true lovers of God, make it together?

I licked shut, stamped, and mailed the envelope to the ashram in Vermont where I'd just been on a two-week retreat. I decided not to make any final decisions concerning my future with Will and his kids until I heard back from this wise teacher who guided so many.

△

Will and I agreed to take it slow, real slow. I think I scared him with my enthusiasm to marry. Both our track records were burdened with horrendously bad romantic choices.

Just as I had foolishly married before, on pure whimsy, when I was very young, Will had married the first woman who came along after his breakup with the film's co-producer, just as he faced the dismal reception of his feature. Immediately after the hasty marriage came the birth of their two children, during which time he discovered the true extent of Debby's limitations; the most obvious being her inability to act as a responsible parent. Still raw from his marital failure when we met, Will figured his shit-detector was permanently screwed up, with Debby just the most recent of a string of partners he'd had who'd blown his mind by ending up hating his guts.

"Just possibly, I attract women who really don't like me after all," he said, his words suspiciously implying I might be the next Will-hater to come his way.

I was less worried about repeating any previous mistakes. Sober, aware and awake, which I hadn't been since a teenager, I was discovering that all that hard inner-work I'd done with the Teacher was starting to pay off, happiness-wise. My thinking had been re-trained through commitment and vigilant discipline. No longer did I think of myself as the victim of a curse, or bad-luck circumstances, as I once thought I'd been condemned to. Unhappiness and misery were no longer my constant companions. Now I was the co-creator of my life. I was a believer now: As I think, so life is.

Now meditation and mind-stilling, constant mantra repetition were my faithful companions. These daily yogic practices, the Teacher said, "strengthen the soul and expand the mind." I was a dedicated yogini, studying Vedic and Kashmir Shaivism scripture along with continuing to practice, as I had since eighteen-years-old, hatha yoga's asanas when I'd found that took care of my scoliosis pain, and my body's racehorse-like, high-strung physical demands best of all.

By the time Will had made that fateful phone call to me on the vernal equinox, I'd become pretty adept at seeing my own part, not only in my previous failed relationships, but in every new one. What concerned me most, truthfully, was whether I had the courage to live in Will's lackluster, so far appearing lack-everything, hometown. I imagined my response, explaining to people who'd ask, "Why on earth did you move there?"—as what I was honestly considering: "To be a mail-order bride." I was head over heels with this sleeping giant of mine (*sleeping* because I knew he wasn't my kind of *awake*), but what confused me most was this: Could love alone entice me to move to a barren black-hole wasteland, as I felt his hometown to be when I visited?

When I went to see him in Lackland, an hour's drive from Tampa, I was walking around a grocery store, placing cheese, fruit, and a long skinny baguette into a wire basket hung on my arm, when an overzealous man startled me by rushing up and saying with unnerving volume and rude urgency: "You're from France, aren't you!?"

I laughed out loud at such whacky audacity. The idea of being taken for a European shopper at the Piggly-Wiggly mega-food chain there in slow-drawl central Florida, was ludicrous. Later though, this incident would be one of a number of signs I'd noticed, but chose to discount, until the day when I fully realized just how alien I appeared to *Lacklanders*: more as a time-warp lark, a foreign and strange-looking, extra-tall, henna-haired woman from someplace like, okay why not? far-off France.

Despite my reservations, when I visited Will's homey scene, it surprised me even more how completely captivated I was, and how inviting this suburban American family was to my taste. Jonny— sturdy in his size minus-three jeans and doll-sized cowboy boots and, of course, the wide-brimmed cow poker's hat—clutched a dull butter knife in his little mitt and challenged me, "Wanna go huntin'?" Kara greeted me in a well-worn dirty-pink tutu with black leotard and tights. She was back from dance class, preposterously pretty, hilariously funny, and energized enough to execute an oblique series of pirouettes. She then rushed to a corner to make more paintings of smiling snails depicted in every imaginable context—racing snails, dancing snails, book-reading goofy snails. Standing a head taller than her brother, she enjoyed bossing him around, never imagining that one day she might be getting something back for her insufferable, constant teasing of him. While Kara wanted to be perfect at everything she tried, Jonny was more interested in greeting the pizza delivery guy with a lavish show of delightful appreciation, handing the startled deliverer each time a small token, one of the boy's own miniature toys perhaps, every Friday night when the doorbell rang promptly at dinnertime at Will's.

Returned home to East Hampton after my second visit to Lackland, I had a serious talk with the deliberating redhead I saw back in the mirror.

"His kids are part of him, teZ. To love Will means an opportunity to face what once was your childhood dream—to help the world become a better place. Only here it's gonna be one person, a man and two kids altogether. Loving this family-man means you'll have to be brave enough, strong enough, to give up your self-centered obsession about freedom. Because that's what it'll take to help him repair his broken-winged, broken-hearted children, who are part of him. You'd better figure this one out quickly because I have a funny feeling that once lovemaking with Will enters the picture, you won't be able to think straight."

If I agreed to be Will's woman, I knew I'd have to step up and become the Better-me that deep-down I recognized I'd always wanted to be, way before the Teacher I'd chosen began to show me how. I knew it'd be worth the work, this family stuff. In a family, I'd have to apply everything the Teacher had been reminding all us students how to circumvent the rackety-roo tricks of our devious monkey-mind, and live in the stillness of our inner Self that tells us, shows us, clearly, that we are all One.

I smiled, hearing once again the mysterious words the Teacher uses to explain, an oft-repeated teaching I still was not sure I entirely understood. She says: "Within all of us is a Better-me, that part of ourselves that is connected to Universal Consciousness, the *One* that has no second. We are all a part of God, and God is part of All. God lives within us, as us."

Every time I get still and meditate—I experience Oneness. In that pristine clarity all conflict, all negative emotion, all separateness disappears and gets reclassified as unnecessary, trivia, not-truth. Problems become simply delusional. Meditating for an hour or an instant, or for one breath's length: Truth becomes clear when it becomes one's experience. Having always believed that angels are really humans showing our best sides, displaying our best, most untainted selves—able to see God in ourselves and in each other—I looked deeper into my dark-chocolate eyes in the mirror.

"The only way I can possibly pull this off," I said aloud to my image, "the challenge of being a wife and Kara and Jonny's stepmom, knowing I'll be in direct opposition to their bio-mom, Debby—is to approach this new role Will is dangling before me, as if I were some kind of angel-stepmom.

Hmmm, I thought, being an *Angel Mom* doesn't seem that impossible. I know it will take a lot of practice. Like learning to fly, for creatures not accustomed to soaring with the wind. Even fledgling birds leaving the nest have to learn. I've always wanted to learn to fly. My earliest dreams showed me, once, that I could soar high, just by willing it so. I can do this too, if I choose to, I said to my reflection.

Off in a distant memory, I heard the favorite old-time hymn my mother used to sing quietly to me as I lay in bed. It always brightened me up whenever I needed to calm down and fall asleep. I heard my mom's far-off voice singing:

> *Shall we gather at the river*
> *Where bright angel feet have trod*
> *With its crystal tide forever*
> *Flowing by the throne of God*

CHAPTER 4

together we plot the course

At another hidden seaside resort on Florida's Gulf Coast, we rented a room a stone's throw from the beach. Lounging in bed together, Will and I listened to the gentle surf lapping the sandy shore in between gorging on the feast of our bodies' pleasures. Finally, we were quenching our fiery hunger for each other, with longed-for ecstasy that cooled our thirst, lovemaking that began again and again, lasting all night long. Beautiful, excruciating, exquisite bliss with our silky-smooth, sweaty bodies. Tapping shared aromas and numbing delights, having light bouts of intertwined sleep, both of us silently awakening, questioning, receptive—to stare in disbelief at the other, still peacefully half asleep. At last, the predawn pewter of another day nudged us awake, with even more reason to enjoy being alive. Love greeting Love, recognizing each other, eye-to-eye, mouth-to-mouth, legs, arms, hair and juices tangled, our bodies claiming each other long after our hearts and heads had.

As much as I'd anticipated our yearned-for sensual tango, I couldn't have expected such cataclysmic explosions that burst kaleidoscope-brilliant in my head, when that day arrived. I couldn't help myself; I screamed, I cried in pleasure; soft moans and loud purring rippled from my throat. Sighs heaved my ribcage while delirious tears streamed my cheeks and neck when Will's primordial lust stroked my yearning to be One. In perfect synch, I joined him when I saw his rapture ready to burst like a tsunami all over his face. Laughter erupted from both of us in waves, accompanying this wildly anticipated vow-breaking dance of ours. All of Will's body parts fit mine as if perfectly made-to-order, finely fitting in and around and through, joyously riveting our dizzying must-have-more-everything horizontal mambo.

From then on, our bodies were compelled to stick like Velcro whenever we spent time alone. His place, my place, any place, we were delirious on the high of sexing, two thirsty wanderers finding what we'd walked life's lonely desert longing for; and we satiated ourselves till we were near drowned on this life's preferred recipe of 100% pure joy. Blindly, foolishly, whenever the kids weren't around, Will tantalized limits of sensations I'd never dreamed experiencing, this man God had made for me, whom I couldn't get my fill of, and he claimed the same for me.

Cast from the same mold, designed by the same die-maker, our ins and outs perfectly matched. Our physical connection was now welded, melded as strong, if not more so than before by our mutual love of Spirit. "Where have you been all my life?" became our sing-song lamentation of past empty searches, looking for each other in too many other human boobie-traps. The harnessing well of our passions, we finally allowed to flow freely.

There was no stopping us.

Yet how bruising—how freaky and how fickle—that such cosmic ecstasy can so easily flip to fear, or worse.

As soon as I was back in Long Island, Will called. His tone, usually of casual cool was now in an unattractive, annoying panic.

"You're going to kill me, teZ. I'm sorry; I have to warn you. I'm afraid you'll soon be getting an upsetting phone call. It's my crazy ex, Debby. She's done it again. This is as bad as when she came after me with an ax, before she accused me of molesting Kara. You need to take what's coming with a grain of salt."

Even with Will's heads-up I wasn't in the slightest bit prepared for the knockdown that the call from the State of Florida Children's Welfare Agency soon brought. A male's monotone, official voice started off with polite southern formality as I answered his call.

"Please don't take what I have to ask you personally, ma'am. This is simply procedure. Sorry, ma'am, but I'm afraid you have to answer every one of these questions I legally have to ask."

"I understand," I said weakly, wishing to awaken from this nightmare.

"Our department has to respond to each and every complaint, even those we know are false, as this one obviously is," he said, his candor surprising me. "We recognized the voice of the anonymous female caller who reported that you abused the two-year-old boy named Jonny, the son of a man named Will ____; you know who I'm talking about?"

"Yes, I know Jonny, and his dad. What do you mean by abuse?" I felt my heart pounding.

"The caller claims you gave the boy drugs with a hypodermic needle; then the report says, ah, that you sodomized him and, er—before or after, she wasn't clear when—you performed devil worship, said some unintelligible words, tortured and sacrificed a dog in front of him and his five-year-old sister, Kara."

"What!" I heard myself shout. "Their father and I are just dating, for God's sake! This is a sick joke! Is this coming from Will's ex, Debby?"

"We know who made the call, yes ma'am, but I'm not at liberty to give you a name. The caller told us crystals, incense, and black magical incantations were involved in the abuse as well, I'm seeing here on my form."

"Good grief," I croaked. Silently, I figured the kids must have told their mother about the amethyst necklace I wore, the one my friend Jane gave me years before, an amulet to protect against addiction to inebriants. And they probably heard me softly repeating my Sanskrit mantra, part of my daily meditation routine. They must have told their mother. And no doubt she mountain-size awful-ized what they'd innocently told her.

The silence on the phone was as large as the arrow that pierced my heart, my soul's altar.

"What horrible things to say about me," I whispered. "It's pathetic."

The man cleared his throat and continued.

"Yes, pretty gruesome stuff she's called in," he said. "Very sorry to have to drag you into this, ma'am. I guess she doesn't know we can now punch onto our phones' keypad, *Star 69*, to identify the last caller's number [this happened just before *caller ID*]. Now we can prove it was she who made this call. We didn't have this feature before, when she made those other calls. Besides, the entire office knows her voice by now. Her reports of the husband's alleged abuse got so thick around here during their custody battle that everyone recognizes her. We have her on tape. By law, of course, everyone is entitled to their opinion, but false reports are illegal. Now, with your involvement, we have proof of her harassment, so we'll warn her: no more calls. Unless you want to make charges against her yourself."

"No, no, I don't want to make any trouble," I insisted.

"That's your right, ma'am. She's phoned in similar sex stuff before, about her ex-husband, but every one of her reports turned out to be untrue after we investigated and the judge ruled against her. She can't make any more crank calls after today or we'll charge her. I still had to follow up though. Sorry for the inconvenience. Paperwork, ma'am. We're required by law to investigate."

"I understand."

"So then," he cleared his throat, "are any of the above statements I've read true?"

"Absolutely not," I said. "Except I happen to own a crystal necklace and sometimes I do softly sing in Sanskrit and occasionally use incense. Everything else is completely off-the-wall insanity."

The official, eager as I was to be off the line, rushed through a few more questions to complete his forms. "It's required," he repeated, apologizing again before ending the saddest phone call of my life.

△

As I hung up, hot lead poison of feeling violated seeped through my veins.

Even though Will and I knew, as the agency now knew as well, that these were all lies—I felt as if my person, my integrity, my life, had been raped.

I paced my East Hampton living room. Outside a chilly rain was falling, adding to the dreariness of the day. My shock soured to disgust, then rage. My head exploded and my guts burned. I wanted to run as far as possible from this insanity, from this repeat of my own messed-up, tormented, abusive childhood I thought I'd escaped forever. My mind was rudely thrust back into the nightmare of my father's booze-fueled cruelty. Suddenly, all the stark horror of his drunken misbehaviors—they were sitting, smirking, right in front of me, present again. The old demons began to whip my mind back into a child's fear-filled tunnel of terror; the old out-of-control forest fire of guilt and shame spread through my soul in five directions at once. A young child's innocence betrayed: mine. Now Kara and Jonny's, too. I could hear my dad's pitiful pleas of begging forgiveness that came as soon as he sobered up. Now I felt the return of confusion around love and parents and trust, things which I thought I'd fled from ages ago all colliding, T-boning my consciousness. My stomach buckled. Breath came in ragged gasps. Happiness? There's no such thing, I shouted silently. Happiness sucks!

"How fucking unfair; how cruel!" I yelled to no one in my empty house.

To have the same insanity, the same sexual depravity of a parent, this unwanted replay of abuse I'd suffered as an innocent child, brought full-circle so close to me, so eerily, creepily, by Will's vengeful, mind-sick, depraved ex. Whom I'd never even met! Accusing me who never hurt anyone, certainly not a child or any animal, accused of such evil. It was a nightmare! My spirit lay in a heap, assassinated. My chest heaved in sorrow.

Will's and my pure love was now forever tainted, enmeshed as it suddenly was with this skin-squirming replay of other people's sins, other's faults, other's ungodliness.

Suddenly, loving Will was way too complicated and much too dangerous for me to consider going one step further. My mind related this fact as if watching a sped-up clip of an actual world disaster—how, as stepmom, I'd forever be mixed-up with this vindictive ex-wife, that I'd never be able to maintain any peace, ever. I would have to be crazy, myself, to continue. I had to turn away from Will, away from his kids, away from that vile psycho moron he'd once mated with. I shuddered thinking of Will and Debby ever having shared such intimacy as baby-making, even fucking. It was too gross. I picked up the phone and called Will.

"Please don't call me anymore!" I commanded. "I can't take this whacked-out drama. Not now, not ever, not after working so hard and so long to rid myself of my own fucked-up demons. There's one too many weirdos in your family. I'm over-dosed on life's painful crap shoots. Maybe I'm too wounded for love, I don't know. There's nothing more to say. Good-bye, Will."

Will sadly said he understood. Then he waited for me to hang up first.

▲

In the days that followed I tried to talk myself out of this great love that no longer felt that great. But after two long weeks of no contact between us, I couldn't help myself; I was an addict, wasn't I? I had to call him. My heart yearned for Will, despite the looming, fearful presence of his kids' obvious nut-case mother. We talked again, and soon we were busy flying back and forth between Long Island and Lackland. I was still scared, but my heart was melting on its own accord. I made plans to move to Sarasota, where coincidentally, I had made some good friends on a previous trip. I was willing to place a bet, a hefty one, on the poker table of fate. My feelings for Will were my royal flush. After almost two months since the false accusations, I decided I was strong enough to handle having a troubled woman, the bio-mom, in the picture. I knew she'd never go away.

Besides, even though my garden design business was booming and I enjoyed working in the fertile soil of Long Island's South Fork, creating live-art with no budget and unlimited plants, ponds and berms, the prevalence of infected ticks had become a threat to every gardener and every kind of outdoorsy worker there. Too many locals had Lyme disease. The move to Sarasota would give me space to decide whether or not to sign onto Will's family's mythical boat I'd invented, and if I were willing to meet all the complications that a journey down Rio Blisso, all of us together, would entail, I now understood things more realistically. I had enough savings to spend months writing that novel I felt bursting from within me, I thought. So, I decided to move, and get one step closer to Will. I was willing to at least try, and that's all I was deciding to do.

Maybe I could coax Will and his kids to join me in Sarasota, away from that boring town of his.

Instead—he and I quickly ran up several speeding tickets apiece rushing the two-hour drive from his place in Lackland to my rental in Sarasota. At a safe distance, I began to slowly take part in more of his and his kids' routine. Our powerful physical magnetism was distracting, but whenever he and I were around the kids we acted like only close friends would, never allowing them to witness anything even remotely more affectionate than fondness between our hot-bodied selves.

△

One day, while visiting Lackland, Kara and Jonny were next door at a birthday party. Taking advantage of the precious couple of hours we had, free of kids, Will and I on-fire-stripped and jumped into the single bed he'd installed in his playroom-like living room for my regular overnight visits from Sarasota. We were in the throes of exuberant lovemaking when suddenly—there was Kara! Standing right next to the bed, silently looking at us with huge glistening green eyes. Thank God, we were under the covers. Zip! We came undone.

Disentangling limbs, I acted unsurprised. Nonchalantly, I extended my arms overhead, saying, "Oh hi, Kara! Your dad and I are doing couples-stretching. This is a two-person lying-down yoga pose we're doing together."

Will sat up, immobile, not able to shift gears like I was. Bopping quickly under the sheet I slipped on panties and blouse I'd grabbed from the floor, then my arms came out on top of the covers and I too sat up in bed. Moving my arms rhythmically up and down, I exhaled, inhaled loudly, counting "one-two, one-two" to add authenticity to my act. Meanwhile, Will hopped out of bed and into his shorts while I distracted Kara with my pretend exercising. Then Will was on his feet. He cleared his throat.

"Sweet pea ... you remember how yoga looks so strange, like that time teZa did it on the beach in Sarasota, how her body got all pretzel-y and tangled up?"

Kara's happy face made big nods, she and Will standing close together now.

"Your dad is really good at this pose, isn't he, Kara?" I said, sliding into my skirt under the sheet as Will pretended he knew what an asana, or any pose for that matter, was.

"teZa's a good yoga teacher, and I'm learning, darlin'," Will added to further our charade.

"That's right," I said, "your dad and I are ...," I now stood up, fully dressed and stretched, to her amazement, in my almost ceiling-high, arms high, tree-pose, "... doing two-person poses."

The girl stared wide-eyed at my strong-oak height. I winked at Will as he tried his best to copy my pose.

"This one keeps us strong and well balanced," I continued.

Kara's smile shone bright like bling, with no trace of concern. "I want to do yoga with you guys, too!" As his little girl attempted to imitate my big girl tree replica, Will quietly left the room.

Like Will, I was a runner too. In the future though, as my knees began to suffer, I upped the ante on my yoga practice, working hard to keep my spine and joints as pain-free as Better-me was keeping my heart-and-mind gates open. Some days I pushed my body harder; other days I needed to rest it. As long as I gave my body as much attention as my mind and spirit, I knew I'd have better chances at enjoying good health. If I didn't pay equal attention to balancing the mind-body-spirit parts—everything would get out of whack. I knew that the closer I got to choosing to become part of Will's family. My always-muscled body would need more maintenance to match the kid-raising energy I'd be expending, I easily foresaw.

The Teacher often said to us: "As spiritual warriors we have to carefully nurture our physical body, the temple of our soul, as well as befriend our unruly mind."

Whenever I visited Lackland, Kara followed me around like a lost puppy finally returned to its rightful companion. She wanted to be wherever I was, doing whatever I did; her delicate little hand holding my oversized one, singing along to one of my yoga chants, or listening to instrumental jazz and world fusion sounds, right beside me. When Will brought the kids along to visit me in Sarasota, I let her mess with my paints, join in with my experimental cooking projects, and ask questions about whatever book I was reading. Her closeness was never intrusive. I loved Kara's curiosity, her playfulness I found as charming as her fanciful snail paintings. Her foxlike spirit was inquisitive, gently prodding yet insistently trusting. I invited her closer and closer into my heart. Unlike his sister though, Jonny kept his distance. Shy and suspicious, totally in love with only Debby, his bio-mom, he crossed his arms over his chest as if shielding himself from feeling connected to anyone not a part of his known world.

Meanwhile, Will and I kept working out our differences, drawing closer to knowing each other. His first Christmas present to me didn't go over so well. You'd think he'd have noticed I never wore T-shirts, ever! So when he gifted me a save the dolphin-and-whale one—conservation consciousness being the only saving grace of this type of garment that I call a *sweat-catcher,* which I haven't worn since forced to in high school gym class—I used it to wash my faithful Yo-truck. My gift to him: a copy of my favorite book, "Siddhartha," which I re-read each year.

together we plot the course

CHAPTER 5

the building of our boat

Will called me in Sarasota. "Can you drive over this weekend to Lackland? My folks want to meet you."

Before we walked up the long driveway, I asked if I looked all right to meet his mother. I'd seen her in glamorous pictures and knew she was way flashier than I. Weeks earlier, before his folks arrived from their summer home in New England, Will had shown me around their impressive mansion of glass and steel, filled with the strong geometric metal sculptures done by his mother, whose work pleasantly surprised me. Her artistic style and finesse matched the best I'd seen in any gallery, in Manhattan, London, or Paris, or anywhere else I'd been for that matter. From her stunning and thoroughly modern artwork I knew his mom was a classy lady. She and Will's businessman-dad enjoyed a comfortable, yet frugal lifestyle. The elegance of authentic Americana antiques, inherited from both sides of their family, was mixed with contemporary art and furnishings added to the beauty of the mother's displayed art, state-of-the-art modern in every regard. I hadn't expected anything like this in backwards Lackland. Will told me his mother had actively exhibited all her adult life and supported the arts as a patron, as well as encouraged young artists. When I first walked around Will's folks' house, unoccupied at the time, I felt I'd stumbled upon a fountain of relief, here in this art mecca of a house, amid the desert wasteland of Lackland's mainstream bumpkins I'd so far only run into.

"You look great, let's go!" Will exclaimed with that unfettered exuberance I found so endearing. I had on a simple top with a vibrant flower-print skirt worn in a style I'd adopted while living in Dominica. With its shin-length hem loosely tied in a knot around my knees, the skirt's material provided a carry-all pouch large enough to be handy for when I had to gather things in the field, orchard, or one of my frequent forays into Nature. Because both of us loved to feel the earth under our feet, Will and I walked barefoot down the long driveway, our well-calloused soles impervious to pebbles all the way up to his folks' stately residence.

Addressing me cheerfully, we were greeted by Will's dad, who insisted I call him Phil and his wife, Claire. Tall like his son, the old man, a spry octogenarian, wore a heavy wool, three-piece suit even though it was eleven in the morning on a Florida-hot autumn weekday. I noticed his maroon silk tie sported tiny yellow Tweety-birds. What a contrast, when I regarded Will's usual getup, jungle-ready attire for business or safaris—cargo shorts and well-worn khaki shirt—then looked down at both our bare feet, carefree and casual as can be, yet both of us completely relaxed and comfortable in this high-class, impeccable residence fill with outrageous modern art and valuable family heirloom antiques. Phil's outdated, formal appearance (suit and tie at home, really?) was opposite to his son's devil-don't-care *Safari-anyone?*-getup. We chatted with the vigorous old man for a few minutes before Will's mother descended the wide staircase.

I stood to greet her. Claire such an elegant woman with a notably slim, full-busted figure. Perhaps a bit younger than her husband, with only mildly wrinkled skin betraying her age, she was stunning. From the rear, I noticed, she had the incongruous figure of an athletic thirty-something. Her whispered makeup was applied so flawlessly you hardly noticed it, or her thick eyeglasses. But her hair style—short and bleached blonde, coiffed in the standard poufy cloud of a teased and sprayed lift that meant weekly visits to the salon—threw me in its over-fussiness. Dressed in pleated and pressed tan slacks, Claire's wide belt perfectly matched her buckled, ready-for-church shoes. Her black turtleneck neatly tucked in at her trim waist covered her neck, dramatically setting off gold blobby earrings and the gold chain collar that shouted Bold Taste was this woman's choice. Her brightly polished, un-chipped nails caught my attention, something hands-on women artists like myself usually can never boast. In all my mingling with other artists—young, old, from many places besides the U.S.—I'd never met a real one who appeared as such a straight-looking culture-maven, especially one who produced impressively strong sculptural work as Claire. For the moment, I was speechless.

"I must be in heaven," Phil crooned in a dreamy, croaky voice, as surreal as his wife making such outrageous art, "I just saw an angel enter the room."

He and Claire chuckled and clucked over this old lovers' shtick of theirs. They looked at each other with unabashed adoration.

Claire was the epitome of good manners and exquisite taste, but her appearance was as anti-artist as an anorexic baker's. Her low-heeled patent leather shoes, were as shiny as those vermilion fingernails of hers. I looked at my bare feet, at my never-varnished nails, my rough but skilled artist's hands, and couldn't help but wonder how this woman stayed so neat while making such labor-intensive, high-tech metal pieces. Prominently bolted in place were Claire's weighty, bi- or tri-colored enameled, starkly minimal sculptures that were suspended on nearly every wall, with other well-known abstract minimalists' paintings hung, plus a neon, and a kinetic piece placed strategically here and there.

One of her works was a stainless totem about six feet tall, starkly angled, flawlessly spray-finished in slickly defined two tones. It was mounted with floor bolts in a conspicuous spot, right in front of the floor-to-ceiling, massive wall of sealed windowpanes; the center of attraction in the immense light-filled room. Genuinely admiring her sculpture, I softly asked Claire how she managed the remarkable feat of their creation, not daring to add what I was thinking: "here in the 'burbs."

"Oh, I have a formula," she said, waving an un-ringed hand agilely, the absence of even a wedding band on her fingers the only outward sign I could see of her being a serious artist. "I work-up small maquettes first, cutting and gluing cardboard. Then I paint the models with acrylics, which I send to the welders where they're referenced to fabricate the monoliths that stand before you. The piece arrives with rough seams, which my assistant who does the painstaking finish work, bless him, takes care of. Then Jim drives the piece, the final step, to the auto body shop where they spray the lacquer of the very sparse use of color I prefer in air-sealed lockers, for that high gloss finish. Just like a car's," she blithely laughed, looking around as if she'd just told a good joke.

Ah, I thought. Hence the perfect hair, perfect nails, perfect everything.

▲

Back at Will's the next morning, he asked if I would write his mother a thank you note. I almost choked on my toast, and asked why. All right, I knew when I came the day before that I'd have to spend the night at his parent's that night, their proximity to Will's house, he'd said beforehand, required me to spend the night in his old-fashioned, so-proper mother's guestroom. "I have no problem with that," I'd said, after Will had explained that his mom was "a stickler for propriety, seeing as my kids are involved." As much as I objected to my own mother's annoying habit of constantly picking on me, she had raised me with proper etiquette. To my mind, writing a thank you note for only an overnight bed was overkill in the Emily Post department. But I humored my gentle sleeping giant and jotted off a sincere thank you.

While I was getting ready to drive my Yo-truck back to Sarasota that morning, Will cleared his throat and meekly asked, "Do you mind rewriting that nice note of yours on better stationery?"

I stood silent for a second, trying to quell the surge of hot shock arising from my toes. Calmly I asked, "Your mother's too good for the yellow legal pad I used from your desk? I didn't see any Crane's under your mess there."

Will sighed. "Mom's awfully fussy. She'll take offense."

"If I'm going to be around," I tried to sound calm as I stated, "she'd better get used to my plebeian ways. That was a perfectly acceptable note I wrote. I used the best paper I could find. If she wants it looking more suitable, then you should have provided me with better supplies. This is who I am, Will."

I could tell Will wasn't happy with this.

"If things work out between us," he said, as if negotiating one of his business deals, "you and I are going to be together for a long while. My parents need to get used to you."

"What do you mean, 'get used to' me?"

Will's silence signaled his unease. "When I asked her this morning on the phone how she liked you, she asked why I thought you came to meet her in bare feet?"

My jaw dropped. "Did she not notice her darling son—he who brought me to meet his straight but sophisticated artist-dichotomy of a mom—also happened to be barefoot?"

"Of course, she did. But she's used to me."

"Oh. And I was supposed to know this about your mother because—I'm what? A mind reader?"

"No, of course not." Will's voice rose a note or two. "Mom's a great lady. She's just a stickler for rules. You know, being proper, and all that."

"Come on, Will. I'm too much my own person to go tip-toeing around, pretending to be someone I'm not, just to please your mother. So, what did your dad think of me?"

"He got on the phone to tell me after he heard mom fussing, like usual. Dad thinks you're super. Likes your pluck, he says. No problem there. Besides, Dad's a sucker for a pretty face any day."

"Well, I'm glad I got at least one seal of approval," I said, as I hopped into my little red pickup and raced back to Sarasota, wondering what the hell I was getting myself into.

Will and I were raised by folks who had not only vastly different socio-economic standards, but nearly opposing approaches to the core beliefs within the Christian continuum. Phil's people had since earliest times been into ships, building and owning clippers and whalers hailing from Kennebunk, Maine, with both sides of Will's family's subsequent generations all highly educated, civic-minded, socially upper-class stock: filled with generations of business, educational, and political leaders going back to when America first became a nation. Claire's people were from St. Louis. Her father had been a university professor. Her mother and grandmother, were powerfully involved early suffragettes, both her parents progressive and involved in bettering society. Claire and Phil had met at a mixer at the eastern Ivy League college they'd both attended, back when it was gender-separated, the same as it was when Will attended.

Aside from being Christian-raised, the similarity between Will's and my upbringing stopped right here.

My dad's family were Welsh commoners, working class people who'd left for America on the second load of Pilgrims; while my mom was a first-generation American-born immigrant farmer's daughter. Both Phil and Claire practiced an ancient, yet today considered esoteric form of mystical Christianity. Even though they attended Episcopal church, they were deeply involved with Edgar Cayce's organization, the A.R.E. (the Association of Research and Enlightenment). Neither Phil nor Claire nor any of their four children ever suffered any indignity from having Church doctrine imposed upon them, as my folks had.

My mom, a devout Catholic, just like her farming Lithuanian-born parents, who, upon marrying my dad, adamantly non-Catholic, was told she couldn't receive the Holy Sacraments of her faith, a harsh reprimand that amounted to her being officially rejected. She chose to marry my dad anyway, a stalwart man who proclaimed being anti-organized-anything, an agnostic rebel, but a breathtakingly handsome, tall and muscular one. In that era—the 1940s and for many years following—any Catholic marrying outside the religion had to face excommunication, or sign a document stating that children from a mixed union would be baptized and raised in the Holy Roman Church. My father, religiously cynical, refused, so at Lizzy's and my births my mother lost the fight for us to be christened in her religion. Without resentment of any kind, though, by ages seven and nine, when my older sister and I officially declared we wanted to follow our mother, she who was everything to us, we decided with our own free will that we wanted to be Catholic, and my father had to relent. Both Lizzy and I were baptized a few days before we received Holy Communion, the Sacrament for young children who'd reached the *Age of Reason*, said to happen at seven. Lizzy's and my conversions automatically reinstated my mother back into the good graces of the Most Holy See.

Immediately after Lizzy and I were baptized and received the sacrament of communion, we attended my parent's re-marriage, at my mother's insistence. She wanted to celebrate the end of her ostracization by receiving the holy sacrament of marriage with my father who could care less about pomp and circumstance, but was by far the most spiritual man I knew growing up.

Why not Catholic? my young self figured. I'd been in love with Jesus from the first time I'd heard of this Mysterious Figure's greatness, his magical miracles, his breathtaking selflessness for the then-pagan world to emulate. The world benefitted, as it still does, from Christ Consciousness being extolled by anyone.

Back then I knew nothing about dogma or that loving God had any rules. Separation in any form from God, which was the source of big magic to my young mind, sounded like a bad joke to me. Yet I was fed the same scary story as all religious progeny: that hell was under the earth and heaven above the clouds, and we only had one shot of this life on earth. Even though I didn't know Christ Consciousness by that name yet, throughout my childhood I felt One with Christ just as I do now with Aum, the All-inclusive name which, of course, includes Jesus the Christ, and all Divine avatars who come to earth to help us during hard times.

Under my mother's abiding love and guidance, because it was she who went to Jesus' holy church, where he stared at us from atop his bloody crucifixion mount, it was natural for me to cherish JC, the magnificent human some devotees call the *only* son of God, the Lamb, the Prince of Peace. Dying for us, Wow! now that's big-time sacrifice! I was told he'd died as a sacrifice for me and all of us lowly humans, so we could live free of sin. But after the innocence of childhood that story didn't make much sense to me at all. Contrarily, it upset me no end when the Church said I sinned, that my soul was doomed to hell, apparently a victim of some other persons' (Adam and/or Eve) sin condemning me, simply by my having been born, depressing News to say the least. But then, the Catechism teachers assured us that Jesus' death made it so we could all live freely, without the curse of Adam and Eve's original sin. How miraculous is *that*!

These strange scary ideas never sat well within my heart. This thing called religion was like a horror story to my young ears. Nasty, confusing business to a little kid.

But, religion assured me that JC saved me when I became baptized. So of course, who wouldn't love such a personage as JC? He who saved me from going to hell! Jesus Christ was now my hero. He was everyone's hero. He was, indeed, the Most Holy Superman in my childhood world, a horror show that was otherwise filled with scary devils and the fear of being thrown into that subterranean fiery, burning-flesh-smelling rotten place, where I might end up for sins I never even committed. The threat of eternal punishment kept popping up like pervasive boogeymen from behind every bush, the more I heard from the Catholic nuns and priests' teachings, shooting pangs into me, planting the need for desperate survival measures as my inquisitive, over-active imagination matured.

Before Lizzy and I decided on our maternal role model's course of faith, pleasing Mom no end, Dad insisted we be exposed to varying Protestant denominations with less rigid dogmas than Catholicism. But when both his little girls chose the pomp and circumstance of our darling mother's faith, with its enthralling Catholic rituals—the candlelit Mass, sweet pungent incense, a musty confessional in which I'd be forgiven for all kinds of mischief I was forever getting into— he conceded. The white frilly dress and semi-grownup bridal veil I'd get to wear at Holy Communion appealed to me in the same way the hoop-skirted rodeo outfit and gun holster did that I wore when I played my favorite character, a rootin' tootin' cowgirl.

My mother had good reason to insist we be baptized Catholic. She wasn't over being traumatized by the stillborn death (her spinal anesthesia was medically blamed), years earlier of her first and otherwise healthy full-term baby, who'd not been able to receive a proper baptism. According to the scare-tactics doctrine of the Church at that time, the soul of anyone not baptized in the Catholic faith was barred from the papally-guarded heavenly gates, doomed to languish outside, outcast forever in an undefined, punitive place called limbo, a place never mentioned once in the Bible. During my entire childhood, I was haunted by a deep sadness whenever I thought about Gilbert, the older brother I never knew, who'd been delivered as a still-born. I used to imagine him forlornly looking down at me, from *up there*, somewhere vaguely between heaven and earth, his forever-baby face wretched, mournfully stuck in nowhere-land, this eternal limbo he was in. As I grew older I thought many of the other Church laws inhumane, unjust, especially after realizing how they afflicted such guilt and shame on my mother, with her marrying a non-believer, then the soul-damnation of my dead older brother. It was cruel and torturous for me to hear about my poor innocent brother Gilbert, my mom and dad's first child, a full-term healthy infant who hadn't been able to draw his first breath and live outside my mother's womb. His soul, I'd been heinously told as a child by the Church, was condemned to nothingness, eternal in-betweenness. Doomed forever to limbo.

Thus, the seed was sown of my early distrust (and disgust) in religion.

Nonetheless, in time I came to see that Gilbert's existence—even though he didn't get the chance to live and breathe a single second on his own—served a pivotal purpose in my life and, no doubt, my parents'. His soul's eternal ambiguity (judged by men in robes who cast him forever out of heavenly peace) fueled my rebellion that was born of injustices I sensed coming from manmade religious doctrine. Perhaps it was Gilbert's soul and my parent's marriage being treated so unfairly by the Church that drove me to become an ardent seeker of Spirit. Adversity always serves a useful purpose, in the long term.

As a teenager, my sorrow turned to rage—over the religion of rule-oriented Catholics, over religions and unjust controllers of all sorts—originating from my brother's unfair banishment and our dear mom's condemnation.

It was this mistrust of religion that spurred me to embark upon a voyage of discovery. After years of searching, and then, attaining spiritual and substance sobriety, finally my path led me to totally trust and embrace the non-religious, non-form and certainly *no-rules* of—Aum.

A few years ago, I sighed in relief when I learned that the centuries-old, hypocritical Roman Church dogma of limbo was exposed for what it is: pure rot, completely made up to scare and keep sinners (the masses, like you and me) in line. In 2007, Pope Benedict XVI issued a formal proclamation eliminating limbo, on the basis of a body of Catholic theologians' recommendation. With this formal decree, no longer could this self-serving fear tactic, this made-up place called limbo, be deemed a repository for unbaptized souls, excluding them from the grace of heavenly assurance that religious folk rely on for comfort.

The papal seal offered no explanation other than limbo was no longer a dogmatic truth.

△

Dad's people were generations of menial laborers, working on railroads or in factories after being merchants upon first arriving at Plymouth rock on an early boatload of religiously-persecuted Pilgrims. Dad was city-bred whereas Mom was raised on a hundred-acre New Jersey truck farm, where my grandfather continued in the same, peasant-style ways of raising livestock and crops of all sorts, and the tightknit family spoke only the old country's Lithuanian to each other. Mom's second language became English only when she started walking miles each way to school at six years old. Sadly, she had to quit school at fifteen when her subsistence farming folks couldn't afford a good enough pair of shoes for her to wear to class, and mom couldn't endure the crushing shame. The depression had hit, so Mom, eager to flee rural life, went to work in a nearby factory, and then a city office. Dad's working-class father had died young so by fifteen, Dad too, was hard pressed and had to help his family survive during that hard time; working as a pin-setter at a bowling alley and later, an intimidating Repo Man. Even as a teen, Dad was bigger and stronger than anyone else. He worked hard to put his little sister through college, sacrificing his higher education to do so.

Meanwhile, I grew to be the ever more rebellious daughter of a autodidact, small town newspaper-reporter mother and a rebelliously agnostic traveling avionics salesman with a budding drinking problem, neither of whom ever appreciated my absolute fixation on the sheer magic of life. At nineteen they stunned me with their disapproval, when I announced my true calling: how I wanted to learn all I could about the supremely magical force, the highest I could find that resonated within me, called Art.

My uneducated, practical parents had always told me, "Art is something you only do after schoolwork and chores are done."

Soon after I declared my intention of studying at a formal Art School they would formally disown me, reading a letter of parental resignation over the phone to me when I began my life as an artist-in-training in Boston. Immediately after their cruel rejection, a very real and torturous physical pain developed in my gut. I would eventually find out it was a reactionary and absolutely psychic result of having been made an official outcast by my judgmental family.

A few days after hearing I'd been disowned by my misguided parents, I wasn't able to even get out of bed. A friend took me to the local hospital where doctors found nothing wrong with me, so they scheduled an exploratory surgery. At that moment I was coaxed by the same friend to try meditation. He helped me lean on him as I literally dragged myself up the sidewalk to the TM center in Cambridge where I was initiated into transcendental meditation and magically, astoundingly, experienced a life-altering mental-physical-spiritual climax of cataclysmic proportion—finding instant and lasting relief.

▲

When I returned to the concerned good doctors who happily cancelled my investigative surgery, they weren't at all surprised to see I'd recovered, using meditation as the sole remedy. They assured me, "We're just beginning to understand how the mind controls physical symptoms. Your emotional distress triggered a psychosomatic reaction."

Before this, I hadn't realized feelings could rule one's life so strongly, incapacitating me as mine had done. The enlightened doctor who spoke next was the first who pointed out to me, "How you feel, emotionally, is ninety percent the result of your mind's incredible power. Don't let stress ruin your health or your life."

It would be close to a year before my parents and I reconciled. Without their support I chose to live freely as an artist, freely a seeker, beginning my explorations of the unlimited world of Art and Spirit and other beautiful people who lived without restraint or judgment.

I continued running from my roots, winding up living as far away as I could from them, as I've recounted earlier. I returned to my family's embrace only for big events, like my father's death, four years before meeting Will, who himself had just recently returned to his childhood faith and hometown after two decades of perilous escapades as a prodigal son, a mismatched marriage, and its horrendous divorce and child custody battle.

That we two natural-born rebels—both of us black-and-blue sheep of our families, both utterly tired now of running away—were considering forging a family of our own, requiring a huge effort on both our parts … was perfectly clear to both of us.

△

Meanwhile, working out our differences didn't stop us from enjoying stolen weekends and vacations out of town, out of state—whenever the kids were away on their court-ordered weekend with Debby. No hassles existed at those delicious love-fest times: no demanding kids, no whack-job ex-wife, no fussy mother-in-law or my mom's unrelenting harsh complaints. No suburban strictures.

I'd done my research. Since having chosen a substance-free, spiritual life, I'd been following the advice of Louise the psychic, whose insights I found helpful after her services were passed on to me by my sober spiritual sister, Jane. Louise's astrological as well as intuitive perspectives, along with my meditation Teacher's and a few other trusted mentors' input, helped uncover Better-me within the messy attic of my former Lesser-me.

As soon as we met, I had boldly asked Will for his personal data, and sent it off to Louise for his and my charts to be compared, as couples do who work with astrology's astute assistance. With her help I was determined, with this man Will, to avoid any more doomed-from-the-start love affairs. Soon afterwards, she and I had a telephone conversation about my new squeeze.

She remembered, as I did too, having forecast six months before Will and I spoke that first time, that "… true love is coming for you this spring." Now she was asking if I thought Will was *The One*.

"That's what my heart tells me," I replied. It was only a few weeks, at this time, into our new long-distance romance.

"Good. Just checking," she said. "Because everything in your and his comparative charts indicates that this relationship has the highest possibilities—on the non-material plane."

"Really?"

"Really. You couldn't ask for anything better, spiritually. But …"

"But what, Louise?" I didn't want to hear any buts. I wanted to hear that her unseen muse advised her we should marry that moment, that night, or tomorrow at the latest.

"Well, I'm afraid you and Will have some work to do."

"What kind of work?" I felt a tightness form in my throat.

"You've heard of the common saying, *Awareness-Acceptance-Action*?" Louise asked.

Her triple-A cliché triggered my glib reply: "We all know that's not a rock band."

Louise let that one fly. She spoke as if she'd recited this a zillion times before:

"It means the introspective, inner work we all have to do to be healed, so our souls are allowed to complete their life-desires this time around. Self-forgiveness and compassion work, darlin', everyone's gotta do it or stay stuck. It starts with forgiving yourself.

If you want this relationship to work, you have to be aware of issues that will definitely come up between you, that's the awareness part; be aware the issues are real, is how to practice acceptance; so then, and only then, you can take whatever action is necessary to not let those issues derail your happiness."

"So … I'm supposed to be aware of —?"

"Your differences. And accept them. Then you and he will have a chance at making it. But you first have to know you have these challenges. You're never going to make it unless you and he both get ready to do some heavy-duty acceptance about your pet peeves, your intolerances. Everyone has them. And that—my job is to tell you—takes work. The work part is the action you take, which only comes after the awareness and acceptance. You've got to make this great spiritual thing you two have going, work for both of you. You've got to accept each other's quirks."

"I think we get along pretty well," I squeaked, thinking more about our pleasure-antics.

Louise further clarified. "It's clear from your charts that you guys have substantial obstacles in the real world that have to be overcome. With Spirit, yes, you're both superb in that area. Even though you have two different paths to God, it's all the same. But mundane everyday stuff? Face it: you know you both come from opposite sides of the ring. But hey, if you want it, you have to work for it," Louise explained encouragingly as ever.

Upon a few beats of my silence, she offered, "Here's how it'll go:

"Once you're aware of something that bugs you, acceptance has to come next. Sounds easy but it takes lots of accepting, and effort, believe me. If either of you don't learn to not just tolerate, but *really* accept each other's differences, you're in deep water, harmonious marriage-wise. Only after you've done the first two steps—awareness and acceptance, over and over, as many times as it takes to accept each other for it to become a habit—can you take healing action, and that's called forgiveness. Only then can you successfully let go of emotional baggage. You'll have to repeat this process of awareness as many times as you must, till acceptance becomes your middle name: that's the action part. That's the spiritual work we all have to do to grow more spiritually mature."

"He can't just accept me as I am?" I said. My old runaway self was kicking in, my *live-free-or-die* mantra loudly resonating in my skull, big time. I forced myself to resist the urge to hang up on Louise, jump up and rush to run away as far and as fast as I could that very instant.

"If you want to make it work with Will," Louise patiently said, "you have to take the lead and start practicing accepting. You want to be with this man, right?"

"I thought so."

"Well, when you're dead sure," Louise said, "you can start the acceptance work."

I wanted to shout Shit! but I kept quiet. Did she think I was a fool? Of course, I'd do it. I wasn't about to throw away the best shot at a great love I'd ever known. I yearned for this man when I wasn't with him. I had to have him in my life. The thought of not being with him made my chest grow tight, my breath shallow.

Louise continued, oblivious of my charged emotions. "A strong person like you has to learn to let go, detach. Don't even expect Will to change. But of course, he will—once you take the lead. For you two to work as a team, your job is to be the most flexible. You're the yogi, you bend easily in more ways than just physically. You can do this; it's not so easy for him. You catch my drift, teZa?"

Compromise, I said. Exactly, she replied. Lots of work, I weakly protested. Love, she corrected.

△

I shared some of Louise's information with Will, who surprised me when he said, with a good-natured laugh, "I'm super selective when it comes to all kinds of weirdo woo-woos, teZ. I've known them my whole life through, because of my family's involvement with the Cayce crowd. So many people out there call themselves psychics, and most are pretty sophomoric. There's only been a few I've ever trusted. I don't know Louise from Adam, but I trust you."

His talking this way was another of Will's giving off mixed signals. In direct opposition to his declared fundamentalism, his reluctant, yet distinct regard for others' extraordinary, prescient powers caused me to reflect on his background. Given that Will's parents raised their kids in an unorthodox, mystical Christian manner, I should have expected as much. I knew about Edgar Cayce's work, that it married the traditional Christian biblical outlook with reincarnation, meditation, astrology, and other metaphysical, unseen-energies beliefs. On the outside, the A.R.E., Cayce's contemporary educational foundation, appeared conventional compared to vine-swilling shamans and people looking for Spirit through every psychotropic means, from L.S.D. available to every suburban kid, to mushrooms, cacti and ayahuasca known to more adventurous mind-travelers of the plant-based persuasion.

A.R.E. members don't embrace ritualized drug-use for divining, but utilize what mystical Eastern thought (and some say, the lost teachings of the Bible itself, re-discovered in the Apocrypha) has taught for eons, from the transmigration of souls to the psychic-mental power all humans innately have. On the surface, Will's parents seemed like upstanding Episcopalians. But Claire and Phil believed in the power within as well, the same as I did, that we are Aum, all One. Belonging to the A.R.E. for half their lives, they were staunch believers and teachers of its philosophy.

Seemingly the antithesis of mystics, on the outside, buttoned-down three-piece-suited Phil, and glamorous-as-a-movie-star Claire were as comfortable using spiritual tools—like dream interpretation, hands-on healing, and working with angelic guides for protection and comfort—as they were having lunch with friends at their local Yacht Club, or playing couples bridge every Tuesday evening. Phil was a born spiritualist. His mother had raised him as a member of the first metaphysically-bent Christian sect, the little-known Protestant denomination of Swedenborgianism. And from the time she married her generous and kind-hearted soul match, devoted Claire embraced everything businessman Phil stood for.

"I gave him my political vote as a wedding gift," she later told me, shocking my feminist stance which always insisted on independence, especially when it came to the subject of politics. "Coming from a strong, matriarchal stance about society, I wouldn't dream of my vote ever cancelling out the political choice of my other half, my husband's, the economic and spiritual leader of our family. I'd just as soon not vote if I felt strongly opposed to his political choice. What kind of spiritual marriage would we have if I negated his vote on my ballot? I'd rather die than taint our marriage, which is based not on being right or financial security but on the best choice of life, our family's, our nation's, and the world's spiritual well-being."

Claire must have noticed my eyebrows skateboarding on my forehead. She chuckled and turned her attention back to the clove and bay infused spaghetti she had going on the stove just then. "Believe me, I take my vote very seriously, teZa," she added. "My mother was a leader of the St. Louis suffragettes."

As an artist and free-thinker, Claire struck me as the most liberated of women. But—to give one's vote as "a wedding gift," as she put it, seemed pretty anachronistic when she first told me. "It's a spiritual gift, to my mind," she explained with a sympathetic smile over my bewilderment. Smart, hip to the happenings of the world even though stuck in Lackland, never appearing sub-anything (certainly not subordinate) around Phil or anybody, Claire fascinated me, as did her surprisingly enlightened, Christian metaphysics. After learning that Will's parents were closely aligned with the teachings of the A.R.E., both of them decades-long teachers at the Virginia Beach headquarters, offering workshops on lucid dreaming, I realized they truly were experts in all areas of spirituality, not merely devout charismatics. So naturally, I listened attentively whenever Claire revealed more about her and Phil's decidedly unconventional approach to their version of Christianity, the interpretation of the God-thing that Will had been raised in.

At another time Claire explained to me in more detail. "Phil had a life-threatening condition in his mid-thirties that was cured by Edgar Cayce giving him a psychic reading. That's when we began to take workshops at the A.R.E., even before Will was born. When we moved to Lackland we began to hold an A.R.E. study group. For over fifty years we've been introducing others here, to the importance of listening to our subconscious, how to work with symbols that arise in our dream state, practice hands-on healing, and of course, Christ Consciousness meditation."

Every time I visited the elderly pair I found myself listening intently. I quickly understood that the esoteric spiritual practices that filled this couple's six-decade long marriage were anything but ordinary. So when I told Will about Louise's psychically advising me, his reaction of acceptance, after first suspecting her to be a flake—made perfect sense. He fully acknowledged her because, and for no other reason—I trusted her.

"Louise's guidance has been an integral part of your personal growth, teZ. I respect her insights."

Sharing another of the delicious and simple meals prepared by elegant Claire, I sat at the older couple's banquet-size dinner table, and asked again about their involvement in the road less traveled.

"Do you believe, as I do," I said, "that all people are born with the ability to develop the Christ or Cosmic Consciousness, to tap their spiritual nature, if only they choose to do so? That we all have the power within to be our own so-called prophets?"

Phil cleared his throat as Claire smiled and waited for him to speak first. "Just because we meditate and work with spirit guides doesn't mean everyone is called a prophet, like Cayce is called the *sleeping prophet*," Phil said, each of his words spoken slowly and distinctly. "Yet if a person works with the innate abilities each and every one of us has, any of us certainly would appear to another, who doesn't work so easily or frequently with these available unseen realms, as prophetic. Whereas we do, don't we, Claire, my darling?"

She looked up and smiled at her man, evidently as proud of him as the day she agreed to forge their lifelong spiritual partnership.

Phil gave her a wink and continued. "We work with signs that are found everywhere, teZa. We pay attention, record, and discuss,

Claire and I do, to the kind of mixed-up symbolism that appears in our haphazard dreams, for instance. And we look for and find signs everywhere, from other sources, like events that occur in Nature. We see so-called coincidences, or what other people dismiss as random and insignificant, as what they really are: signs from our subconscious, which is directly linked to the Divine.

"Yes, of course," he said, his slow choice of words indicating precise use and his obvious enjoyment of discussing this subject. "Every human has a strong sense of instinct and intuition. Yet many people don't understand ... that the choice is ours to develop ... whether we become spiritually awakened or not ... along with how mentally strong and physically fit we are. Claire and I ... we exercise our spiritual muscles," Phil laughed at this, "just like some people ... work hard to develop their biceps, abdominal, calf muscles. It's up to us ... how we choose to use our natural gifts ... or not. People who don't understand ... might label the A.R.E. as a bunch of psychics ... or prophets ... or kooks ... just like Cayce was called early on."

The old man stopped talking as Claire, Will, and I sat at the table deeply listening, engrossed in following Phil's profound thoughts.

"Labeling others as different," Phil slowly spoke after a comfortable moment of silent reflection, "helps some folks ... explain to themselves ... why they can't, or won't, develop their own ability ... to access this totally human, completely ordinary ... ability to expand one's own thinking. Their consciousness ... Everyone can tap the information of ... the Akashic Records, or Universal Wisdom ... if they just desire to ... Cayce showed anyone ... who wanted to know, how. Knowledge of past-present-future ... insight into whatever affects us ... is available to anyone ... just by connecting ... with the unlimited Christ or ... Universal Consciousness. Claire and I ... we do this daily ... through paying attention to our dreams ... and regularly meditating ... listening to God ... instead of yapping to him ... which is prayer ... Which is okay ... in small doses.

"It's all in how ... we see things ... or hear ... or feel them," Phil said nodding his head as his slow words flowed like nectar over a cool stream. "When I was a young man ... I said to a friend ... how I had *aging parents* to take care of ... and he shot back, alarmed ... 'What? Phil, what the hell are you doing with *eighty parrots*!'"

Phil sat chuckling, thinking over this long-ago exchange with his friend who definitely heard things differently, and maybe saw and felt things from a much different perspective than his more insightful friend did, as well. I caught Will winking slyly at me. Claire remained silent, her amused smile revealing more than words ever could.

I relished listening to this interesting couple, especially Phil. Will's folks were even more out-there than I was! Just as I thought this, I looked over to see Will again wink and nod my way. I thought how much he was like his old man. Always the jokester, the clown. I could never tell who this man Will was, not really, other than it was he alone, I somehow knew, who could replace that thirteen-man harem I once considered the only way I'd ever satiate the urge, the need I had for variety, amusement, electric wit.

Claire was speaking now. "Being spiritual means knowing that every single one of us has this higher ability, this access to expanded thinking ... if only a person chooses it."

Hmm, I said to myself. This is exactly what the Teacher tells us: "The power within is the same in all."

△

I found Will's parents—the straightest-appearing but well-disguised, metaphysical Christians—to be compelling. And charming. When later, Will explained more about his family's involvement with the A.R.E. I would find out that in the early 40s, Phil "had been chronically ill and his life saved by Edgar Cayce," Will explained. "From a distance Cayce journeyed *psychically* into Dad's body," Will stated as plainly as if giving a weather update. I asked him exactly how Cayce *did that*.

"From many States distant, using only the street address and exact time Dad had told Cayce in advance where he'd physically be, so Cayce's trance-Self could find him, Cayce—however he did it—used soul travel, teZ. Supposedly we can all do it, but I've never been successful. Anyway, Dad was six hundred miles away, in Boston, while Cayce lay in a trance in Virginia. That's why they call him the *sleeping* prophet."

"I've never met anyone who's been personally healed by Cayce's readings," I said. "That's phenomenal." I was awestruck.

"Cayce willed his consciousness, as it was explained to me," Will said, "to travel out of his body to where Dad had previously written Cayce where he'd be that day, at that time." Will spoke as if he were giving simple directions to the shopping center around the corner, not relating how one man's consciousness was able to invisibly travel hundreds of miles away, and, with the other's permission, enter into another's body-soul-mind essence, what Cayce always referred to as "the entity."

"Cayce calls his subjects *entities*, not bodies, or people even," Will said in a measured manner, as if remembering something he'd read or heard once. "I think entity encompasses the past, present, and future of whomever he's giving a reading to, from what I can tell."

Will smiled and continued. "A few days after his *Life Reading*, as the A.R.E. calls it when Cayce did his thing, Dad received a typed-out transcription of what Cayce spoke aloud, taken down by his secretary Gladys, during his trance. That information gave Dad implicit instructions for his condition of hypothermia: things like changing his diet, and certain aspects of his negative thought patterns. He did those recommendations, and Dad got well right away. Of course, Dad was intrigued. He started studying with Cayce, who unfortunately died not long after they actually met. Classic case of the physician not able to heal himself. It didn't help that Cayce smoked several packs of cigarettes a day and exhausted himself trying to help everyone else, selflessly neglecting his own health.

"To this day the A.R.E. carries on his life's work. Helping to disseminate Cayce's teachings became Dad's passion. He and Mom practice Christ Consciousness, in meditation and through other disciplines they recommend. They're considered Christianity-influenced metaphysicians. Everything is centered around the Bible, including the *Search for God* prayer group he and Mom started in our Lackland house before I could even read."

"It helps to have a trusted teacher," I said. "I'm lucky to have mine."

"Sure, if you feel she's right for you," Will said, with no judgmental inflection, disbelief or disrespect. "I don't know her or her teachings, but everything you've told me about what she's into so far, jibes with the A.R.E.'s beliefs and what I know to be true in the Bible, the Word."

I must have made a face without intending to.

"Except your group doesn't believe that Jesus is God incarnate, born of a Virgin birth," Will quickly added.

Again, the sudden gust of Will's unexpected belly-punch intolerance, knocked the wind right out of my sails. This blasted Jesus-only issue of Will's, again. Awareness. Okay, here we go, I said to myself. Acceptance. So I took another stab at explaining myself.

"I'm sure my Teacher would agree, and Jesus himself, and Cayce too, if they were all here, when I say we're all part of the same, nameless energy source I happen to call Aum. What different people call God, their personal Divine Source, has become so highly charged and contentious in our world today; why, it's ah ... a little incendiary, don't you think, Will, to be intolerant of others' ways of speaking about the Sacred, in any of its myriad forms and names? That alone is why I prefer to use Aum. So nobody thinks I'm talking about some certain religion, or path, or philosophy. The Mystery is—for most of us—difficult if not impossible to describe."

"I'll accept that, teZ," he said, "if you accept that I speak to Jesus when I address my true Source," Will stated as if I didn't know that already.

"Yes, of course, Will. Let's agree, as many times as we need, to accept how each of us calls our own Source. And maybe, one day it really won't matter anymore. I accept Jesus, and you accept Aum, okay? Can we agree on that much, so we can both feel comfortable? I'm sure we'll get better that way, at cutting the other guy some slack. About how we call the God-thing, I mean."

By now I was wondering how Will—who believed with all his mind and heart that Jesus Christ alone, is God manifested on earth—could be the son of a founding trustee of the A.R.E., a learning institution whose sole purpose is to help people of all beliefs realize their dormant spiritual powers, their God-Self within. Will was becoming more of a mystery to me with each new discovery I made about him.

How surprised and elated I was, each time I conversed with them, to learn that Phil and Claire's enlightened Christ Consciousness views, that we are all sons and daughters of God, echoed exactly the same ancient Eastern-mysticism, Buddhist-Vedic-Sufi philosophy I'd been studying for years with my yoga-meditation master, the Teacher. Will's more spiritually-attuned Dad said to me in an early conversation: "We passed our Christian mysticism on to our kids, as the holiest wisdom of the Divine that we feel is available to humans." Will, as outspoken as a TV evangelist, the recently-returned prodigal son, the wildest of Phil and Claire's four grown children, ironically was also the one who most closely followed in his parents' paranormal-friendly footsteps, I noted after hearing about his early involvement in the A.R.E.'s Egyptian and Bahamian explorations. His other three siblings were not as involved: one adhered to his wife's Catholicism; one remained Protestant like her folks but a more mainstream version; and the other was an unaffiliated, intellectual Freudian shrink who would, late in her career, introduce using altered states like hypnosis and past-life regression to her heretofore clinical analysis. Even though Will adamantly, nonsensically, declared himself to be a born-again, he was as mystical as Phil and Claire.

Acceptance, I reminded myself.

Will told me he believed in reincarnation, as I and all of the Eastern-mystic bent do, he also acknowledged the latent spiritual power within every human. He did gentle hands-on with his kids, on sick animals, and himself when he felt out of sorts; and now he laid his powerful healing hands on me too. Will never denied any aspect of Cayce's esoteric teachings he'd been raised on, even as he continued exploring the more conventional path that attracted him since returning to the embrace of his familial Christian faith.

Will's biblical fundamentalism, he claimed, was leading him to the same spiritual enrichment as his parents' charismatic, and my all-inclusive mystical approach, did—that of a person achieving his or her highest spiritual potential in this lifetime: right here, right now. To me, the difference between Will's and my spiritual outlook was insignificant, but Will couldn't see that.

He kept asking me, "Aren't you worried about what's going to happen to you after you die? How are you going to be with me in heaven if you don't believe in Jesus?"

And I'd answer in complete confidence, "I don't worry about that, Will. I see God everywhere, right now. This is heaven right here, and I'm certain of that because my addicted life used to be hellish."

I wasn't trying to be facetious. I was simply telling him how life truly was heavenly, this moment I was living in, right now. My messed up past didn't bring me down; and I tried not to worry by projecting into the future. But when I did, I caught myself and said a few silent mantras to keep my awareness focused on being present. The magic moment of the present was my happy spot.

"The trouble with you and this religion thing," I once said to Will, "is you want it both ways. You say you believe in reincarnation yet you're worried about not going to heaven. An afterlife is antithetical to reincarnation. Why do we need a heaven or hell, if our souls keep evolving? You want to believe in everything, and that's cool. You're a spiritual glutton! Just admit it, you're one crazy mixed-up dude, and that's why you're you, and why I adore you!"

I threw my head back and roared, deciding right then not to take Will so literally about this religion thing anymore. This guy, I thought, wants his bases loaded no matter what, with three homeruns coming up—his sure-fire ticket to the paradisiacal promised land—for when he hits his out-of-the-ballpark homer, good ol' death.

For me, it was simpler. I believed I was already in heaven. Being in hell was behind me, I made sure of that one-day-at-a-time. *That* was my inebriated life before embracing Better-me. But now, I'd learned to love myself and that took a lot to accomplish. Getting sober and meeting the Teacher, both, showed me how my own choices make or not-make living on earth, *the real* heaven and hell, that's right here, right now.

Since returning to religion and taking his beginning steps back to his folks' enlightened version, having been happily dunked in a gator-pond some years back by Preacher Joe when he declared himself born-again, Will was now more suspicious than he used to be about self-proclaimed spiritual people. He couldn't deem them all, kit and caboodle, airy-fairies, now could he? Because ... where would that leave his own folks? He joked about the "whack jobs" he'd met in his childhood, the off-the-wall visitors, his parents' A.R.E. comrades, none of whom ever would be suspected by Lacklanders of being mystics due to their eminently ordinary appearances.

Will mentioned many times how he wanted—no, *needed*—the assurance that I wouldn't be bringing any more grief into his kids' lives by being "as flakey as some of those out-there spiritual nutcases who hung around my folks since the God-squad, the Cayce prayer group started meeting at my house back when I was around Jonny's size."

▲

Soon after Louise advised us about accepting each other's differences, we found ourselves sitting in the office of Dr. C, Will's kid-friendly family counselor. We were nervously awaiting the results from the compatibility test and psychological evaluation she'd done for us. I hadn't wanted to do this clinical stuff; it was Will's idea. All I ever needed was our two astrology charts interpreted by Louise's clairvoyant gifts. For years I'd been seeking her advice and she'd been right on target, helping me resolve leftover issues from my childhood traumas. As a result of Louise's direction, Will and I soon came to realize that we needed help if we wanted to make it as a couple.

Will stated as soon as we arrived at Dr. C's for our test results, "I need to know that marrying teZ isn't going to backfire on me like it did with Debby. I need proof that my feelings for her aren't just another bad-relationship trap I'm falling into."

Sitting relaxed in a cushioned chair, I listened as the pleasant mannered shrink spoke to us. Watching her open, kind face I knew I could trust her.

"Straight off," Dr. C said, after clearing her throat, "you both definitely have to make some major changes if you want to be happy together."

I noticed Will sit up straighter, as if he hadn't bargained on hearing that. This was no news for me, thanks to Louise's forewarning.

"What sort of changes are we exactly talking about, Doc?" he asked.

"Okay, let's start with teZa," Dr. C said. "The test shows that, on a scale of one-to-ten, concerning the issue of control, she's a seven—"

"I knew it! She's a control freak!" Will practically jumped out of his chair, excitedly pointing an accusing finger at me. I laughed at his jester-like contortions but squirmed under his unjustified accusation, wondering if this was an act, always the clown; or could he possibly be that knee-jerk reactive? I consider myself to be strong-minded, sure: artists usually are, more easily seeing what's a waste of effort than some others can. I wasn't prepared for Will's aggressiveness, having prided myself in always before, choosing conciliatory and compassionate companions.

"Hold on, Will," Dr. C clucked. "Take a seat. Now it's your turn. Your test results showed your control issues are off the charts."

Dr. C's tone was firm. Will instantly looked deflated, knocked right off his high horse.

Dr. C continued. "For the two of you to have a peaceful union, teZa—afraid I'm the one who's got to tell you—you have to learn to demure to him if you want to make it with Will. You have to not be so strong, so unbending when you and Will get into a standoff. I'm not saying give in. I'm just saying, soften your stance a little. I know you hate hearing this. But the test shows you need to do it. Otherwise you and he don't stand a chance for happiness."

Bolts of outrage raced up my spine, hearing Dr. C mention an attitude that'd always been demeaning to me as a self-proclaimed liberated woman. The word, let alone action, of me interacting with this *demure*-shit was not even in my vocabulary. That feeling of restraint I'd thrown off as *not-me* since deciding long-ago, as a child who felt trapped in her own family, when I vowed to believe in *me* even when others insisted on tormenting me; when I threw off those early frustrations about my deepest desire to learn to fly, high in the sky, safe and secure in my humanity, and the only way I found to do that was by promising myself to be free and beholding to no one.

"I prefer to compromise or cooperate, than be demure," I slowly formulated, not happy how this counseling appointment was going. "Semantics aside, exactly how would you suggest I do this, if you say I must? Give me a for-instance?"

"Well, to start with," Dr. C said, "listen to him. Will has clearly stated, many times over, that he can't be with any woman—not after Debby, his ex, made him *feel* a cuckold—unless she makes him *feel* sexually secure. And that, my dear, means—to him—as he's said before in our previous sessions, ahem, that means he needs you to wear a bra."

"She's right," Will shot out. "It's a deal-killer for me if you don't!"

"This again?" I couldn't believe it. First Jesus, now *the bra*. Another of his exasperatingly dumb issues—yikes! I had to restrain myself from running out of the shrink's office that very second. Nervously I tapped my foot and sat on the edge of my chair. Next to justifying my deeply profound relationship to JC to Will, his bra-thing was my personal crown of thorns. Since we'd met, Will had been harping like a soapbox preacher going on about, "Men get distracted by publicly displayed boobs," his favorite rant, since he realized I never wore a bra, and couldn't care less if other females or well-nippled men or trans, did or did not. Bras were not my thing, period. More athletically yogic trim than Kardashian-endowed, I'd always been a free and loose, no-bra kind of gal since I threw mine away, like every other self-respecting feminist, especially flat-chested ones like me did back in the sixties.

"I'm not going to ever feel cuckolded again," my suddenly serious, formerly goofball boyfriend stated. "Dr. C is right. It's a deal-killer for me. Debby never respected my needs. With her big tits loose, flopping everywhere, getting all the men's attention, my life with her in public was miserable from day one. I'm sick of feeling that way. I'm never going through that again for anybody. It hurts too much. I don't have to explain myself. I've told you what I need. Not a chastity belt. Not for you to become born-again. Just wear a flimsy sports thingie like you do in yoga, so guys don't see any more than they should, okay? Is that so much to ask? Call me old-fashioned, call me square, I don't care. I can't stand seeing my woman's treasures out there for everyone to ogle."

"I'm afraid he's right, teZa," Dr. C said, nodding her head. She looked from Will to me, and back again. "You have to give Will this one concession if you and he stand a chance to be happy together. This is what I mean about being demure to *him*."

I moaned, sinking back into the chair. "Like living in suburbia isn't enough of a sacrifice?" Suddenly I was furious, feeling unjustly put-upon.

Will firmly stood his ground. "Wearing nothing under that see-through stuff you like, I just can't hack it. I've seen people stare at you. And don't forget, I remember that time in Boston when I first met you, even if you say you don't. No self-respecting woman of mine is going to show her tits to the world. Unless we're skinny-dipping with trusted friends."

Wearing a bra, to my all-people-free way of thinking, was an even more extreme clash of ideals than living in suburbia *or* the JC-*only* issue. I no more believed in women being told what to do with their bodies by others—especially by the mostly religious, self-righteous white men who considered themselves the vanguard of conservative America—than I thought my soul was going to a place called heaven or hell after I died. To me, a bra represented much more than a piece of optional underwear. To me, the freedom of no-bra signaled true liberation.

"I see it as other people's problem," I reiterated for Dr. C's benefit. "If someone judges me because I have untethered tits, that's their hang-up, not mine. You've made it your problem now, Will," I said, turning toward him.

"I disagree," he calmly stated. "We men can't help ourselves. We're animals. Women don't understand how dressing provocatively messes with us; we're males, not moral-weighing calculators. You didn't have brothers, you don't know crap about us. My male sex-driven head has been consumed with wanting-to-get-laid since I've been ten-years-old. Call me fucked-up if you want, I don't care. Everything else is do-able about you and me. The way I see it, all the woo-woo spiritual stuff, the chanting, the Eastern instead of the Western God, the Christian one you were born into." Will spoke as matter-of-factly as an impartial judge, "I can accept. But you wearing a bra is my one non-negotiable."

Dr. C looked at me. She looked at Will. None of us said anything. Dr. C sighed and relaxed her hands on her lap over her notepad. Her chest heaved noticeably.

△

Another breakup with no contact between us. My heart went flat. The spring in my step collapsed. I felt halved, plagued by questions for which I had no answers. How could I possibly cooperate with this strong-willed person, half straight, half way-out-there? How could I, having fought my whole life to be free as a bird, relent by buckling myself back into some boob harness? Seriously, I couldn't imagine wearing a brassiere any more than restricting my desire to know Aum. Could life really come down to being this stupid? I wondered. Do I have to prove how much I love this man by going backward in my fight for personal freedom? Isn't love supposed to be easier, loftier than this?

Two weeks crept by without hearing Will's voice. Without his gently lisping Ss tickling my ear as we cuddled, without feeling that tingling resonance his deep voice instantly charged in my body, awakening all the sleeping parts I'd never known. Whenever I thought of him, which was almost constantly, I felt lighter and noticeably more energized. Without his presence, his titillating voice, I felt heavier, somehow off-track. Finally, I picked up the phone.

"I guess I can try to let you lead this crazy dance we're having."

"Thanks, teZ, I miss you, too."

"But you have to give *me* something *big* back," I said.

"Name it."

"You have to promise you won't make me stay in that wretched town of yours one minute longer than we absolutely have to. When I left my parents' home, I swore I'd left suburbia forever."

"Okay, that's fair. I love you. I want to be reasonable. We belong together, I know we do," Will said. "What do you need?"

"Tell me," I said, "how long *you need* to stay in Lackland."

"I need five years at least, to get financially secure."

"Five years!"

"To get on my feet again after the divorce, after the movie drain, I need that much time."

"Okay here's the deal, man. If I give my word that I'll wear the loosest, most un-bra-like, mammary torture-device I can find, and you give me your word of honor you're getting me out of there not a moment longer than five years, max, I'll agree to this insane hang-up of yours—as long as it's quid pro quo we're talking. Agreed?"

"It's a deal," Will said.

I could feel his grin on the other end of the line.

"We've been through all the breaking up I can stand. I need to be with you," I said. "That's all I know."

△

It was during a visit soon after this when I thought of another solution to our differences regarding the God-thing. Why neither of us hadn't thought of it before, or Dr. C hadn't suggested it was because Will and I had been so freakin' busy butting heads over bras and JC, each of us trying to control the other's version of what's right, we'd missed seeing the obvious solution to our other big issue: the God-thing.

"If you're so worried about my beliefs being a bad influence on your kids," I suggested, "after we're married we'll continue raising Kara and Jonny in your tradition, whatever Christian denomination you choose, I don't care. We'll simply keep my spiritual preferences out of their day-to-day. Don't ask, don't tell-ish," I said, referencing the then-favored method of how to publicly deal with the gender revolution that was breaking out in American society.

Will's look of surprise equaled my spark of hope. "And you'll back me up?" he said.

"Sure," I exclaimed. "Gladly. Loving and respecting the God-energy is all that matters to me. I don't care how other people choose to honor or call theirs. I just don't want anybody telling me how *I'm* supposed to do it."

"Fair enough. And you'll agree to come along with us to church on Sundays, so it will be a family event?"

"Of course. It'll be my pleasure."

"And you'll at least feign solidarity with me, in Jesus being the only Son of God, even though I know you don't feel that way?"

"Absolutely, daddy-O. These are your kids, Will. You get to choose how you want to raise them. I'll totally have your back. I'm stoked to be with you. Each time we've broken up I'm a mess. Let's stop testing ourselves. Let's go for it."

"I agree," he said. "Let's do Us."

"I'm more interested in being One with Aum, Will, than arguing how to do it correctly. I feel Aum everywhere, within everyone, everything. God isn't just found in a holy book. Words are outside us, spoken or written; they help some of us connect with Aum on the inside, that's for certain. For me, the God-connection is inside and outside; it's not about a building or a book or a story that's been told, which all might work for others."

"Okay then, let's do it," Will proclaimed, apparently satisfied.

CHAPTER 6

setting out at last

A year and half quickly passed after Will's equinox phone call. We'd had a few short but bitter breakups, then wildly passionate reunions with persistent vacillating on both our parts. And now—we're booking a mutually acceptable, all-inclusive-type, Christ Consciousness minister for our ceremony. Immediately after making arrangements to marry next month, I am walking into Will's home office.

"Oh, look," he says, "here's something for you, teZ. I just found it under this big pile of papers. Must have gotten lost on my desk, sorry."

He hands me a beautiful cream-colored, square envelope with a certain weighty feel. Its distinct look I instantly recognize. Eagerly, as I take the letter and see it's been posted from the Teacher's ashram several months before. Typical. Surrounding Will's desk is a mound of his mess. My heart starts skipping. I open the letter's seal. I'd given up getting a response from her. Not knowing what to think, really, about the delay of her answering my question about marrying him. I'd given up, truthfully, not knowing what her silence meant ….

Did she disapprove so much, is that what her delay meant? Of her spiritual student marrying a nihilist-gone-fundamentalist, now outspoken lover-of-Jesus such as Will? I opened the envelope and glanced at the words I knew the Teacher dictated to her secretary:

"If this man you have chosen to love also loves the Source of all Power, God, as you say he does, it doesn't matter if his path is different than yours if he respects yours and loves you. The strongest connection two people can have in this life, is to both have a similar level of intensity with however they understand God's Power to be, within all. How one does this is a personal choice. You have my blessings for this union, teZa."

I laugh out loud. Or course she'd approve! How could I have imagined anything but? I'm such a spiritual dumbass. No, I take that back. I won't sow any more negative thought-seeds.

I allow myself about two seconds to wonder what, exactly, I'd have done if she hadn't approved? In a flash, I knew this would never happen. She's too evolved for judgment of that kind. I laugh again and Will looks up from his paper-strewn desk to see what's so funny.

"The Teacher says she approves of me marrying you, Will."

"How could she not?" he smiles, confidently. "You and I, we're the same. We both put God above all else. Any other way doesn't make sense. We've both tried life the other way, the no-fun, no-God way. We both know ourselves now. She probably recognizes that, if she's as good a spiritual teacher as you say."

I smile back, loving the serendipity of having discovered this important letter, but not before both of us had agreed to join our lives forever.

"I see from the postmark this letter arrived over six months ago, Will," I said, feigning exasperation.

"Oh yeah? Gee, guess I'm a bit much, eh?"

We both laugh, he with obvious insouciance; me, with a great deal of acceptance.

△

How did I know I was meant to be Will's life partner?

Because my insides were peaceful whenever I was with him, and in turmoil every time we were separated for too long. After my crazy, partying, Lesser-me period of ignoring these kinds of kicking, shouting gut-feelings, I knew better. I had to follow my inner compass. I had to honor the great love this man kindled in my heart.

We were married on his parents' expansive lawn in front of Claire's twenty-foot totem-tall, sleek steel sculpture that she'd told me earlier, "honored the sacred joining of a couple."

With an acceptable minister found at the local New Thought Christianity church, Will and I spoke aloud the vows we'd meticulously composed. In attendance were Kara and Jonny and a few neighborhood kids, a man whom I managed to drag away from his lawn-mowing job, and a couple of local childhood pals of Will's we'd invited, who were speechless and nonplussed at our casual, but ritualized affair. Claire and Phil were still up north, and my widowed mom either couldn't or wouldn't make the long drive across the state. ("I don't approve. She just doesn't know anything about raising kids," Mom had sternly warned Will.) On the phone, long-distanced Lizzy tried warning me: "Where there's smoke, there's fire," referencing the child-abuse charges Will had to fight during the custody battle, and said she'd pass on my iffy-wedding. Neither Will nor I cared who was or wasn't attending.

The kids didn't have to dress up. Jonny's favorite blue shorts, clean white top, and orange flip-flops worked just fine. Having heard his dad and me tell others, "We're getting married," when the big day arrived I overheard Jonny telling Debby on the phone:

"No, I can't come to your place today, Mama!" his squeaky voice proclaimed. *"We're* getting married today, remember?"

Kara and I had gone to the Goodwill store beforehand and picked out a hand-stitched, soft and fancy pink affair, some other little girl's special-occasion dress from another time, another world. I made my own dress from a length of an artist friend's hand-printed raw silk design. On our special day, from the look on Will's white zombie face I could tell he didn't appreciate my ankle-length purple-lace stockings, or anything about how I looked or acted that day. He almost passed-out when I jubilantly starting singing the 60s tune, "Go-ing to the cha-haha-pel and I'm gon-na get ma-haha-ried." Barely able to talk or button his shirt, my husband-to-be spent the entire morning in shock, still not entirely trusting that marrying me was the right thing to do, his eyes stuck in bulbous, self-doubt mode. But he obeyed me because I'd told him, without a shred of ultimatum attached to it, just after getting the Teacher's letter, "Marry me, you won't regret it," after waffling myself for the thousandth time, afraid both of us were making a terrible mistake. Our indecision always revolved around what was best for the kids, not us. In our hearts, we knew we were destined to be together.

I accepted my fate was to be Will's wife. I'd tested myself with the too-many times I'd run away from him. I resigned to never run from his love, after the tests of fire ours already had had. Call it a compulsion, I had to follow he who'd once passed me up, like the ship in the shadows, but he'd returned for me. Just as the saying goes: *the teacher appears when the student is ready*, my partner-match reappeared when my heart was ready. Will and I solemnly pledged—to each other and to God—to spiritually nurture ourselves, Jonny and Kara, and all we encountered together, declaring ours to be nothing less than "a sacred union."

Throughout the short ceremony I'd designed, reciting the vows we'd composed together, I kept assuring myself: I am here, I am present. With an open heart and mind, I accepted my role with this man and all that his blended family represented.

In the back of my mind I kept hearing the Teacher, whom I'd heard so often say: "When life brings us the gift of love, fine-tuned to our own needs and temperaments, it's our courage that actually lets us fulfill our spiritual obligation, and go for it. Be courageous. Believe in love."

△

Right beside our bed was an old-fashioned rocking chair, comfortably upholstered for the inveterate rocker I am. Here I had been bringing frightened little Kara to comfort during the frequent nightmares that came to her almost nightly, which had started well before Will's and my meeting.

Dr. C and Will both assured me Kara's troubles had nothing to do with my arrival. When Kara's blood-curdling screams erupted (after everyone had fallen sound asleep), my sailing-days alertness kicked in. I was always the one who jumped out of bed and rushed to her room down the hall. There, I held the sleeping, terrified sweet girl in my arms as she shook and cried uncontrollably, unconscious still. When she awakened, I'd carry her to our bedroom where I held and rocked with her until she calmed down.

Whimpering in my big arms in the rocking chair, I told my little Angel Girl over and over, "You're loved, and you're perfect, Kara." Along with each of my long and slow in-and-out breaths, I'd say such things as, "You are surrounded by protecting angels, us, your parents. I am here now, along with Dad." I whispered encouragement to her after every nightmarish attack, until she fell back asleep while an exhausted Will continued to sleep right beside us, grateful for me, out of gas from previously dealing with Kara, before I took over our family's interrupted nights. He'd been doing this long before I showed up as the newest member of our boat's crew.

Kara also had occasional daytime anxiety attacks. Out of nowhere, her consciousness would fall, like a nameless malady, out of the blue, to repeatedly grab her. It was as if she suddenly tripped over a pebble and fell into a deep and dangerous, unseen dark well, sometimes several times a day, but always, absolutely wide awake. During these daytime fits, her eyes would pop wide as she'd freeze in fear. I knew when these attacks began because she'd start hysterically clawing the nearest smooth surface with her clenched fingernails, hyperventilating, a sight frightful to see, absolutely terrified out of her skull. During the night terrors she suffered after being sound asleep for a few hours, she'd lapse into God-awful screaming bouts that awoken everyone else, before herself. Night and day, the poor thing was besieged by invisible demons. My heart ached for her discomfort and I swore to do whatever I could to help her.

I asked again, and Will assured me: "These terrors of hers started long before you and I met. They are definitely not associated with your arrival, teZ."

I read up on the clinical facts in some stepparenting books. There, I learned about *the psychic break* that commonly happens in girls whose mothers didn't or couldn't bond with them in early childhood. A girl like this, the texts declared, has a damaged psyche that starts to demonstrate cracks around Kara's age, seven.

"I'll help heal Kara with my love," I said to Dr. C, with whom I discussed everything instead of my own mother. Dr. C was familiar with the dismal diagnosis of an anxiety disorder, given our daughter by earlier visits to custody-court-ordered pediatric shrinks.

"Just as delicate land masses are profoundly affected by the earth's tremendously powerful seismic tremors," Dr. C offered in explanation, "severe disruptions happen in newly forming psyches of every young person. Trauma has an enduring impact, I'm afraid. Kara's mom not giving her much loving attention as an infant has severely affected Kara."

Will told me that Debby rarely held her baby daughter back then. "What kind of mother could do that?" I implored of Dr. C.

I asked Claire and other mothers I respected about what to do, to help heal Kara. I spoke to everyone about it but my own mother, whom I knew would only use this information to torment me about being inadequate to solve any of my new marriage's many challenges. Sure, both of Will's children had serious problems. Show me a kid who doesn't after a bitter divorce. Kara had non-specific anxiety issues; Dr. C. told us Jonny had a separation disorder. And there was their crazy bio-mom hanging in the air, like a dreaded virus, affecting us all. After hearing how Debby clung to Jonny all during his infancy, the opposite of how Will said she'd treated poor Kara, my heart ached for my Angel Girl.

Determinedly, I set out to help Kara. Willingly, I gave her as much physical contact as she wanted, as much eye contact, hugs and holds of all variety and at any time. I encouraged her to be what I saw her as: my new lightness-and-laughter Angel Daughter. From our first meeting when she said she'd seen me in her dream the night before, I took it upon myself to be her totally surrendered, surrogate Angel Mom, a transmitter and fountainhead of the unconditional love a good mother naturally gives her natural child.

So I spent an inordinate amount of time with Kara in that comfy, clunky old rocker next to our bed. Rocking her, holding and cuddling her doll-like bundle in my lap. Keeping her close to my strong heartbeat, speaking softly, helping mend her fractured being. Her own heart so raw, so tender, frozen in fear at unpredictable times during those fits, that I had to remind her many times every day, to breathe:

to slow down her race-car mind. I couldn't deny that this great love of mine had brought me another, inadvertent mission: to help heal these two other shattered young beings, besides my own recovering, ruptured self.

I had loosened my anchor in the solo life I'd had, and cast my fate. Aboard our family's boat as we set off on our journey upon Rio Blisso, whose gentle waves radiated and reflected love, what I had faith in could heal anything: kids, adults, the world around us. Our crew set off to travel this uncharted river of shimmering waters.

CHAPTER 7

batten down the hatches

Will and I discussed many times how we were the ultimate partnership, much more than romantic love, magnificent sex, and raising kids. "Let's make ours a true spiritual union," Will and I promised each other. We vowed to work hard, pray and meditate, live and love from our core center—celebrating the awareness that God-is-everywhere—so that our marriage would be an exciting commitment to last the rest of our lives. We agreed that the wonder and magic ignited by our coming together was a sum much greater than our two lives lived separately could ever match.

This vow of making ours a spiritual marriage was essential, given the challenge posed by Debby, whose poisonous, early complaint about me to the Children's Welfare authorities nearly destroyed our relationship at its onset. I finally got my first glimpse of her when she came to pick up the kids for a weekend visit shortly after our marriage. She was late, and Jonny, whom she always fetched before driving to pick up Kara at her nearby grade school, was close to tears. But then his sad little face instantaneously brightened when he saw Debby's big blue pickup turn into our street. Worrying that Mama, the sunshine of his life, would never come, he lit up like a Christmas tree when her truck noisily pulled into our quiet neighborhood street.

Peering from behind the curtains of a second-floor bedroom window, I watched rough Debby get out of her enormous beat-up Ford and take a swill from a can right after hugging Jonny. Among discarded beer and soda cans rattling in the bed of the truck were three monster-sized, slavering, barking mongrel dogs pacing in the back, ready to bite off anyone's head who approached.

A short and stocky, tanned woman with a wrestler's physique, wearing short cut-off blue jeans, she looked like one of those hard-living Roller Derby queens that had fascinated me as a kid, the kind that elbowed or shoved hard, then laughed uproariously as her opponent crashed sidewise onto railings or the floor of the rink. Debby was a veritable cowgirl Ringo, wearing silver on every finger, and as many turquoise necklaces as a First Nation woman could accrue in several lifetimes. Her many noisy bracelets clanged as she raised the can to her mouth again. Then tossed it into the truck bed hitting a random dog's bony head, before bending to pick up her beaming son at her side.

Okay, I admit it. If anyone ever saw the two of us, Debby and me, side by side, we'd probably appear more similar than I'm comfortable admitting, both of us altogether unconcerned by current fashion trends and ready for action anytime. While she was small and bulky, I was tall and lanky and wore no jewelry other than my home-made wedding ring and an amethyst crystal at my neck. Debby's cutoffs were skintight; my baggy gym shorts were splattered in paint. Spying from the window, I saw that Debby sure wasn't wearing anything under that well-filled elastic tube-top of hers. By then I had already surprised myself, over how enjoyable the colorful sports bras I wore under my own skimpy tops actually were. Aside from a few minor details like hair color (mine purple-red from years of using henna; hers, bottle-blonde), it's true: we might have passed for members of the same ragtag caravan of natural and no-makeup, strong working women; gals who don't give a royal flip about what others think of us. Yet after our rough 'n' ready shared physical aspects, we parted ways.

How odd, I thought. Had Debby not made that slanderous report about me, and were I not committed to cultivating only healthy friends these days, this country gal might have been someone I'd have found genuinely interesting, in a perverse "let's check out the seedier side of life" way. I recognized her blatant indifference to honor and esteem; I used to have it too. From above I watched her greet Jonny and then, a moment later, take a swill from the next can she'd just popped open. Soda or beer, I couldn't say. This gal's southern country bit wasn't at all like my gal-pals from New England, New York, or the jungle hillsides of the Caribbean. Instead of wearing all black like we artists do, or colorful bright dresses like West Indian ladies, in more humid Florida I mostly wore shorts and skinny tops, just like Debby here, when I wasn't getting sweaty with backyard gardening, when I wore a muddy bikini, a wide-brim hat with Wellie boots and protective gloves.

△

We had a plan, one Will and I discussed with Dr. C beforehand. I would be civil, but Debby couldn't enter the house whenever she arrived to pick up and drop off the kids. Dr. C helped me realize the value of maintaining boundaries to preserve the loving environment Will and I intended on creating in our home.

To make clear where I stood with our blended family, I always called myself Angel Mom. The main reason for this was that I hated the word *stepmom*, which had such a bad rap. Wanting to distinguish myself from the kids' bio-mom, I told them I was, "your Angel Mom," to remind Jonny and Kara, and me, that loving-kindness was my intention, more than most stepmoms had to offer to counterbalance their bio-mom's mean-heartedness that I faced. My nurturing would be nothing short of Angel Mom-terrific, I determined. Exceptional. Extraordinary.

I envisaged morphing into a real live Angel Mom-version of myself, not as some kind of a saintly cloud-sitter but as a joyful stepmom who shopped, cooked, did laundry and filled in for maternal-everything with a glad heart. I would be a go-for-it, cliff-jumping (if need be) kind of nurturer, with yoga headstands and twists my instruments of flight instead of soft fluffy wings. I'd sow positive thoughts as easily as other moms prepared meals with microwaves. I already knew that Jonny needed joy and playfulness and the constant presence of a grownup female's presence, while Kara needed all the healing love energy that I could pour into her.

They both needed me to be a love-bug kind of Angel Mom, not an average, everyday kind of stepmom.

I watched from behind my curtain as the strange creature the kids called Mama threw her next empty on the pile of other rattling cans rumbling in the rear of her truck, laughing as she again hit one of her hapless dogs on its snout. I cringed, hoping she wasn't driving and drinking, but powerless, because I knew Debby was oblivious to the law. And dangerous to my sphere of fragile nest-building.

Will had told me much earlier how it was with her. "We started off fine. But right after Kara was born, she went out and got drunk every other night. At the end, well, all she cared about was hanging out with her lowlife cowboy pals and doing crank (that's redneck for crystal meth, speed) the whole time Jonny was in her womb."

Remembering this, my mind instantly dismissed the idea that she and I were any more alike than the work clothes we both happened to be wearing that day. I considered going downstairs to greet the kids' bio-mom. After all, this was the first time she was in my immediate presence. But I was still wary, and pissed off—sure I admit it—by the heinous lies she'd told the authorities about me abusing her kids. Maybe some other time, if I knew she was sober, I'd greet her. Maybe never.

△

Our blended family had many other differences, besides two radically different moms.

After college and the Amazonian jungle, Will ended up in New York City to pursue a filmmaking career, while I ran as far as I could from cities. Now though, Will and I viewed our differences as assets, not deficits—which, we agreed after doing many sessions with Dr. C, was the best way to offer our kids a more expanded view of life. Early in our joint counseling sessions I insisted he stop calling them "my kids," and say "ours." Fat lot of good it did. No matter, we agreed that our crazy-quilt family was challenging, but we saw it also as more fun, our unique kind of diversity, than anything we'd known before. Thankfully, both Will and I liked the offbeat and thrilling, preferring to be challenged rather than accept the status quo.

Besides nurturing my own Better-me, my role in our family dynamic was helping my man and Angel Kids to heal from their woundings. Serving the family became my new *seva*, a Sanskrit word that translates loosely as *doing one's sacred duty*, connoting an offering of work as a way of honoring others. "Next to meditating and keeping good company," the Teacher said, "seva is the most important thing you do on the spiritual path." My duty as Angel Mom, I believed, was to continue healing myself first, then do my best with my three beloveds. I started calling my new homemaking routine, my *household yoga*. By convincing myself that this approach, doing seva by performing household yoga, would lighten the otherwise art-devoid suburban world I now found myself in I became more spiritually content, far beyond any other time in my life.

Nurturing became my new, live-performance art medium. I traded in my studio's paints and brushes for band-aides and lots of soothing hugs. Surrounded by suburban people with whom I hadn't much in common, I did my seva, religiously. Household yoga was my new ongoing, interactive, environmental art-performance piece. As Angel Mom, I would subsume my personal desires to help counterbalance the psychic damage the kids, and Will and myself to lesser extents, had suffered up till then.

Gradually I came to test and learn to accept that part of myself the Teacher called "every person's Inner Self, their Better-me." Returning to suburbia was going back to my roots. That meant that I too, could now heal from whatever residual wounds remained unresolved in my seven-year recovery process from a lifetime's worth of addiction.

Right away I made an important decision.

For a year, at least, I would willingly trade-in using my studio's tools and materials for those used in a householder's domestic arts. I'd forego creating two- and three-dimensional objects for concentrating on culinary alchemy, and having a forgiving sense of humor. I'd trade possibilities for public exhibitions for spontaneous dancing, wrestling, tickling, and clowning around; willingly giving up my airs of being a great artist for the humble new role of being a puppet in my household yoga-act. I determined to make our everyday family routine the joyous carnival I wanted my new life to be. As Angel Mom, I promised myself to never feel burdened by helping to raise Kara and Jonny, or ever regard them as any kind of inconvenience.

I knew I needed a year to learn how to do this, how to nurture them, my Angel Kids. They were now as much my kids as Will's. Nobody could tell me any differently. I worked hard to make this performance piece of mine—as Angel Mom—my sacred duty and honor.

▲

To fortify myself for this strenuous role I started doing aerobics at the gym, pumping up my yoga-derived stamina with three-mile runs, and added more challenging poses to my regular hatha home practice. Being around Jonny and Kara and their friends meant I had to work triply hard to keep my vitality level high, especially since I'd had no experience with kids since babysitting as a teen. And even if I had, our situation was unlike any I'd ever seen or read about.

All children suffer in breakups, but it seemed as if our kids had gotten more wounded in their mother's angry bitterness than most. During the custody battle, after Debby and her mother were caught red-handed by a guardian ad litem, a court-ordered observer, coaxing Kara, who'd just turned four, to lie about "Daddy touching you down there," traumatized Kara was taken away and forced to live for three months in a group foster home run by uncaring strangers. After the judge's final ruling awarded full custody to Will—who of course was completely exonerated from the false charges brought by his vindictive ex, who consequently was deemed "unfit" by the judge—Jonny, who was a one-year-old, barely a toddler, was sadly yanked away (per court order) from Debby's arms to go live full-time with Will, the parent found most responsible. And so, especially after Debby's blatantly public drug use was reported, he became the sole custodial parent.

As a result of all this trauma, both kids acted like scared little bunnies when I first met them.

Fully realizing that our kids needed more care than children raised in a healthy nuclear family, one in which both parents were present and mom wasn't drunk or, as court witnesses reported about Debby, "high on crank even during her pregnancies"—I prepared for the hard work of repairing what was broken. All of us, my three fellow crew members and me too, all of us aboard our family vessel sailing on snaking switchback curves of Rio Blisso—were varying degrees of emotional wrecks.

Behavioral scientists tell us our personality patterns are set for life within our first seven years; some say by age four. Kara was already seven when Will and I married. Her intense personality, negatively influenced by Debby's anger and paranoia, had already been programmed, I knew, yet I was committed to showering Kara with overdoses of love, hoping to fill some of the cracks that had been inadvertently created by her mother, deep within her. Aiming to help heal four-year-old Jonny, because he wasn't yet in school like his sister, I had more time to influence him. His worldview wasn't nearly as fully formulated as Kara's was. With this in mind, I set about creating a positive, nurturing bond with both my Angel Kids.

△

Although I instantly felt at home in Will's sexy-spiritual-soulmate embrace, and his family was totally mine now, there was no debate that I was the last to arrive at the kids' party. I did what I could to accustom them to my permanent presence. Admittedly, there were times when I felt like the odd guy out, but I learned to shake off that persistent, shabby old insecurity of mine, telling myself I shouldn't take things so seriously. I tried to remind myself that I wasn't being shut out on purpose. In private sessions with Dr. C, I shared my perceived *them-versus-me* dynamic in our household. After our discussions, I realized that my *feelings of being left out* were the re-experiencing of my own deep childhood wounding. Suddenly, being Angel Mom began to take on more weight than I'd foreseen. I was forced to face old insecurities head-on. Forced to heal my own psychic scars.

Occasionally, I'd notice how that *left-out* feeling arose from what Will said, and at other times what he didn't say. He was an over-protective dad, totally unconscious of how he excluded me. Whenever I called him on this annoying trait, he admitted he still wasn't sure about me, saying he was "still wary of your out-there God-stuff, it's too much for my kids to handle, after all they've gone through."

What a bummer, I thought. I argued how he needed to trust me. To our credit, he and I continued to attend sessions with Dr. C to address our obvious deficits. Will tried to accept my weird quirks as much as I did his. Even though we were now married, after a year-and-a-half courtship we were just getting to know each other.

▲

In my own family of origin I had to fight for the right to discover who and what I was, and then, to speak about my own Truth. Raised in a home where chaos and denial reigned, neither Lizzy nor I could ever dare say what was on our minds. As the youngest child of a dear-when-sober man who masked his fears with Canadian whiskey, by the time I reached ten I never knew if Dad was going to be nice, mean or creepy, since trust had been lost early on between us. Mom appeared not to notice all the bizarre behavior, having shielded herself within the cocoon of denial, alcoholism's sad sibling along with enabling. Consequently, my childhood in the 'burbs had been so painful that by early adulthood I'd come to trust no one and nothing.

As a kid, afraid of being punished for my boisterous behavior, I learned to never share any of my deeper feelings. Until I found art, I kept my overly imaginative thoughts and feelings safely hidden. I learned to never speak of my rich and colorful dreams that took me far from those pursuing demons in them, and how I learned to fly away from their angry grasps. My earliest aspiration, like all children's, of saving the world, was revealed to no one but my secret pals (I had many) in hard-to-find places around my neighborhood: in the woods, by a stream, hidden between big boulders, where we met up—in my imagination. I cultivated an enthusiastic fantasy life, focusing on adventures waiting for me, as soon as I'd grown up, rather than accepting the dull dread of my childhood's suburban atmosphere. By adolescence, I was so good at fabricating a pretend existence that I lived almost exclusively in a state of perpetual daydreaming.

My haunting, vivid dreams segued easily into narratives I taught myself to draw and paint, I began to create stories with characters and imagery. Eventually I found it difficult to separate real life from these, to me, realistic flights of fancy. To avoid mom's constantly reprimanding me, and dad's regular drunken harassments, I'd do just about anything to avoid replicating the suburban hell that was my childhood's reality. In adolescence I trained myself to shut down all feelings entirely, awakening my emotions only when creating images. When teenage escapades involving booze and forbidden sex entered the picture, when real-life risky behavior (the adrenalin-pumping kind) started showing up—I dove into addiction feet-first without stopping to think.

But it wasn't until deciding to be a real artist, and even more so after embracing Better-me as a sober woman, that I learned to truly be free. At a steady pace that accelerated after finding the Teacher, I began to heal. Now my husband, children and I, in our weird and wonderful journey down Rio Blisso, each in our unique way, were healing in the safety net of a blended family. I felt strongly that the best way for all four of us to become whole—and thrive—was to always speak the truth to one another, despite how hard that might be.

We called a Family Meeting whenever anyone had something to say. I knew FMs were vitally important to successful parenting. The instructional book Will insisted I read and follow, taught us about FMs. Every family needs a safe place, it said, a forum to share, because otherwise it's too easy to end up stuffing one's confused or painful feelings. How true. Having been forced to do that as a child, I understood all too well the negative consequences of suppressing one's real self. Being free to express the truth, each of ours vastly different from the next guy's, was pivotal in this Better-me way of living that I'd been shown first by sobriety and Jane my sponsor; next, the Teacher, and now by the stepparenting guide Will had given me as a how-to.

Will and I agreed to hold regular Family Meetings. With them, our kids would never have to carry around in their souls any more fear or sadness brought on by the hardships they'd already endured. Our regular FMs, and the frequent visits the kids were making to Dr. C, encouraged Kara and Jonny to let out their feelings so their spirits could soar high. Freedom-to-be became the essential soul medicine in our family's get-well bag of tricks.

A sweet-natured boy who was more heartbroken than anyone his age ought to be, Jonny pined for his Mama all day, every day; just as a lonely fish in a bowl longs for bigger waters. But the judge deemed Debby "unfit" to share even joint custody, which meant that Jonny and Kara were allowed to visit her only every other weekend. Being disconnected in this way from a mother who genuinely loved them—despite her shortcomings—is hard for any kid to accept.

By the second month of my permanent presence, Kara's nightmares thankfully stopped. Able to sleep more soundly now, she became immersed in her schoolwork, gymnastics and other fun activities, and less worried about her bio-mom. Of the two kids, Jonny was by far the sadder, outwardly. Refusing to pity him, I accepted that separation from his birth mom was the harsh but painful truth of Jonny's young life right then, as well as his sister's. Instead of feeling sorry for them, I determined to love them back to a happy, balanced childhood, to help them play the hand each of them had been dealt in this cosmic game of life.

To do this I had to acquire some basic new skills, not the least of which was cooking healthy meals from scratch. My first reaction to this part of household yoga was: "Breakfast, lunch—and dinner? Really? C'mon, guys! Three meals? Everyday?"

I'd never been a foodie but a healthy, if irregular eater when left to my own lonesome-me devices. It didn't take long for me to realize that nurturing begins with good food. Kids need soul-healthy meals to nourish mind and body. As fast as an empty stomach grumbles, I discovered that Kara and Jonny were far less cheery if any of their three daily meals were late or forgotten, which happened often at the beginning of my performance-piece mothering.

I noticed that Jonny got antsy whenever he stood before the opened fridge door, right after returning from a weekend at Debby's. He got nervous when the milk jug or the mayonnaise jar got low; just as he grew agitated when blown-out light bulbs weren't immediately replaced. I didn't want to add to his distress so I made sure we never ran out of basic supplies, something I'd never given much thought to before, unless I was stocking up for a long cruise back in my deep-water sailing days.

Having two different homes is complicated for kids. Whenever Jonny returned from Debby's country place, he would notice right away any change that had occurred during his absence. Everything had to be just as it was when he'd left for the weekend, or Jonny became uneasy.

Kara didn't appear overly stressed by externals like Jonny was. Her back-to-suburbia self-preservation ritual was to remain in a semi-twilight zone for the first few hours after Debby returned them to Lackland. Everything about Kara during this in-between phase—the way she held her mouth; her uncustomary use of *ain't* and other redneck words; her unfocused, dazed gaze instead of her usually sparkling clear, wide eyes—all appeared altered, discordant when she arrived home from a weekend with Debby. Acclimating from one radically different household to the other took a few hours for the kids, so Will and I gave them space and patience during this wobbly transition period.

When it came to kid-matters, I couldn't turn to my own mother for advice, sure as I was of her overly critical response. Mom was too quick to judge to have a conversation with, so I just didn't. Our rapport had always been next to nonexistent. If I wore blue, Mom would say, "Why not red?" If I baked a cake, she'd bark, "Why not a pie?" Instead of her to confide in, I came to rely solely on Dr. C for advice about how to be a loving mother, a patient wife, and the best nurturer I could be. Thanks to Dr. C, I came to understand that for kids, "Discipline means love, not harsh criticism and one-sided judgment." As for any spiritual questions, I relied on a regular mailed-letter correspondence with the Teacher.

Thanks to my meditation teacher, I'd become pretty good at calming my chaotic mind that once plagued me, that used to feed on my fears and anxieties like a starving simian devours bunches of sweet ripe bananas. Seven years before marrying Will, right along with getting sober, I'd learned from her pure, unaffected teaching of ancient spiritual practices, the yoga of constant, silent mantra repetition, which kept my wanting-to-chatter mind, my inner beasty monkey-mind, busy, and oddly, wonderfully ... satiated.

The mantra my Teacher offered was *So'hăm* (pronounced *SO-hum*). The first time I tried silently repeating it, I experienced the same instant relief I'd had when I'd been initiated into TM meditation twenty years earlier, when the Divine inner light saved me from that psychic pain in my gut I was experiencing, right after my parents disowned me, simply for being who I was. The Teacher showed how to use this sacred phrase silently, coordinating *So'* with each in-breath, and *hăm* with each out-breath. She taught us how seekers had used this mantra for eons, to guide them, and how repeating it calms the mind anytime, anywhere. So I began the practice of *japa*, continuous, silent mantra-repeating whenever I could.

I trained my mind, like a deep-sea diver trains their muscles and lung capacity, to hold onto the steady sureness of this mantra's invisible power. "This *chaitanya*-mantra," the Teacher said, "is alive, and when repeated with intent, is the same as our own inner Power, our Kundalini; the same as Aum, the name of God." In short time I was going to bed repeating the mantra, replacing the oftentimes scary feelings that gripped me then, as I fell asleep, with the sweet solace of this holy sound. Whenever awake, I trained myself to repeat the mantra. In between talking or listening to others, I repeated the mantra. When I was upset, I repeated it fervently. When I was calm, I did so in a more relaxed fashion. In short time, japa became my main yogic-meditation practice.

The Teacher told us this ancient Sanskrit mantra translates into the concept of what is known as *universal consciousness*: called by some, the great *I am*. Since recorded history, *So'hăm* has been used in the East to identify with the unlimited aspect of expanded consciousness. Wanting to still the agitated mind is a common human trait. "Silently repeating this mantra soothes the troubled mind," she told us, her devoted students.

Whenever awake, I did this user-friendly practice with dedication and consistency. Now that I had a family to hold together, I was even more thankful for this assured relief from my lifelong assault of mental agitation. Even though I still had some inner work to do, serenity not yet entirely mine even after prolonged glimpses of it, the technique of japa was my favorite yogic mind-stilling tool, my greatest relief from mental disturbance. Especially after realizing that finding time to sit in quiet meditation, the usual way of meditating, was virtually impossible with two young children afoot. But I could do silent japa practice 24/7, at whatever time I was awake. I repeated it first thing when I awoke. I watched it immediately change my agitated mind whenever I remembered to silently repeat it during the day. And falling asleep with the mantra, I clung to it as a child clings to their teddy bear.

Haunted since childhood by a wave of paralyzing fear that seemed to strike me each night as I began to fall asleep, pushing me into a dark chasm that felt exactly as I imagined death must be, watching myself slowly sinking, falling, being swallowed by an unnamable dread—this feeling had been neatly blotted out by my having used booze and drugs for so long—now when it unpredictably erupted, but only when I was falling asleep, I only had to remember to silently repeat *So'hăm, So'hăm* and … I tumbled into the velvety peace of sleep, thanks to the mantra, each and every time. Thankfully, once the Teacher taught me, I trained my mind to repeat *So'hăm, So'hăm* instead of the useless, often destructive chatter that used to fill it. Using this mind-stilling technique, my reality became calmer as slowly, day-by-day, Better-me began to take charge of my everyday awareness.

By the time I married Will, my family got to benefit from the peaceful center my spiritual practice had wrested from the former menacing demons that had haunted me since early childhood. The old me, drunken and druggy Lesser-me's obsessive, runaway freight-train brain had been slowed, and sometimes was even semi-tranquil, thanks to the previous years of daily meditation and japa I'd done. By the time I married Will, my monkey-mind was well trained to silently munch on the soul-soothing sound, the yum-yum ancient sound of *So'hăm, So'hăm*.

Taking the helm at Will's side, as the confident co-captain of our family's boat, navigating along Rio Blisso's swift currents, I felt more content than ever. Nobody was more surprised than I to discover how family life could be such a thrilling, satisfying adventure.

CHAPTER 8

strange and distant shores

I was a dolphin out of water. These frolicking cetacean cousins of mine that I love to swim amongst, or watch them playing freely, happily in the sea. As a vagabond artist, I prefer to live surrounded by water, living or working on boats, dwelling on islands, whether in the Caribbean, Manhattan or Iceland. But not since growing up in a Chicago suburb had I felt as alienated, as out of place as I did in landlocked central Florida. For now, we had to stay. Will was restrained by the custody agreement to stay for the kids' formative years in his hometown where he was within driving distance to Debby's, and he had family and community support, so the kids could best adapt and recover from the vicious divorce.

The women of this strange alien place stared at me unmercifully. I could only presume it was because my style was so different from their outdated formality, their stiff-teased hairdos, pastel pantsuits contrasting my New York artist attire. I wore my long henna hair loose around my shoulders or up in a ponytail, and sported workout-skintight spandex on the street when no one else did there, in that 90s cultural black-hole. Let's face it: I didn't resemble any of the Lackland lassies, especially when I went to church, which I did every Sunday in accordance with Will's and my spiritual agreement.

Often, when I stood close to another mom or a granny in a park setting, watching our charges romping on swings and slides, or while waiting in line at the bank or the supermarket—on numerous occasions completely out of the blue, one of these buttoned-up women would turn to me without any preceding greeting and ask: "Have you taken Jesus as your personal savior yet?" It happened so many times there in central Florida's tightly buckled Bible belt, I finally had to ask Claire's advice how to respond.

My impeccably proper, Art Forum-informed mother-in-law made me laugh with her smartass answer. "It took me a long time to figure the best way to handle that imposition. You *must* immediately reply, Why yes! of course! Haven't *you*? And then right away, look away."

Smart and sophisticated, always non-confrontationally kind, was Claire and Phil's style.

In short time our three generations became as tight as a blended tribe can be. Funny, but I related more to Phil, a retired businessman imbued with a solid New England work ethic, interested in discussing dreams and expanded consciousness, than I did to Claire, a serious spiritually-motivated artist. Maybe it was her pouffed, salon-blonde hairdo, or her hardline abstract art, so opposite to my naturalistic style. Claire proudly claimed herself, first, a Christian wife and mother, then a cutting-edge sculptor, committed to pursuing original ideas. Since her early motherhood days, she'd exhibited her work, choosing to show regionally rather than pursue the art world's international web of collecting patrons.

Claire wasn't the hands-on, "Let's hug up and bake cookies," type of gramma, nor Phil, the "Hey kids, curl up here on my lap and I'll tell you a story," kind of gramps. In their magnificent home, Will's folks set the tone of formality for our family's regular visits. We'd speak quietly, have low-key interactions, but feel comforted, well-fed, always listened-to, and peaceful. The rule was: adults talked while the kids were sent, corralled in the grandparents' newly built, well-separated but spacious play room, complete with a brand new computerized upright player piano and club-size pool table. Above all, both Phil and Claire insisting on having it relaxed and quiet in their private space. Theirs was the old-fashioned approach in which grandchildren were required to behave, and that meant our young ones being expelled to the other, well-secluded, sound-proof room. The antithesis to the free and easy, laid-back democratic way in which Will and I had agreed to raise our kids, using weekly FMs to nicely sort out things like grievances or complaints.

Everything about our two generations' methodology was opposite. Phil and Claire's dramatic designer-home, with decorated and numerous rooms large enough to display their valuable contemporary art collection placed museum-like throughout, was exquisitely lavish. Copious shelves in hidden nooks boasted thick musty books and shiny crystal, delicate Chinese ceramics, or one-of-a-kind artifacts from the couple's worldwide travels. Theirs was a modern version of an urbane, sprawling mansion of refined taste and demurely stated old-wealth.

In contrast, our home, located at the end of their long driveway, where suburban sprawl insistently tried to encroach upon the older folk's isolated, field-surrounding estate, was an adequate but rowdy, kid-friendly suburban split-level: a boisterous whirligig free-for-all, plainly outfitted but cramped, and did I mention yet?—average Americana. Father and son's abodes reflected their different lifestyles and bank accounts, about as similar as a small calm lake is to a vast chaotic ocean.

▲

They say that instead of a shrink, all a person needs is one good friend, and I certainly had that in Will. Thanks to the premarital therapy we'd done with Dr. C, ours was a solid, honest friendship, deeper even than our insatiable passion for each other. It helped that I accepted my mate's annoying idiosyncrasies, and, however difficult and only because it was temporary, tolerated the all-too-familiar suburban crunch of our current situation. Surprisingly, I quickly became neutral about wearing a sports bra, being now a regular member of the PTA, soccer field, and church activities to which I'd committed, embracing wholeheartedly my righteous-mom persona. Per our bra-pact, I made no demands on Will other than that we'd be leaving this barren town after our five-year agreement was up.

Whenever I grew scared that we'd somehow be stuck forever in the too-square 'burbs, Will assured me: "As soon as we get our finances sorted out we're out of here. Maybe it'll be sooner than five years. So stop bugging me, will ya. I don't like it here anymore than you do."

Okay, being thrust into motherhood is a monumental change for anyone in their mid-forties, granted, but being a Lacklander was beyond any grueling test I could have foreseen in my future. Yet I rose to meet each new challenge demanded in this performance piece of mine. I became a fabulous actor, playing my least favorite character, a middle-class mom who arts—and played it convincingly, with all my heart.

With this goal of becoming a super Angel Mom from the start, I consciously decided to set aside my studio work for as long as it would take—a few months, a year at most?—to learn my new role. With gusto, I threw myself into being the best nurturer, the most fun stepmom I could. More than anything, more than recognition by my artist peers, or exploring far-flung corners of the globe, I wanted to succeed in this challenging role, not just for my sake but for these three other souls I was now responsible for. Yes, it meant a million different obligations I'd never been concerned about before, including the complexities of creating and maintaining a permanent home. Who'd ever think I'd come to know about kitchen appliances or mole-crickets ruining lawns, for golly-gosh sakes. Let's face it: more than creating art, Jonny and Kara's brokenness held my undivided attention. To care for them I decided that studio work would just have to wait—until I sensed both kids felt secure and I had this caregiving thing down cold. However long that would take, it would have to be.

Like a petri dish, our house was alive with nonstop activities. Projects multiplied before my astonished eyes. Not a cool or hip artist's lair, but a home devoted to rough-and-tumble play, filled with broken-down used furniture and kids' stuff strewn everywhere, this was my new stimuli. Gone was the endless string of groovy out-there friends, and other risk-taking environments of my former years. Instead of edgy art, on display in our homey house was an entire wall filled with kids' paintings, thick gooey posters and fragile drawings of cut-out-paper butterfly wings. Playing in the grownups' bedroom was off limits, but Kara and Jonny had free rein everywhere else, space enough to grow healthy and free. We wanted them to feel

Strange and Distant Shores

comfortable expressing themselves, as long as they didn't break any of the three guidelines I'd soon have to come up with.

If Will's and my home was a galaxy removed from the grandparents' launching pad, Debby's was, to me, an undiscovered, far-off universe requiring time travel. The kids thrived on living full-time in our relative normal, grace-before-meals and apple-pie family setting, with two former alternative, freak parents, presently living incognito in well-clipped, well policed, sugar-pretty Lackland. Will and I both cleaned up our piratical, curse-filled language too. Daunting at first, I changed in so many ways, behaving more ... decently ... in order to fulfill the demands of caring for young Christian children.

Every other weekend though (and any free-of-kids time in between), Will and I jumped into the sack every Friday afternoon, as soon as Debby's truck pulled away from our oak-lined street, after picking up Jonny and Kara. These treasured afternoons in bed were so needed, so pleasurably animalistic that I had to put a muffler on my uncontrollable screams of delight, afraid our too-close neighbors might hear. Yes-sir-ee, when the kids were gone for the weekend, visiting their off-the-grid bio-mom, all bets were off concerning propriety and restraint ... and decency ... in the lovemaking department.

Every other weekend the kids left on Friday afternoon for Debby's spread, deep in cowboy (the famous Florida "cracker") country. Traveling there, one passed endless acres of pastureland filled with grazing cud-chewing cows and ultra-long-horned bulls that dug big holes in the sandy soil they rolled in to rub off feeding insects from their backs. Miles of dusty and narrow, straight and mud-slick roads led to her place, interrupted now and then by a solitary house, a no-frills doublewide or a trashed-up trailer, and occasionally a red-bricked or pre-fab one-room country church. Flung from her cowgirl's pickup onto anyone's turf, Debby's ever-present Pabst Blue Ribbon empties landed in ditches at every dusty crossroads. Every other Friday she left her twenty acre property—set in a clearing in the midst of cypress hammocks and tall pines, too unmanageable for any single person to handle, even a woman as nail-tough as she—her sights set for those kids of hers in Lackland who were, in her own spiteful explanation to them, "bought from the custody judge by your miserable, good-for-nuthin' father."

Her dilapidated house—twice as large as our split-level suburban—was an old, three-story clapboard, a former rooming house in the nearby town that had been originally built for nomadic cowhands. Back when Will and Debby were giddy-high, beer-swilling newlyweds, Will had bought it for a feather. He'd cut the three-story residence in half and had it transported down the road twenty miles away in the dead of night, with hired workers moving the telephone and utility wires ahead of the rolling house. At the final destination, a cleared site in the middle of nowhere, they reattached the two sections smack in a swampy woods.

When divorce ripped the couple apart six years later, Debby got the country spread and Will got the kids—a godsend, in our estimation. Now, Debby's place looked more like Tobacco Road than Will originally planned it as an exotic wooded retreat for making more features from. With debris and dogs' messes strewn everywhere, the current decay and neglect had erased any vestige of Will's vision for a rural filmmaker's Shangri-La. Situated miles from the nearest village, with its one-room post office and five bars nearby, the closest country corner had a couple of competing evangelical churches, plus a convenience store that sold beer and cigarettes and not much else. Besides Debby's many barnyard animals, most untamed for playing around with, the kids had no friends other than Bruno, our black-and-tan dachshund, who obligingly made the trip every other weekend with them.

Suspicious of strangers, and even one another, the locals around Debby's provincial world all carried guns, concealed "for protection," as I was told by one of her neighbors. While once waiting for Will to pick up the kids from Debby's, I decided to stroll along the two-lane stretch of lonely country road in front of her dismal place, visible only through thick trees. Will drove our station wagon down the long lane to Debby's house as I began to walk slowly on the empty road, reading a paperback. No cars were to be seen in either direction on the miles' long straightaway. Suddenly, a gray-haired woman in a dark mini-truck appeared. She slowly, cautiously passed me, gawking as I walked and read on the far side of the macadam. I was surprised when she braked, and then slowly backed up to pull alongside me. Why not? No other car was around. The two of us were the only humans on that long length of hot road. She stared at me incredulously, unsmiling.

"What on earth you doing out here, honey?" the woman demanded.

I gave her an abbreviated version of how my man was picking up my stepkids, and pointed to Debby's place, hidden by a copse of trees. The old lady pulled back, regarding me with a no-nonsense, ice-blue-eyed squint of disdain.

"Sugar," she drawled, "there's strange folks in these parts. You don't wanna be caught out here without one of these."

She reached over and patted, like it was her best friend, a mean-looking, un-holstered handgun that lay beside her on the seat. It was a western-style pistol right out of *Bonanza* or *Have Gun Will Travel* episodes I used to watch when a kid. I vigorously shook my head and told her not to worry about me. She gravely *tsk tsk'd*, her wire-haired silvery head swaying side-to-side, muttering as if in disbelief as she looked right at me.

"Have it your own way, sweetheart," she growled. "But you're in some big-trouble territory here." She gave me a shrug and no wave as her pickup crept away down the road, her head still shaking.

I stood staring after this apparition, wondering what upset the old bag so much. Then I resumed walking, reading my book on the empty road.

CHAPTER 9

learning the ropes

I wanted to focus on cherishing the kids, adoring their father, and continuing to love and respect Better-me—plus get back to work in my cobwebby studio. I preferred not to acknowledge the fear and loathing I couldn't shake for Debby. It wasn't any fun, diving into that dark place of imagined fear where my aversion for Debby lurked, well beyond the real peace I'd found with my new family life. But I would be a phony if I didn't fess up that the kids' bio-mom scared me out of my wits. If her falsely reporting me to the authorities wasn't enough, I grew even more scared of her after Will told me Debby had shot her first husband—in the foot—and more fearful when Will mentioned how she went after him with an axe, trying to kill him, just before they divorced. I couldn't help imagining the worse: Debby aiming a pistol at me, blasting me right through our front door. One day without warning, she'd shoot me in the heart, I feared, even though I kept telling myself, "Stop it! This kind of paranoia doesn't help anyone, you fool."

Debby was a transplant from Arkansas who was living out her dream in the gator-infested backwoods of cattle country. At her and Will's keg-o'-beer wedding, she was a gum-snapping western-style bride, wearing a plaid polyester, yoke-fringed shirt along with shiny new boots and brand-new starchy Levis to match her groom's. Suspicious of God and anything else not in her trailer-and-beer tribe, pint-sized Debby drove the Florida back roads in a gigantic deep-blue pickup with its own portable TV installed on the dash. Regardless of the law, she drank can after can of Pabst while driving, at the local saloon, and everywhere in between. She dreamed of having a facelift and a brand-new double-wide, and she'd soon get both, right after she sold her too-large spread that as young'uns, Kara and Jonny called Mama's place. During the custody proceedings, she denied having done crank during her pregnancy with Jonny, but several witnesses claimed otherwise.

I'd never known anyone like Debby—savage and brutish in appearance but right at home in a mid-sized mall. I was repulsed by the numbing constancy of her self-centeredness, memories of which I've locked forever away in my forgiveness drawer labeled, "Never to be Mentioned."

Repugnance is a terrible thing to suffer, something no sane person chooses to feel any longer than a scant few seconds. So right now, I must turn away from this repulsion of mine for the kid's birth mother. I tried to be civil to her. But she never returned any of my smiles, waves, or attempts at being decent, respectful, and kind. Never.

From the start, I chose *not* to dwell on my ill feelings, regardless of how often the monstrous desire of loathing tempted me; I never let myself feel the justified hatred my Lesser-me held for Debby. Sure, it was tempting. But earlier, when she'd so viciously reported me, I'd felt the poison of aversion seep into my heart. And from then on I forced myself to not feel the leaden emotion of loathing that resentment brings, knowing by then it was more destructive to my chance at real happiness, even, than Debby's insane behavior toward me ever could be.

Instead, I tried, over and over, to accept her for who she was: a mentally unstable person who made strange, completely inscrutable choices. Whenever I couldn't fix something she'd done to the kids—all the lies, all the "teZa is a witch" stories—I commanded that sinking feeling of wanting-to-hate to *shutthefuckup*! In the early days of journeying on Rio Blisso, I had to work hard not to imagine her dead, I was that threatened by her. As Angel Mom, along with nurturing, I took upon myself the righteous decision of not giving any energy to this blackness, the sickening feeling I fought so hard against that I felt toward this poor soul Debby, so lost, so sorrowful. So fully living in destructive addictions, as I once had been.

Before she made her vile accusations about me, when Will first told me about her, I had determined to have only true compassion toward her. As I would for any man or woman who'd lost the legal right to raise their children. I could easily imagine how Debby must have agonized over that insufferable loss. But after purposely attacking my character, wounding me in the deepest spot of my soul when she accused me, a victim myself of childhood sexual abuse, after I'd worked so hard for so many years to shed being the victim and embrace my Better-me—I no longer held a shred of sympathy for her. What she'd accused me of was, to many besides myself, unforgiveable. The idea of ever trusting, respecting, or empathizing with Debby got killed by her making that so-called anonymous phone call.

I told myself if she ever had the balls to apologize for having done her stupid trick, things could be different. But I didn't hold my breath. Instead, I learned about the kind of forgiveness that entails acceptance of another's loathsome behavior, the only kind of forgiveness, I would find out through experience, that's necessary in order to heal from pain inflicted by others.

But—she never spoke to me, period. She barely looked my way when I would call out a greeting of "Hello Debby!" or wave when she arrived for the kid's pick-up. I never spoke to her about how incensed she made me, by the little regard she seemed to have for her responsibilities as a mother. People would ask Will and me, "Why do you let such a bad mother like her spend time with the kids?" And the answer we gave was always the plain truth, hard to believe for any outsider: "She truly loves Kara and Jonny. And that's enough for us."

I never saw or heard of anything she did for them that faintly resembled a snippet of a child's edification. Besides the regular expensive steaks the kids said she fed them from the grill, along with microwaved scrambled eggs and canned beans, it seemed everything she did with them was for her own pleasure: dragging them into bars, onto overcrowded party-boats, never reading a storybook or mouthing a soothing prayer before meals or bedtime. Where was the nurturing? Where, the guidance? But we knew she genuinely loved them. With Debby, we realized there was just no sense at all, to how some people demonstrate their love. With Debby, her brand of loving the kids Will and I foresaw as looming challenges they'd later have to deal with in adulthood, and how fortunate they'd be to be so well equipped to overcome life's adversities, as we all have to do, sooner or later, as grownups. Neediness. Codependency. Guilt. Lack of the God-thing. That's what she taught her kids. Watching their mother drink beer, tossing cans out the car window, never having heart-to-heart talks, loud Jerry-Springer TV everywhere, being yelled at, thick-headed never hearing or listening: these were Debby's ways of showing her sad brand of motherly love. Painfully remiss in the outer ways of demonstrating positive role-modeling.

Her love for her kids was genuine, however. And it taught me how to not judge what, to me, makes us most human of all: the way we love, or hate.

Sadly, Debby never came to visit them in Lackland on the midweek day allotted her in the custody agreement. Kara and Jonny said she never read to them, neither at bedtime nor any other time, telling them, "I don't want to waste my visit with y'all doing that dumb stuff!"

Homework that was due for the kids' classes the very next morning after the Sunday night when she returned them to us, perpetually too late in the evening, never got done. Instead, she dragged them to the mall or the Am Vets with its cheap drinks, making the kids wait hours, sometimes late into the night, while she had her fill at the bar. Whatever the kids wished, she'd buy: unlimited candy, soda, crappy cereals crusty with sugar; video games (discouraged at our place), expensive toys and gadgets incongruous with her meager income as an "antique dealer," her euphemism for being a glorified junk dealer on eBay. In place of offering the kids comfort and support, the woman instilled her values of mistrusting God and cleanliness, a fear of water, foreigners, and anyone but her closest drinking pals.

She laughed with them (and they in turn, laughingly told me), "I love ya, you little turds!"—which, I guess, was her way of making light of a bad situation. It seemed to me she dished out only hurt and confusion, like poison candy. To onlookers, her mothering style didn't make any more sense than it did to me. So many people told me, "You shouldn't let them be with her" to which I always replied, "I know it appears weird, but she's their mother. It would be way worse if she didn't love them, trust me. Will and I are just glad she didn't abandon them."

In time, Debby's insufficiencies, sadly, would become her children's liabilities. Catastrophes were always on this woman's precipice. Once, a young son of a friend of Debby's cornered Jonny in the pool and, in our son's words, "rubbed himself up on me." Kara came home one Halloween wearing a scanty, provocatively sheer belly-dancer costume, showing way too much flesh for an eight-year-old. Every other Friday Jonny would tearfully wait at the end of our driveway before Debby showed up, predictably late. The rest of the time Jonny kept his feelings of dismay, for the most part, well hidden, but Kara had learned by age seven how to argue back at the top of her lungs with her bio-mom. I had to learn to let Kara be like this, I was advised by my chosen mothering authority.

Dr. C helped me understand. She said in one of our sessions, "If Kara can't yell back, Debby will overpower her and refuse to do anything she or Jonny need or want. Let her scream at her mom. It's her only defense mechanism, for now."

The kids' total adoration for their mama was never in question. "She don't mean nobody no harm," Kara told me, making me cringe as she imitated Debby's backwoods grammar. I solved that by making Thursdays the kids' special *Ain't Day* so then, if they wanted, the kids could speak all the redneck they wanted to, at least that one day each week without receiving any correcting from grammatically-anal me.

"Me and Jonny says *ain't* around her a lot so's Mama don't feel bad," Kara explained, still in the short-term verbal and psychic twilight upon her Sunday-night return from Debby's.

To Kara's credit, all it took was that one time, when I corrected her saying, "Why sweetie, did you know that ain't isn't actually considered a real word?" and Kara never misused the word again—unless purposely imitating her mama.

Another time Kara told me that when she asked, "Mama, why you be throwing that beer can out the window like that?" after Debby had taken the last guzzle while driving them back to her country place, her response was to laugh, pop open another and say: "Why, you little turd! Don't you be worrying none. It's the can man's job to pick them suckers up! Ain't it?"

I admit, living so close to such insufferable lowness infuriated me. I'd worked so damn hard to change from my own former wasted self, from that vagabonding wild child I'd been to the straight-arrow Angel Mom I was now—and here was heathen Debby making no noticeable effort to recognize, or mend her lowlife ways. These were her kids, dammit! Why couldn't she at least cool it with the booze? Will and I chose not to report her or make any more trouble with the court. But he did keep issuing stern warnings to her privately. Why couldn't she try to participate in their school? Come to after-school events? How about giving them a tad of much-needed mama-support with their homework, instead of self-centered zero input? He'd implore his ex, to no avail.

The kids told us how Debby frequently called me *Big Foot* or *Monkey Arms* to anyone instead of using my name. Her refusal to parent Kara and Jonny instead of simply love them, her idea of sufficient motherly effort—drove me nuts. I worked extra hard to accept her, realizing the only peace I'd ever have in this blended family was to think of her as Will's regrettable choice of a baby-machine. I tried to remember, with gratitude, that it was Debby's womb that had delivered these two wonderful kids to Will's and my loving care. After all, she'd done what I was incapable of doing, having kids.

My only choice to achieve acceptance about her presence in my life, however distant, was to change my way of thinking.

"If someone in our family had cancer," I reasoned, "I wouldn't shun them. For me to live without constant outrage over Debby's insane behavior, I'll start thinking of her as one gigantic, dangerous tumor our family has to endure. I just have to live with it, and not be upset every time her toxic ways create the next, always the next, disaster. I can't hate her for being a chronic, incurable disease, that's pathetic of me. But I have to protect myself from her. From now on, in my mind I'm going to accept her as if she's a lethal disease another person in our family might have. Anybody can get sick. It's not their fault. It's not like she's the personification of Satan. She's just not well. Her mind has an infirmity of some sort. Poor woman."

Still, I found Debby as dangerous, as unknowable as that pop-eyed green-scaly monster of a gator that lurks in all Florida ponds. I never got any closer to her than a quick friendly wave from a window, or a southern greeting of "Hey!" from across the yard. To expect pleasantries between Debby and me, I accepted as futile. The kids wondered why their Mama was never allowed inside our house, to use the bathroom or view their bedrooms. We never told them about Debby's lies and accusations, never hinted to them about her being a mental case, either. There'd been too many crises, though, and far too many lies for me to do anything but learn to tolerate her. My job was to protect the four of us, and that now included regarding her as an incurable blight, constantly striking awful close to home.

I made light of their repeated requests, saying, "Her house is hers. Mine is mine. We don't mix well, that's all."

Dr. C advised me about safe boundaries. With her advice, I emphasized to the kids how lucky they were to have such different homes, Debby's and ours. Ours was in town, nestled at the end of a tree-shaded, no-traffic cul-de-sac, right next to Phil and Claire's many-acre'd estate. Debby's was a remote hideaway where the kids had a pack of barking dogs to play with, plus an old horse, a cow, some ducks, geese, chickens—and a silent gator menacing the fetid pond, patiently waiting for its next victim. Although the kids desperately wished their Mama was a part of their Lackland lives, Dr. C advised us not to give in to their pleas. At first I found it hard to deny the kids. But my gut told me to follow our family counselor's eminent wisdom.

Debby's dramas seemed cartoonish in their lunacy, their sheer unbelievable mania. The kids told us about the places she took them to where they "had to watch Mama play darts and drink beer all night." How she drove them to scary spots deep in the woods where her truck too often broke down, and they ended up spending a sleepless night "in the strange noisy wild with creatures roaming all about." She refused to clean up the ton of dog crap, sharp glass, and broken junk strewn about her messy yard and front porch, even after we threatened, once more, to call the authorities, right after warning her about drinking behind the wheel. The fleas in her house made the kids appear as if they were wearing black leg warmers, requiring that they and our family dog Bruno be immediately de-bugged as soon as they returned from Debby's always-infested house.

All this insanity! Will and I only knew one thing as undeniable fact throughout all this unacceptable shit of hers—and we knew this only because she kept showing up—that in her own weird, and to us, sick way, Debby truly loved her kids. Perhaps not in the selfless way healthy parents do. So, reinforced with Dr. C's advice, we decided time after time that no matter how bad things appeared, Will and I would honor Debby's more primitive bond with the kids, and let her have her time with the kids. They were her kids too, after all.

Strangers, family and friends often challenged us on this. "I wouldn't let my kids near someone like her," I heard countless times. But we stood firm.

"Jonny and Kara need their bio-mom, despite how unkind and thoughtless she appears to others," I calmly told them. No other proof of her love for her kids was needed by us, other than she kept showing up. Will and I agreed: love is stronger than morality. And human love comes in as many flavors as there are people.

Watching her drive off with the kids beside her in the truck's wide front seat for their bi-monthly visits, I'd utter a silent prayer of protection as Jonny and Kara merrily waved goodbye. Debby's big scrappy dogs hanging on for dear life in the rear of the pickup, barking at the wind. Her truck roared up our quiet street, then silently swerved around the corner of our once-again undisturbed neighborhood, disappearing from sight.

CHAPTER 10

the See-er

Floppy, sweet-smelling and needy puppy-like, Kara followed me everywhere. Each morning I awoke to see my Angel Girl's still-unbelieving wide eyes as she knelt right beside my side of the bed, my cheek on my pillow, facing her as she patiently waited. Waiting for me to awaken and open my eyes, when I'd see her face filled with wonder, at my actually being her new Angel Mom. It was the same rapturous face Kara had when she looked at me that very first time we met in Sarasota, when she said she'd seen me in her dream the night before.

Yet her dreamy openness hid something unsettling. On other occasions, without warning and for no apparent reason, she would suddenly lose it and start freaking out, in one of those fits of hers again. Her bright eyes would go darkly bonkers as she shivered like a bad wind suddenly was blowing right through her. She'd stand or sit, frozen in place, her irises expanding to enormous black orbs, her breathing becoming as rapid as if a pack of unseen monsters were chasing her. Diving in to rescue her, I'd attempt to relieve the overwhelming fear that obviously tormented her during such time. I'd watch helplessly as she reached out to claw her clenched nails in anguish at the nearest surface of wood, glass, metal, the hard-plastic dash of our car: anything that was solid to the touch and within reach. With glazed eyes and not able to speak, it looked as if she was trying to scratch her way out of an invisible ambush taking place deep inside her.

Whenever I saw Kara unexpectedly freak-out like this, I rushed to her side. I'd hold her, or pick her up and, if I could, rush her to our rocking chair where I held her body close to mine, in a tight bundle. I wanted her to feel and hear my heartbeat and know my strength was hers as I softly whispered in her ear: "You're safe, Kara. You're here with me, with Dad, Jonny, all of us. There's nothing that can harm you anymore."

I wanted her to focus on her breath instead of her unknown torment. So I kept repeating, "Breathe in, breathe out, try more slowly, watch me," over and over until her slim, small body finally began to relax, sometimes in five minutes, sometimes in half an hour.

"Feel your breath filling you, Kara. Feel its goodness. Slowly let the air out. Slowly, bring it back in. Pump your belly up and down to gently ease the air in and out. You're here with us, we love you, Jesus loves you, Great Spirit too," I murmured.

Gradually Kara's tightly clamped fingers uncurled from their talon-hooked freeze. Her hazel eyes would begin to shimmer in waves of recognition. She came back to the room. She felt safe again, back from that unseen briar patch of mental terror to where she'd been kidnapped.

As if these daytime attacks weren't enough, Kara's old nightmares, though much less frequent, were still occurring, less so with each passing month of my arrival. Now it was me alone, instead of Will, who had for years before, gotten up in the middle of the night to comfort her, jumping to the girl's sleeping form at her first high-pitched screech, the wailing signal of this odd, unconscious torment that could be heard from our bedroom down the long hall. More than anything, I wanted to relieve Kara of her nightmarish hysteria. So I held her tightly and rocked with her for as long as it took, giving her comfort.

I'd already been told of the sad fact that Debby had rarely held Kara when she was an infant and a toddler. Despite Will's pleading with her, Debby chose to often leave her baby girl to go drink with her cowboy pals. Just the opposite to how she would later cling to infant Jonny, when she filed for divorce, Will said. Each nighttime we rocked, I willed my strong love into Kara's heart, directing my strength to mend her brokenness. More than anything I wanted to reverse whatever had traumatized my Angel Girl, long before we'd met. Her precious soul's hurt went so deep, and my love for her was already so strong, that we did a lifetime's worth of rocking in just the first year we spent together, during which I made no art, but focused on learning household yoga and how to nurture others. Whispering until she regained her surroundings, we then laughed softly together, as Kara and I continued to rock. Being comfortable with silence, we two, our heartbeats melded rhythms, united in motion. Angel Mom-and-Daughter, our bond was forged in the undulating motion of deep healing.

△

I sat in the rocking chair with Kara snuggled tightly on my lap, both of us enjoying our closeness, until she no longer contracted or convulsed in fear. Like this, I would share stories with her until she quieted.

"Once upon a time," I said, "there was a girl named Kara who sometimes got very afraid."

"That's me," she giggled as I hugged her closer. "Bad wolves chase me in my dreams."

"Wolves? That's sure scary. Well, this little girl named Kara," I began again, "sometimes got so frightened by these wolves inside her that she would shiver and shake, because she felt trapped in the terrible world she saw in her own mind. Then one day, her Angel Mom came along and taught her there was nothing to fear, outside her own mind, and how Kara could see that her mind was making up frightening stories, and she could see that now and not be afraid anymore."

"You did?"

"I am," I said. "Listen, the next time you feel something scary begin to happen inside you, remember this fear is, these *wolves* are, in your imagination *only*. They're not real. Fear is a made-up thing, did you know that? So when you start to feel it, try to remember to breathe deeply like we do together. That way your mind will keep busy and not be bothered by the scary wolves. And you'll not fall more deeply into that made-up fear of yours."

"I'll try," Kara said, enthusiastically nodding her head.

"Yes, you're a brave girl, we all know that, Kara. You're very precious."

"So what happened to me in your story?" she asked.

"Kara remembers," I said, "that there's really no wolves around. She remembers to breathe every time she feels something weird inside her, when she begins to think a wolf might appear, like smelling it, or hearing it panting ... and guess what?"

"What?"

"When Kara remembers to slow her breath down, her mind slows down, too. And then she knows that whatever bad thing is starting to happen, it's just her mind's own make-believe powers of invention, appearing so real they are actually happening, not real life! Slowing her breath on purpose, helps Kara remember there are no bad wolves or any other kind of monsters chasing her. And no bad people trying to hurt her, either."

"That's a nice story," Kara smiled as her body eased more deeply into my welcoming lap.

"When your breathing slows and your mind gets free, then it's easy to remember about being the See-er."

"What's the See-er?"

"It's the part of us that sees what isn't easy to see that our fears aren't real—like when bad things feel they're happening but they're really not. The See-er inside us knows this, and also how bad things, when they do turn out to be real, don't ever have to upset us, if we choose not to let them. The See-er inside us lets us know what's real and what we imagine, and what's the best choice to make. One's imagination can create really beautiful things, or really awful situations, like wolves chasing us. You know about the wonderful things you can create from your mind, like the funny snail drawings you make so wonderfully. Every person has to choose for him or herself, what is or what's not real. We can choose to be happy or choose to feel terrible. All of us can."

"That sounds hard."

"It's not so hard. Just start slowly. Start by wanting to be happy."

"That's not hard at all! Everyone wants to be happy."

"You're right. And after that easy first choice, keep making other choices, one by one, until you get really good at seeing yourself, as if you're watching yourself, Kara, living your life. As if you're sitting in a movie theater, and the story up on the screen—is your own life."

"A movie! That sounds like fun!"

"And interesting because, like any movie you haven't seen before, you don't know how it's going to turn out. Viewing your life as if it's a real movie, and you're a real actor in it, is way more fun than being scared of stuff that isn't really there. Right, Kara?"

"Right."

"If you remember to be the See-er, you won't be scared. That way, you'll be sure to have more fun."

"You mean I can choose to not get scared ... about anything?"

"That's right. I've been practicing this choosing business for a while, and you know what? When I remember that I'm just a character named teZa in this movie called *my life*, and that's how I learn I can quit feeling scared, or wanting to be the boss of my life, because that's God's job. When I let God, one of the See-er's other names, do his job, then I don't feel awful when bad stuff happens. It's just what God wanted to happen. I get to be a lot happier when I remember to be the See-er, and I'm watching a movie called *my life*. Sure, bad stuff happens to us sometimes, but lots of good stuff does, too."

"I want to learn how to do that," Kara said.

"You can. The first thing, like we've been doing, is to watch yourself breathe in and out, as slowly as you can. When you remember the breathing part, the rest comes naturally. Your busy mind, even with wolves chasing you, gets calm. Being the See-er just takes practice."

Soon an excellent opportunity came to put this See-er stuff into practice. Will and I had driven to pick the kids up from Debby's place, an unusual event because she usually insisted on both getting them and bringing them back to our place. But this time the schedule was different.

We pulled off the lonesome country road and went up the muddy, quarter-mile driveway at the appointed time. Four of Debby's dogs—all of them mangier, rowdier, skinnier and scarier than average mutts—aggressively surrounded our car. Debby's truck wasn't there. She, the kids, and her fifth dog, a Chihuahua who habitually lived inside her bra-less blouse, hadn't arrived yet.

"Debby not doing what she said she'd do, how extraordinary," Will said with a sigh.

It was another shirt-drencher humid day. No breeze stirred the air; the surround-sound of cicadas pounded our ears. Close by, the gator pond's surface trembled with a green slimy patina, hiding the hungry reptile that lurked beneath its depths, like everywhere in swampy Central Florida. Will busied himself looking around the old property. While he nosed around in a corner of a falling-down shed, I walked up the wraparound porch of the three-story clapboard house.

"Think she'd mind if I went in?" I shouted to Will.

"Probably. So make it quick. If I hear them coming I'll give you a shout."

The glass panel of the back door leading to the kitchen was so opaque with grime I couldn't see in. It squeaked loudly as I gingerly opened it. Two steps into the place, I stood shocked senseless. I felt dizzy from the stench. I dared not inhale deeply. I stood not moving a muscle, just observing. Such chaos I'd never seen in my life, except when I'd gone to a dump somewhere. Not in the poorest shack in the back country of the third world where I used to live, had I ever seen such repulsive squalor. In that wretchedly filthy kitchen were piles of garbage, stacks of old moldy food, layers of grease on every surface, dirty kids' toys mixed with baked-on slop everywhere. The stove was buried beneath years of grease, dark spills reeking and putrefied, every square inch filled with burnt, sticky, crusty cooking pots and mounds of what once might have passed for something edible.

My stomach did backflips as I stood in a gargoyle-gawk, taking in this deplorable place. Human horror flashed on my mind's movie screen; an unspeakable terror gripped me. In that instant my breath got knocked away. Right then, I understood completely why both kids had such a hard time with my particular ways. Suddenly everything became clearer to me: why it was such a stretch for them to do chores, wash a dish, help to pick up their messes, as my Better Housekeeping-mother had early on instilled in me. I suddenly flash-realized: Why it was so hard for them to admit liking me, when their hateful, depressed mother despised me so for raising them my way, instead of her doing it her opposite way.

My ordered environment, including home and studio, aided me to stay in the Light, to feel centered, and inspired me to make beneficial ideas manifest in my art, and perform my duties of household yoga, like preparing healthy nutritious food. Not like this fearsomely dank and dirty hell-on-earth I was witnessing before me. I'd never seen the likes of such depravity before, not in any human's or animal's haunt, not in my worst nightmare. This, to me, was an unfortunately ugly glimpse into another's undeveloped, anti-love, anti-God sensibility.

As silently as I'd slipped in, I retreated. Feeling like retching, I closed the kitchen door behind me as I uttered softly:

"Great Spirit, help me to be patient. Help me to always remember the complicated lives Kara and Jonny have, juggling two such different homes, with such different moms: the two entirely different ways of being we have. This one here, God help us! is beyond what any child should ever have to endure. Help me remember it's no accident I'm their Angel Mom. And that my job is to teach them to balance the good and bad of life."

From that moment on, after witnessing the truth of Debby's scrambled mind—as each of our environments reflect whatever state our mind clings to most—I recognized and accepted, as learning to Be the See-er allows a person to do, that I'd come into Will's life not just to know real love for myself, but to save these kids from the harmful shadow of their bio-mom's grim neglect. Without my arrival and the consistent guidance I gave them, Kara and Jonny's most influential female otherwise, was the creator of that rotten mess back there, that abysmal place where our kids spent way more time than I cared to think about.

green scaly monster

CHAPTER 11

green scaly monster

Will was no disciplinarian, which meant I had to tame the kids' unruly beasties all by myself. But how? My mother had taught me to mop floors, do dishes, sew straight lines, bake a pie, tend a garden, and never tell a lie; but since her approach to child-rearing lacked the spark of freedom needed for my wild-child spirit, I never sought her advice on other maternal guidance issues. Some days I floundered in the Sea of What-to-Do, facing the formidable feat all alone, of how to rein in someone else's traumatized, undisciplined kids. Reading manuals and asking friends can only get you so far.

Lucky me to have Dr. C as a mentor. A grandmother many times over, she'd divorced her alcoholic, lawyer-husband, returned to school and learned to be a shrink after realizing her former degree in piano performance wouldn't pay the bills when she found herself raising nine school-age children on her own. Gladly I threw myself into her expert hands, my ignorance on mothering so absolute, and Will's laissez-faire approach so ineffective. Gratefully, I let Dr. C guide me every step of the way. She urged me to be the chief kid-boss of the house, to trust my judgment over Will's less orderly, less self-inquiring approach. She encouraged me when I faltered, and assured me I had to be the strong one for the job of instilling some basic life skills in Debby and Will's near-heathen children.

Since becoming a single dad, Will had taken Kara and Jonny to Dr. C to help them adjust to the split of their parents. Although to the kids he called her "The Talking Doctor," Dr. C used predominantly a nonverbal approach to help deal with problems that can't easily be articulated, the case especially with young children. SandPlay is a Jungian-based therapy intended to portray one's inner state by creating a scenario, "rendition" of one's inner state at any given time, in a miniature sand box. Painted blue inside, to represent water when sand on top is pushed aside, its proportions duplicate the so-called Golden Rectangle. Choosing from a wide range of tiny objects, either Kara or Jonny, separately, had fun making a tableau of their own from a basket they were handed by Dr. C and that they filled with tiny figurines they were attracted to that particular day. Each in turn, would then stand aside the waist-high box filled with fine white beach sand as Dr. C asked Kara or Jonny questions, like "What's this figure doing; What's this one's story?" Afterwards, she'd make suggestions to Will and me, and of course, the kids based on her keen observations.

Helping me was a different story altogether. I needed straight-talking advice; so Dr. C and I talked non-stop during our many private sessions together. Will and I continued visiting her as a couple too, on an "as needed" basis, whenever we needed a "tune-up." The good doc helped me design the three *guidelines* to use for helping teach the kids the basics of disciplined behavior. I called these three tools Dr. C and I made up, our home's *non-rules*. Using them instead of other methods, I crossed my fingers that my man, rebelling still against the overbearing strictness he'd suffered from his so-proper mom in his childhood, might not balk at these user-friendly kid-boundaries as any kind of a restriction. My hope was for him to see the three non-rules as a means of providing more pleasant interactions in our chaotic anarchy, as I first saw our family's boat trying to maneuver down Rio Blisso.

After many private sessions with Dr. C we came up with these three strategies to make performing household yoga more manageable when it was my turn to be at our boat's helm. They are:

See God in Each Other: the all-important Number 1 non-rule.

Listen and Do: Number 2 non-rule. For what's the point of guidance if a child doesn't learn to listen?

Hands, Feet, and Words to your own Self: non-rule Number 3. As in no hitting, pushing or other kinds of violent intrusion or disrespect, including name-calling and bad-mouthing of others. Ah, if only the world could follow Number 3, all of humanity would have a chance of someday living in peace and harmony.

These three non-rules became my lifeline to sanity. To give some examples how I made the handy trio work I would say, "That's Number 1!" instead of telling the kids they weren't being nice; or I'd say, "Number 2!" when they refused to do something; or "You just forgot Number 3!" when they were pushing or fighting, which all kids do, constantly if left to their own devices, I quickly had discovered. Doc C urged me to use *ye olde* reward system: a Star Chart to record each kid's use or misuse of each non-rule, laden with shiny-star gains or stripped of bemoaned losses or demerits. The kids' bright-colored poster-board chart hung in the kitchen, filled with accumulated stars for all to admire. A successful, competitive reward-based system that worked wonders at bringing control to my untamed wild things.

Of course, Will never used the non-rule system, and shook his head in mockery whenever I did. But I didn't care. Someone had to bring a semblance of order to the imploding chaos surrounding these children.

Despite this easy, indirect method I devised—rules that weren't rules, a system only used by me, rewards of applause, praise, prizes and special privileges connected to this brilliantly blazing, star-studded poster the kids made themselves—Will refused to ever assign either of *his kids* a simple chore, like take out the trash or the compost, and never dished out a single consequence to them. He was simply incapable of it. He didn't buy into Dr. C's opinion that children need and want structure. To his mind, he'd turned out okay not having had any house chores. He told me Phil hadn't allowed Claire to give the boys any household jobs at all, only the girls. Still, he couldn't help being a product of overly tidy, nit-picking Claire. So as a parent, Will railed against any rebuke whatsoever, when things weren't done "right." Maybe it was guilt over divorcing their mom?

Dr. C hinted at that to me. A repetitive subject of my counseling sessions with Dr. C was how I had to accept not only the kids' but my man's severe limitations about not being disciplined. A big deal I had to accept about my otherwise, near perfect mate.

As important as learning to nurture was to me, I had to remember Will and I weren't just parents; we were lovers still getting to know each other. Like all busy parents, we had to remind ourselves to make time to have fun together. Still, we didn't have time to take a honeymoon, not until months after marrying, and when we did it was just a weekend at a nearby resort. A dinner and movie date on a week-night seemed impossible; we didn't want to leave the kids with a babysitter so soon after my arrival. Dr. C helped us sort out everything in time, yet Will's refusal (or inability) to discipline the kids remained the biggest hindrance to our smoothly functioning household yoga.

I couldn't help but notice the uncomfortable dynamic begin right away, of me being "the bad guy," another common drawback every stepparent has to deal with. Was it my feeling overly criticized, or was it, in fact, how Will created an "us against her" atmosphere in our blended family? I wonder to this day. Without his support, whichever way it was, it was true: I was soon perceived, and rightfully so by Kara and Jonny, to be the only one who enforced any kind of order in our anything-goes house. Will's constant complaint in our joint counseling sessions was that he thought I was too tough on *his* kids. Dr. C disagreed.

"Somebody has to show them," she said, "that discipline is love, Will."

"But teZ gets all serious on us, Doc."

"Confronting misbehavior is something your own folks were either overkill about, or not any good at all," I defended myself. "Naturally, I'm the one in our house forced to do it. Otherwise, our household is like an upside-down ride, or horror-house at the carnival, for me at least. You think I'm being mean but it feels to me most times as if I'm the only grownup in the house."

"Someone has to do it, she's right, Will" Dr. C said. "Be glad you have a partner willing to teach your kids basic habits, like personal hygiene, and how to balance their time between work and play."

"Well yeah, teZ is good with all that," he concurred in a low voice.

Other than his concretized resistance to correcting the kids, Will was the most attentive father ever, a great friend to me and generous in all ways. Jonny followed closely behind his dad in the kind and compassionate category. Almost to a fault, Will always stepped up when needed, for anyone, friend or stranger, when something was needed. His caring heart was unparalleled, in my experience.

However, he did what needed to be done when it came to correcting Debby's bad mothering. Once, nearly seven, Jonny came back from Debby's and casually mentioned something we'd never known.

"Me and Mom fall asleep watching TV in her bed every night. I don't know why I can't have my own bed. I'm big enough, and Kara has her own bedroom down the hall. But Mom says I have to sleep with her because she's lonely."

Will immediately called Debby in outrage and told her if she didn't make a separate bedroom for Jonny by his next visit, out of the many empty rooms available, he would call Child Protection Services. As they spoke I could hear Debby screaming from across the room out of the phone's receiver, but Will stood his ground.

"We'll check with Jonny after his next visit, Debby, so don't try any funny business. If you don't get that kid out of your bed, you're going to lose what few privileges you have left in your kids' lives!"

At one of our joint sessions with Dr. C, Will and I discussed Debby's attempt to interfere with whatever the four of us tried to plan, a feeble method of sabotage she was sure to pull. This time it was our long-planned-for winter trip to the Bahamas when she scared Jonny for no reason, proclaiming, "They'll be bringing you back in a body bag!" and to Kara she related *When Animals Attack* stories about man-eating sharks and getting drowned by paralyzing, stinging jellyfish. Of course, she wanted them to stay behind with her—always the bottom line—to have her kids all to herself.

"Dr. C," I blurted out, "sometimes I get so furious at Debby I call her the BM, short for both bio-mom and *you know what*. I know it's not PC, but that's what she is to me—a big stinky bowel movement, her actions always like excrement, fouling the air of our happy family atmosphere."

"That's a disgusting image, teZa!" Dr. C made a sour face.

Will piped in, "Well we both call her the BM, because she is one." He laughed unabashedly.

Dr. C thought for a moment, then said, "It's not what I'd recommend. But it's probably needed, even healthy for you both, to call her that, privately, of course. No doubt it does bring comic relief to your challenging situation. As long as it's strictly between you and Will, and you never let the kids hear you call her that, I think it's okay."

Will reassured the good counselor, "Sure, it's only when we're alone together we call her the BM. We know it's an awful thing, but she's so off-the-wall, that annoying woman. And half crazy."

The hideous nickname we privately called Debby did help blow off some steam; a silly reprieve, we agreed, that Will and I shared to lessen the miserable reality of ornery Debby that we had to face every damn day.

▲

One Friday evening I was lying exhausted beside Will in our bedroom, too tired to even think about lovemaking before we had our customary kids-gone nap, to regain some energy. Debby had just picked up the kids and we were worn out from a week's worth of *normal*. Will was done-in from his demanding job and nonstop kid-play. I was dog-tired from all that entailed household yoga (the endless chores), along with going to the gym, doing yoga at home, and at that time, right after marrying, spending all day, every day with preschooler Jonny, who needed constant supervision.

Day-by-day I was trying to keep improving Better-me—having gratitude instead of attitude, recognizing fears and trying to be the

See-er of my old anxieties. Yet still, there were times when remnants of those old negativities still knocked me right out of that boat I crewed on, as we meandered along Rio Blisso, despite all the counseling and constant repetition of *So'hăm, So'hăm* I was doing.

Out of the blue and for no apparent reason, instead of the longed-for lovemaking we usually did as soon as the kids were gone on Fridays—besieged by some recalcitrant old fear of Lesser-me's—I found myself leaping for Will's throat, attacking him for no reason whatsoever!

Some unknown part of me, a small-voiced demon that still lay hidden within me—in one crazed, irrational lunge of this mind-monster of my own making, like Kara's wolves—for no logical reason I became convinced that my wonderful mate was a dirty rotten bastard. In an instant, my former stinking maniac-me took over and reared its nasty head! The dragon within—the one that turned me into a self-loathing addict instead of the seeker I truly was—rudely awakened, who knows why? Thank goodness Will, in that horrible moment, was a quick-acting, instinct-sharp athlete, as always. This colossus of a man reacted to my surprise attack by reaching out one of those cannonball arms of his, and gently knocked me onto the soft carpeted floor, startling me awake from this seizure, hallucination, or whatever disguise fear wore that day, which had bubbled up from within me, causing me to mistake my darling man for another mean-masked demon. Startled, I sat on the floor, wondering what the hell just happened. Had I just attacked Will? Was I absolutely nutso crazy? I was as much in shock as Will, yet fully present and immediately remorseful. Shocked. Horrified. Ashamed.

Had I really just done that?

Had I actually just imagined—in one flash, like an old acid flashback—my giant-hearted Will to be the evilest person I'd ever met, who was taking advantage of me for his own needs? He, the most sacrificing, kindest person I'd ever known? The man who took one of our sick chickens to the vet and waited in the lobby with her on his lap? How could I have just attacked my heart's desire, the man I loved more than air?

Thankfully, by this time Will had begun to understand me better than I did myself. This kill-or-be-killed behavior of Lesser-me, a throwback to my old addict-self, he'd never seen before, he'd tell me later. But he knew something within me was off as soon as I went for his throat. That I wasn't myself. He must have seen the feisty demon still lodged within my soul, because that day, Will allowed me space to gather myself, to shake my head in disbelief, to shake my seizure of fear away. Ancient fears and insecurities, those destructive and deeply-rooted traits that had once driven me to madness and then to the numbing forgetfulness of addiction, were obviously still working their way out of my psyche. Will couldn't have known this then, but I figured it out later, when I recovered from this inexplicable, instantaneous possession by those ugly gargoyles within me, still. My fear's revival, for no apparent reason other than perhaps, that my life was finally in a happy place, showed me I needed to work harder to heal those remaining inner wounds of mine. They obviously went deeper than I'd ever suspected.

This harrowing episode that took place in the privacy of our bedroom, taught me that I had to be patient and kind, not only with the other three in our family's boat-size communion, but first and foremost with myself. Now, I understood. Even though I was committed to change and had thought I'd fully embraced Better-me, I realized I had lots more self-healing to do, healing inner and still traumatized Lesser-me, whom I desperately wished would grow up or go away. I had to extend mercy to my wounded inner Being. I had to admit I had mental imbalance of my own, not just my Angel Girl or her brother or her mother. Whether this imbalance of mine came from the traumas of childhood—or before I was even born—honestly didn't matter to me. This flashback to my former lower-self forced me to commit even more to practicing what the Teacher offered: "Diligently embrace Better-me, the part of God, the See-er within you," I heard her singular voice in my head. "Never give up in searching for God within."

Will agreed to let the embarrassingly violent incident go. "But it better not ever happen again," he warned. We were both working so hard to help our kids, our melding blended-family, there was no room for any personal freak-outs on my part. "I won't subject my kids to another mental case, teZ," he admonished, and I quickly said, "Fair enough."

Better-me was still in training mode, I had to admit. My true, sober persona wasn't yet fully formed; this bedroom scene proved it. More episodes of my inner Dread breaking out of my soul would arrive, but thankfully in private, away from everyone, even Will. The twisted thinking that originated in my old-patterned brain, that monkey-mind of mine, caused me so much torment when it occasionally bubbled up, sometimes once a year, or every other, it was all I could do at such infrequent times to retreat somewhere private, and lie on the floor in a fetal position, alone and terrified, shaking in unknown gripping fear. I'd hug myself and wait and shiver—repeating *So'hăm, So'hăm*—until this next Lesser-me fear-episode dissolved. Which it always did. Until … one day … these erratic episodes—which previous to sobriety I'd masked their daily take-overs by the mindless numbing-ness of chemicals—disappeared altogether, many years later.

Until finally, in the grip of another rare occasion of deadly fear trying to consume me, I had asked, and been given advice by the Teacher about what to do. When the fear "naturally arose on its own," I was told, "go somewhere alone, then allow Better-me, your meditative state to enter this scary realm. Don't be afraid."

It would take me several years after the bedroom incident, but I finally did what the Teacher advised us, her students.

"Be courageous, and dive deeply into that fear in the sacredness of a meditative state. Let your fears, your tears, your shortcomings show you who you really are."

I only had to do this fear-diving once. And it was, indeed, one of the scariest experiences I've ever had, but—when I came out of that deep place, in which I hadn't turned away from the fear but met it head-on, allowing my soul to merge with the fear—I somehow, after many shakes and shivers and buckets of tears with my eyes still closed and in meditation—I came out the other side. And I never experienced that soul-gripping fear ever again.

But this didn't take place until several more bends and crosscurrents and going over a bunch more fearful waterfalls, after the bedroom scene that day.

I never let the kids or Will see me in that state, not after that first and only time the demon-within-me attacked Will. When yet another "brain fart" would arise from my thankfully increasingly less-predominant Lesser-me, I'd seek out privacy, eventually my studio, where I told myself the exact things I'd instructed Kara to do. Breathe. Let go. Know this fear was just made up by a restless, unfocused mind. Be the See-er, I said to myself just as I was teaching Kara. Because I too, needed to learn to not give into my inner fears, my demons. In See-er mode, I could believe I wasn't actually dying when fear struck and besieged me. Practicing being the Witness, the See-er, I could lie still and breathe deeply, comfort myself, rock myself, curled on the floor in a fetal ball, silently repeat the soothing vibration of *So'hăm*, until the paralyzing darkness that gripped me, not the menacing wolves Kara had—left.

Please, I'd pray, grant me peace.

So'hăm, So'hăm, So'hăm.

As I grew to embrace more fully the See-er mode, Better-me gently overpowered self-destructive Lesser-me. In time, I'd learn how to do the deep meditation technique I've just described, and my inner battle stopped. I learned how to become One with the See-er. Gradually, I lived undisturbed, my newfound peaceful life as Angel Mom.

Exactly as I told Kara. Breathe each mental roadblock away, as each one arose. Never sharing these secret panic attacks with Will, the kids, not even Dr. C, I trusted my Better-me version to be the stronger of my two selves. No longer hiding from the pain of who Lesser-me was, I committed to releasing its pain and suffering, one hurtle at a time. Meeting life head-on with the armor of breath and mind-stilling mantra, I had all the tools I needed to fight the shifty demon within, that old sidekick of mine who'd been nothing but trouble, and took a lot of effort to eradicate. But I never took any Prosac, Zoloff, or any other anxiety-reducing drug, ever.

Teacher, heal thyself: this was my true savior, my lifesaving motto.

I knew those attacks, however random and consuming they'd felt in their moment of siege, were not related to anything in my past or present. I'd already done all my forgiveness work, all the letting-go I needed to cover my getting-sober recovery steps. The only "bad thing" I was facing—nothing compared to famine, flood, or murdered children in Africa—was living in suburbia. But that wasn't so bad that I couldn't slap myself back to ease from any degree of *dis*-ease.

As Will played hide-and-seek with the kids, I watched our *CBD*-dachshund at play, an animal every bit of the acronym I coined for him: *Cute but Dumb*. These slices of suburban sweetness could tease anyone out of their worst funk.

One day I looked inside myself and found no remaining demon, none whatsoever. It had disappeared, ever since I'd done the spiritual work my Teacher had advised. I'd healed whatever unnamable fears I'd somehow accumulated.

▲

I took both kids to an outdoor park close to our house. Except for us it was empty, so I let Kara and Jonny roam from swing to seesaw, free to explore the many different fun opportunities of the playground. I sat by myself on a bench and watched these two towhead charges of mine, for whom I felt protective in ways I'd never felt with anyone. Sure, I'd had close connections with lovers, two earlier short-lived marriages, dogs and cats, but only one other time had I bonded with a child. Many years before, I'd invited a motherless wharf rat, a lonely, underfed boy of ten, to come along with me on a long sailing adventure on the Caribbean Sea.

As I was sitting and musing on these things, I watched the kids—my kids!—running, skipping, making joyful noises. Looking over at me occasionally for confidence, showing off how high they could swing, how fast they could run, it was obvious they were secure with me there, protecting them. I felt satisfaction ooze out of my every pore. A smile stretched from one ear to another.

Suddenly I saw danger. Two other kids, a little older and a lot bulkier than mine, came from out of nowhere. They walked right up to Kara and Jonny and began talking to them in what clearly was a threatening manner. I sat straight up on the bench. From their changed expressions I could tell my kids were in distress. I heard Jonny shout, "Leave us alone!" And Kara cry, "You better shut up!" I leapt from the bench and ran the twenty yards to the confrontation that was boiling over.

"Hey! What's going on?" I demanded, looking straight at the two interlopers.

"This kid's mean," Jonny said in his succinct way.

"He's gross," Kara added, pointing at the larger one.

That boy, the tallest of his gang of two, might have been a little older than Kara. He looked at me with a scowl on his distorted, nasty face. I wondered which of his parents taught him that unfortunate grimace.

"Leave them alone," I demanded.

"Lady, I'm allowed to do what I want," the boy threw back.

"Listen," I said in a low voice, my face coming real close to his punk-sized one, my eyes in slits, "you leave my kids alone or I'm gonna make fresh meat out of you, buster. You got that?"

The bully and his accomplice looked wide-eyed at each other, then high-tailed it out of the park. We never saw them again. Sometimes being half-thug, half-Angel-Mom comes in handy. We three laughed all the way home about the mean kid's cowardice, opposite to his blustering act.

▲

I spent every day that first year with Jonny. We took endless strolls, visited neighboring playgrounds, or just stayed home doing fun activities together. Jonny and I grew close in ways only a child and a pretend-grownup can: without many words, without needing goals or reasons, just being together. This is how we learned each other's ways.

Whenever Jonny and I went for a walk in the nearby field, we brought along Bruno, our family's ever-entertaining CBD. The frog-catching, skunked-often, eagle-thwarting, horse-chasing wiener dog was a great source of joy for all of us, even if he was a dummkopf who'd used up enough lives for a cat. Jonny especially delighted in the mischief that Bruno always got into. The two were constant companions when Kara was at school and Jonny was a preschooler. The dog patiently played every game with him, like Rider in Jonny's laundry-basket caboose when the boy would choo-choo him all around the house and backyard.

One day Bruno got the idea in his obstinate mind it would be fun to chase the cows that grazed peaceably in Grandpa's pasture, right next to our house. Since they were familiar to us, we always felt safe walking near the herd, on our way to the pond behind Phil and Claire's house. We never feared Mr. Bull, the tan-colored, monstrously proportioned but gentle-as-a-lamb patriarch of his tribe. Mr. Bull never did anything but look our way when we walked close to his dozen cow-wives and numerous offspring as they all stood in the same direction, as cows do when they're grazing.

For whatever reason, Bruno decided to chase them that day and nothing we could do, no amount of yelling would sway him from his mission. Usually complacent Mr. Bull met the challenge by charging flea-sized Bruno several times. Later, we'd find out that the old bull was uncharacteristically cranky because he'd just had a shot of antibiotics for an infection in his hoof.

No matter how much Jonny and I shouted at our dog to stop, emboldened by his audacity and far more interested in harassing bovines, Bruno ignored us. When I finally got within arm's reach, I grabbed him. The pink plastic shopping bag I had with me for bringing back plant specimens on walks, I filled with lemon-sized field rocks, and tied it to the collar of our crazed dog. Encumbered by the heavy weight that cramped his style, his leaps haltered, his energy soon drained, Bruno and his obsession slowly deflated. All the barking in the world couldn't make the twenty-odd head of cows fear the pipsqueak CBD with his diaphanous pink bag attached like an extended goiter on his neck. Frustrated after a few feeble leaps, his tethered rock-balloon many times larger than his head, anchored-to-earth Bruno gave up the chase. He settled down and stayed close to us as we made our way to the pond, two people and a dog lugging the heavy pink anchor behind him that I would unharness when we were out of sight of the cows.

△

Other days, we'd wander over to Grandpa's pond, not far from the older couple's big house. Jonny and I liked to take Bruno and sit in the grass and just stare at the shiny water where we'd pluck a few pieces of duckweed from its surface with long sticks, or throw in cherry-sized pebbles and watch the ripples spread on the glass-like surface. We three picked a floating plant or some field bush, vine, leaf or splashy-hued wildflower that we'd later look up in our plant books. That's why we needed that plastic bag.

Like every other interminably hot summer day, the katydids and cicadas were as loud as the brass section of a philharmonic orchestra. The motionless air could be sliced like honey pie, thick and pungent with sweet smells rising up from the pond, from the rich soil of the surrounding pasture dotted with cow-pies that, whenever rain came, sprouted overnight with purple-tinged psilocybin mushrooms.

We three, Jonny, Bruno, and I made our way to the windless, silent and silvery pond that was three times bigger than the average suburban front lawn. In its middle was a two-cars-length island with a cluster of tall cypress trees growing crowded and lonesome, smack in the middle of Grandpa's all-flat pasture. In summertime, most of the pond's surface was covered with a sheet of thick green algae and weed slime. Except where the wind cleared occasional patches, nothing could be seen of the murky water below.

As soon as the pink plastic bag was untied, Bruno flew, made a bee-line dash and dove into the pond, as he always did on hot summer days when near any kind of water, including swimming pools and cattle troughs. Today though, just as our CBD took a boisterous running leap into the pond water—

Strike! Spray shot high up in the air!

Gator!

A tangle of dark slippery nefarious intent tossed about, rolling ferociously on the surface, half-furry-black, half-scaly-green. Jonny and I froze for a heartbeat before we realized what was happening. In that split-shot instant, I saw the water slice angrily; a young gator about four feet long had snapped up Bruno, half its length, in its vice-grip juvenile teeth. The dog struggled for his life. With no sticks or poles, with nothing long enough to reach the attacker or stronger than a pebble, no oars, no rocks big enough to matter—there was nothing to do but yell and scream, and that's what Jonny and I did at top volume.

As abruptly as the attack began, it was over.

Bruno got loose and dragged himself onto shore, huffing-puffing drained, startled senseless. He lay in the grass, exhausted from his desperate wrestling match with death. Blood gushed from tooth-size puncture wounds on top of his bony muzzle and under his fleshy throat. Jonny and I caressed and soothed our pal, hoping the worst was over. I kept looking over my shoulder, worried the big mama of that baby gator might pounce on us. When I looked back at Jonny, I saw he was silently crying, hard. I gathered up both shaking boy and bleeding dog in my arms and hurried away from the pond into the tall grass, shielding the three of us from any other attacking beasts.

As soon as Bruno was breathing more normally, I carried him and Jonny followed, straight back to our house. With the outdoor hose, I rinsed the swamp stink off Bruno, who now shivered uncontrollably from shock. He whimpered in pain as I inspected his wounds while Jonny spoke calming baby-talk to him, just as he'd seen our country-style vet do with his animal patients. Later, we'd take Bruno to Dr. Wilson for a checkup. And forever after, along with being our CBD, he was called the "gator dog" at the vet's.

I went in to make a cup of tea for myself, leaving Jonny to comfort Bruno. Minutes later, I came back outside to find Jonny and

Bruno both gone. I called for them. No answer. I ran upstairs to see if Jonny had gone to his bedroom through another door. No Jonny. I whistled for Bruno, who never ignored that long-range signal I'd painstakingly trained him to obey. No Bruno. I began to panic. Never before had Jonny left me or disobeyed me. Outside, inside, front yard, backyard. Over the pasture fence I made out Mr. Bull and his herd in the far corner of Grandpa's thirty-acre pasture. No small Jonny, no minuscule black Bruno.

Suddenly I understood.

Racing up the drive to Grandpa's, I rushed toward the pond. As I came around the big house I spied Jonny coming toward me from the direction of the water, now-recovered Bruno leaping in the tall grass behind him. My Angel Boy was bawling inconsolably, carrying what looked like two skinny sticks. Rushing to his side I realized what he'd done. He'd snuck in while I was in the kitchen, to where Will kept his prized Amazonian Indian hunting spear, in a special spot in his office. They were meant to have been locked up, but weren't, thanks to Will's lackadaisical precautions. Jonny held the deadly sharp spear, now broken in half, wailing at the top of his lungs. I held the boy in my arms and got the story in gulps and spatters. He'd taken the spear and run back to the pond "to kill that stupid gator for hurting Bruno."

"Well," I said, hugging him tightly, "next time, please tell me so I can go with you. So we don't worry what might happen to either of you, okay?"

Jonny said he would, even though we both knew he needed to have this fight for himself. It would be the only time Jonny ever took off without me. If I were a five-year-old who'd just witnessed a murderous attack on my best friend, I'd have tried to kill that gator too.

CHAPTER 12

old salts

Claire was way more interested in making her unswerving steel totems than in baking sweets, granny-style. Whenever someone asked what Phil thought about his wife's abstract, non-representational work, he was known to joke, "Oh, give me another drink and I'll understand it better." From time to time Grandma Claire invited the kids up for milk and delicious store-bought, gigantic chocolate chip cookies; and once a month she had our family over for her famous clove-infused easy spaghetti dinner.

Early on she'd told Will and his three siblings that their children, her grandkids, were never to call her anything but "Aunt Claire," and their grandfather, "Uncle Phil." Will just pooh-poohed his mother's well-accepted tendency of harmless affectations, never telling Kara and Jonny anything of the sort. When he was a kid, his mother had insisted that her kids say "rest-auh-*rant*" French-accented, never pronouncing it just plain restaurant like the whole of the English-speaking world did. She even insisted that Will pronounce Mick Jagger's name *Yag-ger,* believing her unique interpretation more correct, as she did with *Pon'-ceh* De Leon, instead of Americanized Ponce.

No one was allowed to touch any of Grandma Claire's sculptures or anything else that was shiny in her cathedral-ceilinged, many-windowed house, greasy fingerprints being anathema to her. Off limits also were touching the see-through shelves holding china and crystal, and the hot tub-sized glass-and-steel coffee table that took up half the living room, which had a panoramic view of the surrounding pasture, pond, and adjacent woods, a mind-stilling sight that commanded everyone's attention. The studio for her sculptures' messy finishing stage, where only her assistant worked, was conveniently out of sight; a knocked-around old trailer mounted on cement blocks, grandly dubbed the Claire Mahal that stood regally beneath a grove of tall oaks. It was astonishing, really, that Grandpa and Grandma's estate, with its impressive, modern manor house set amid a semi-circular acreage of cow pasture and citrus orchard, including the house's several acres of mowed lawn, lay smack in the middle of Lackland's city limits.

One day I was invited to her sparse main studio, altogether different from her assistant's ugly one filled with the discarded remains of grinding and polishing Claire's metal pieces. In a show of her self-effacing good nature, she jokingly dubbed the trailer where the untidiest process surrounding her work took place, the Claire Mahal. But I was going to her other, more orderly main studio that was attached to the big house. The atelier's loft-like space was entered by its own separate door, and where surprisingly, it too had a spectacular floor-to-ceiling window view of the serene pasture just as the living room did.

"I trust your artistic expertise," Claire said as we stood side-by-side, artist-to-artist. "I'm a little nervous because I've never done curves in a three-dimensional creation before." Her arm swept before her to indicate the stainless-steel finished sculpture before us. "What do you think, teZa?"

She knew my background included silver- and gold-smithing, cabinetry and woodworking, graphics and printmaking, and that I also made both paintings and sculpture using mixed media. As a hard-edge artist, she was also aware that my style rarely contained a straight line, since that's hardly found in Nature except in crystalline and rock strata formations. She was also aware that my work was aligned with naturalism rather than her purely non-representational work.

I was honored that Claire, such a seasoned artist, valued my opinion. We stood together looking at the shoulder-height piece she was working on, part of a series intended to capture the uplifting feeling of humankind striving for connection with the Divine. A subject as close to my own heart as it was to Claire's.

"I think it's nicely balanced," I said, always honest yet tactful whenever asked to critique others' work. "I like the way you've introduced a curve in the middle of the other sharp angularity. It pleases my eye too, its reversal, how it curves back on itself. Very intriguing. It adds engagement to the metal's surprise flow, more energy, more interest."

I paused, thinking: If she were a different kind of artist, not so formal, and not my mother-in-law, I might even call that opposing-directions curve, downright sexy. But instead, I took a deep breath and said, "That neat bend, expertly angled, adds a deeper, mysterious element for me, Claire, than your previous, strictly all-linear pieces."

She smiled. "I appreciate your insights, dear. Not only are you an artist comfortable working with metals, but more importantly you understand the work is about acknowledging Spirit. I don't have to explain its premise to you. We can cut right to the technicalities involved in the work. I like that."

△

More often I visited Phil. I sat on a short stool so I could be as close to him as possible to hear his whispery-voice, as he relaxed in his favorite green lounge chair in the living room. That's where he usually was while Claire worked in her studio. Times like these, I asked him to help me understand a recent dream of mine that troubled or puzzled me. A taciturn, humble gentleman, Phil liked to crack one-liners, throwing out punchy witticisms just as much to rattle pretentious people as to put simpler folk at ease. Yet when it came to dreams, Phil would wax scholarly serious, discussing their significance as long as it took to unravel the secrets of a dream's hidden symbolism.

In one particularly unsettling dream I shared with him, I clearly saw myself: alone, crashing headfirst into a chain-link fence in a runaway speeding car I'd somehow lost control of, and BAM! I'm dead. At least it felt that way. And then I awoke.

"What do you think it means, Phil?"

"What do *you* think it means?" he said, reminding me that he didn't give answers, but helped others to find their own meaning.

"Well, I don't know. That's why I'm asking you."

"All dreams are about ourselves," he gently reminded me. "Even if it appears there are other characters in them. Dreamt characters, each of them, all represent different parts of a person's own psyche. So, what part of you drives your car—your life—so recklessly?"

I stopped to think. "Everything in my life is going pretty well—except my shelved-for-the-moment passion for making art. You might know that I put my studio work pretty much on hold this past year, so I could learn to take care of the kids. I'm only dabbling in ideas in my sketchbook, nothing serious. But now that you mention it, I think this dream might be about me needing to get back in and drive my car, my own interests. It's been a year since Will and I married. Right now, I've gotten used to all that nurturing the kids requires. I guess the dream's reminding me it's time to regroup and redirect my efforts—before I end up killing my need to make art. I know I can pull off both mothering and making art now. I've boosted my energy by regular aerobic workouts besides my regular yoga practice. I'm ready to get back to serious studio work. Find some new galleries in which to show."

"Sounds right. Maybe that's what the dream is showing you."

"That my art career is in serious jeopardy, not me?" I winced, remembering the bad feeling the dreamt crash and my own resulting death, how it made me feel so awful upon awakening.

"Well," he quietly offered, "do you think that sounds right?"

"But Phil, the feeling I had was, really, *everything* in me went dead."

"Well, then, try it on to see if maybe the dream's message is a beforehand warning. It's telling you it's up to you to pay attention. If you don't, maybe you really will end up, not necessarily being, but feeling dead inside."

No matter how I felt—on this day somewhat annoyed with myself, realizing I hadn't been listening to what my subconscious was trying to warn me of—I always left these brief-but-insightful conversations with my father-in-law with a better understanding of what my confusing dreams were trying to tell me.

Thanks to Phil's help, the death dream shook me out of the domestic reverie I'd found myself in, or rather, had created for myself in order to learn about raising kids. Determined to become as passionate an Angel Mom as I was about making art, I'd sublimated my own needs to work in my studio, and exhibit my creative output. I knew when I'd decided to put art-making on hold it wouldn't be for very long. Being a nurturer had never been an aspiration of mine, before that sober wish list, when, right afterwards, Will and my instant family arrived.

Domestic stability in itself, I'd always told myself, went against the prophetic voice I'd heard at, again, that magical age, seven. I was standing at the sink doing dishes, mesmerized by rainbow-colored soap bubbles. "This life," I'd clearly heard a voice inside myself whisper, "the kind your parents have, with kids, in a place with too many rules, isn't the one that's waiting for you."

Once I finally arrived at art school, I instantly knew I'd been born to create new ideas. To share original and inspiring pieces; not just make beautiful and provocative work, was my aim from the beginning. To help others experience the subtle connections I'd found that turn me on, became my mission. After the car-crash dream though, I knew I had to stop focusing solely on mothering and get back to sharing my ideas with the world, before I started feeling so damn angelic I'd be useless to anyone but my needy family. Clearly, from this dream's emphatic message that Phil helped me interpret—I'd go dead inside if I didn't soon change.

Then I remembered what the Teacher often said to her students.

"Our thoughts are powerful magnets. Thoughts are the seeds of our life's actions. Each of us plants our own thought-seeds. And then we reap our destiny from how well we tend our garden of intentions."

Immediately I went back into my studio. With a fury I made art, planting thought-seeds about this next stage I was in, a spirit-artist. The thought-seed of *me-as-Angel Mom* had worked, so I trusted this next seed I was sowing would successfully sprout as well. If I nurtured it, exactly as a gardener tends fragile seedlings into healthy plants, I knew I could juggle both parts of myself, artist and nurturer. I'd become pretty adept at the family-nurturing business, the respectable discipline of household yoga, which didn't come naturally to me. Confident I had my dual lifestyle down pat, I returned to creating objects instead of focusing only on my live, straight from suburbia, performance piece.

I shared many other dreams with Phil, looking forward to our continued dream-work together. Phil now became the next of my many teachers. He seemed to like my company, and I was grateful for his. He and I passed many an hour quietly talking as Claire, in her studio most times of day and night, focused on making massive metal totems, while Will and the kids were busy elsewhere.

One afternoon I went to Phil with another of my crazy mixed-up dream-puzzles.

"Last night I dreamt all my teeth became loose. I wasn't doing anything special, just hanging out. I don't know if anyone else was there or not. All of a sudden, my teeth started swimming around in my gums. I panicked. It felt like they were going to fall out if I opened my mouth too wide. Then I woke up."

Right on cue Phil softly asked, "What does it mean to you, teZa?"

"That I should keep my mouth shut? So my teeth don't fall out?"

"That sounds probable," he chuckled. "You do like to talk. What else?"

"Maybe I need to not be so chatty about what I need to do—and just do it?"

"Sounds right."

"Yes, that must be it."

"Well," my favorite old man said, wiping his face with the white handkerchief that was always in his breast pocket, an unconscious habit he did whenever he dove into the deep terrain of mapping the subconscious, "the trick, for all of us, is to do what our message-dreams tell us to do. Once we figure them out."

"Oh, I will," I said, thinking Better-me wasn't a fool, like Lesser-me was, to shun such blatant signs from my dreams as I'd done for too long.

△

It was the year that Jonny went into first grade when I went back to full production in my studio. Will supported my endeavors, even accompanying me on a series of scouting trips to major art centers, as we made an adventure out of searching for venues in which to show my pieces. Soon I had solo and group shows lined up for the next two years. My focus shifted from large paintings on wood that I called Dreamtimes, shaped and textured to look like slabs of stone; to multi-media freestanding sculptures, a series named Recycled Souls, which were fabricated from bones, crystals, feathers and metal constructions, held together by dark earth-tinted papier-mâché. These sculptural pieces included figures with wings sprouting out of cow skulls, mounted crystals dangling from skull-like forms, trunks replacing tails; and a next series of paintings on textured boards featured iconic human and nonhuman figures depicting made-up or actual myths.

Making the work now became easy to manage, along with guiding the kids and practicing household yoga with Will, what I'd been doing exclusively before that death-dream woke me up. Now I was in balance, able to make time for my own needs as well as attending to those of others. I was on a roll in the studio, depicting ideas designed to awaken higher consciousness. By learning how to share center stage with equally depicting Spirit and caring for my family, I became as capable of drawing from the deep well inside me, the creative art-making place, as I was at loading the washing machines or putting out a mean plate of quinoa stew. But I couldn't have done this juggling act if I hadn't taken off that entire year from art-making to learn giving loving-kindness to others, full-time. I needed that much time to get used to my demanding new role as co-captain on our self-contained little boat sailing down Rio Blisso.

Jonny came home with a project. In class, they were now talking about people's *standard of living*.

"Our teacher said all people have different ones. She wants us to talk about our own family's *stand* of living. I told her I have two families. She said I need to talk about both of them, Mama's and ours."

I chuckled. Jonny's lispy singsong voice barely got this new phrase out, *standard* of living. I was pleased Jonny's teacher had asked the kids to share their own, real experiences rather than just telling them about others'.

Jonny and I talked about how different folks have varying standards.

"Like us for instance," I said, "we're ordinary people who keep our house and yard neat, have a few nice things but not too much of this or that, possessions-wise. We enjoy an average but good standard of living."

After a few more minutes of talking, in which we discussed how his environment was at Debby's, for comparison sake I then asked: "Which of your two families do you think has the higher standard of living, Jonny? Debby's or ours?"

After a few silent moments with his brow wrinkled in thought, he said with complete confidence: "Mama's."

"Oh, and why is that, Jonny?" I asked with a straight face.

"Because her house is three stories high all around and ours is only two in some places. Hers is higher!"

I chuckled. Then I gently agreed with him that Debby's house was indeed higher than ours, but that wasn't exactly what the phrase "higher standard of living" meant. We talked some more about the differences between his two homes. I asked for his thoughts.

"I guess Mama's house has a lot of messy stuff in it, more than ours."

"So I've heard. What else is different?"

"At her house she has a bunch of TVs, one in every room. And a portable one in her truck. And an even smaller one for the basket of her bike where she keeps Bernice, her Chihuahua, for her to ride when Mama hasn't got Bernice stuck inside her shirt. We only have one TV here in the living room at our house."

"That's right. What else, Jonny?"

His face scrunched up in thought. "Mama has papers all over the dashboard of her truck, flying out the window all the time, and we never have messy papers around except on Dad's desk." He thought a moment more. "There's always a bunch of empty beer and soda cans in the back of her truck that the dogs trip over. One of them, Scrappy, fell off the truck and Mama never even noticed until she got back home. Scrappy never got found. With you and Dad we only have Bruno. We recycle bottles and cans, and you guys never have any beer. Mama gets funny when she drinks beer. Once in a while we have a can from that tomato stuff you use to make soup or spaghetti sauce. And we recycle, we don't use the can man like Mama does."

"That's right. What else is different?"

"Mama doesn't wash the dishes hardly at all, so we never have to do any work when we're there. Here we have to do dishes after we eat, take out the compost and the recycling and a whole bunch of other chores, like making the bed and picking up all the time."

"Doesn't Debby compost?"

"Naw. Dogs eat everything up."

I thought silently for a moment, then asked, "What did your teacher say about how to figure out if people have different standards of living?"

"Mrs. McClellan says that a higher standard of living is about making right choices. She says being clean and peaceful is important, no matter how fancy a house people have."

"That's smart of her," I said, thinking how insightful this teacher was.

"Yeah. I guess I forgot." Jonny's voice dropped a note. "I guess that's not Mama's house. Dogs run all over her place, tearing everything up. And there's dog poo all over, on the porch, all around the yard. She doesn't clean anything up either. It's not very clean and peaceful, I guess. The TVs are always on, tuned to different stations in each room. And the fleas inside are a bummer. Their bites hurt."

"Let's try again," I said. "Which of your two homes, Debby's or ours, do you think has the higher standard of living?"

Jonny looked down at the floor. I knew the truth was hard for him to admit.

"I guess we do," he said in a soft voice. "Dad went to college. Mama never reads. You don't shout like Mama does; she yells a lot. Our house here doesn't have bugs. There's not so much dirt and stuff."

"That sounds more like what your teacher told you to help figure out living standards."

"Yeah," my little guy said, his head sinking to his chest. "Mama's real nice but her house stinks."

△

Down the street from us, the standard of living skyrocketed. Surrounded by the pristine horseshoe-shaped pasture of Mr. Bull and his many wives, stood the fortress-like modern castle of our kids' upscale—yet frugal to the extreme—grandparents. A royal crown in the fife-dom of its surrounding middle-class conformity, Phil and Claire's residence, set apart from the rest of suburbia, shouted the earned privilege of its occupants' focused lives. When Phil wasn't at his office, where he drove to everyday even when he was over ninety, he and Claire either played bridge at their club, or attended one of the various cultural and philanthropic boards on which they sat. Will, however, for reasons he never could reckon, always felt more comfortable with common working-class folks than his parents' elite tribe.

Unlike his three siblings, Will didn't want to retain a speck of what he called "that uppity class crap." He totally rejected the high-society etiquette his mother attempted to instill in her young offspring, forcing them to learn manners, formal dance steps, behaving like proper gentlemen and ladies of their privileged background. Will never cared which utensil he used to eat fish or steak, or other such peculiarities not necessary for survival in jungles or on tugboats. But for Claire, who often advised me in private, "It doesn't hurt to be a little square," propriety meant everything.

I disagreed. "I'm afraid it *does* hurt to be even a tiny bit square," I told Claire every time she offered that annoying motto of hers. It felt like she was prodding me to tame my too noticeable wild streak. Not for a moment did I entertain the nauseating notion of squaring anything. Will's and my bra deal that hinged upon our relocating from Lackland, was as far as I was willing to go.

Every time I left home, I was uncomfortably aware of the fact that I represented Claire, the town's grand dame of Art & Culture, one of the most respected and affluent women in the county. She remained a walking paradox to me: a serious artist who had her hair and nails done every week at a salon, wore matching-everything, but made incongruously of-the-moment monumental sculpture. For Claire's sake, as a member of her esteemed family, I felt pressed to dress appropriately, and fix myself up with at least a smidgeon of conformity, whether at the gym, grocery store, or the kids' school, so she wouldn't feel shamed by her rebel son's new wife. Reluctantly I put aside my usual tropical-island skimpy getups, the antithesis of Claire's pressed pantsuits dolled up with exaggeratedly bulbous, gold flashy jewelry. She never said, but I knew she appreciated me not showing too much skin or yoga spandex, her eyes only imploring, *Lose the ponytail, puh-lease, teZa,* because she'd never be caught dead criticizing anyone aloud.

One day I was working in our tropical-lush backyard wearing my customary dirt-digging uniform: bikini, knee-high wellie boots, wide-brimmed hat and gloves. As usual I brandished the only tool I ever need to garden, a big sharp machete that can do everything from digging up rich humus earth and dividing plant clumps, to poking around delicate roots—when I heard our front door bell ring. No one else was at home that day. Will's business revolved around packages being delivered to him in a timely fashion. Suddenly I remembered how he'd asked me to be on the lookout for a certain package before he left the house earlier with the kids. In that moment's recollection, I decided to forego my usual kowtow to propriety. Paying no heed to the teeny bikini I wore, I left our secluded, high-fenced backyard, figuring FedEx or UPS had arrived with the expected parcel. Quickly

I calculated I'd chance freaking-out the unknown-to-me delivery person by my muddy, sweaty, machete-wielding self, and for once, just this once since arriving in Lackland, wouldn't give a hoot about my appearance. Claire was nowhere in sight. I figured what she didn't know wouldn't hurt her. Figuring the signing operation would take all of two seconds, I kept ahold of the machete in my gloved hand as I walked out the garden gate onto the front driveway of our suburban home, calculating this would take only a moment and I'd avoid offending any neighbors … or next door in-laws.

When I rounded the corner from our driveway to the front door—I saw them. Too late! I couldn't hide. I had to greet them.

Two Jehovah's Witnesses, a man and a woman, oh God! Their jaws dropped at the sight of me. The middle-aged man who wore a light-colored suit and a dark tie drawn tightly to his throat, instantly sunk his chin to his chest and cast his eyes to the ground to avoid the sinful sight I was: a nearly naked Amazon smeared in garden dirt, with boots and hat, and something really sharp and shiny in her gloved hands. The similarly matched woman nervously clutched the big black Bible she held tightly to the bodice of her full-skirted pretty cotton dress, her mouth twisting in dismay. I felt bad how agonized this couple's embarrassment made their faces look.

Yet I did not apologize. You see, I was as shocked as they were to see these two, so buttoned-up. Without waiting for them to say anything I gave them my customary door salesman's rap: "You didn't see our front door sign? The one that clearly says: *Solicitors DO NOT ring this bell! We DO NOT discuss God or politics at the door*." And I quickly added, "And we don't in the driveway either."

I knew these two folks were mortified about my lack of shame, so I said no more. Standing in the driveway in mud-splattered bikini and boots, I didn't want to add any more pain to the already deeply-aggrieved couple.

Without lifting his sight from the tips of his shiny tan shoes, the man crept away alongside his upright partner, both of them silent, and nevermore to return to our house at the end of the cul-de-sac.

I found out later that before we'd joined our lives, Will used to invite the Jehovahs into his house to discuss the Lord's holy scripture, which this earthier encounter put a quick end to.

△

Claire said she liked my whimsical sculptures. And I was relieved she never felt pressed to comment on my paintings, quite sure the blue-skinned (depicting people's spiritual bodies), clothes-less creatures of my works' anthropomorphic narratives weren't anymore to her liking than my multi-textured, vari-patterned attire that led her to hint at my needing to be "more square." As two committed artists from consecutive generations, we had nothing more in common than a shared passion of our work's theme: depicting humankind's relationship to Spirit. Notwithstanding, the manner in which we expressed the search for Oneness was as opposite as our choice of materials and our stylistic interpretation.

Claire's work was all symbolic icons of sharp angles of stainless steel (except for that lone, brave curve of hers, signifying a new direction), glossy car enamels, and uninterrupted straight edges. My two-dimensional works were explosive brushstrokes of colors, shapes, and forms; and my naturalistic sculptures were made of voluptuous clay-like earth tones, and curvaceously organic objects and patina'd silver, brass, and copper.

The work in my studio celebrated life's riddles using rough wiggly textures that were designed to provoke the mind's engagement. Juxtaposing two or more incongruent things in a composed, character-laden narrative, I meant to engage the viewer's questioning. My aim was for each person to discover his or her own answers to their thirst (if the inner life was still unknown to them), or quest (if they were a seeker already) for Spirit. Claire's art honored the Divine via smooth materials in union with intellectual acuity. Her work: no contours, no deceptive textures. To Claire, too much information, or symbolism equaled misleading messages. She preferred no stories, in art. Her premise: pure symbolic abstraction, no delusions of metaphorical reference of any kind. My approach—based on the stimulus of balancing order with presenting choices, wedding disparate living creatures of the natural world—utilized chaos and haphazardness. I loved mimicking the randomness of Nature to create drama and tension in my work. My goal has always been to heighten the dream-like qualities of this world by documenting the surreal perception of reality. Even though Claire's work honored mankind's desire to know the heights of pure spiritual Truth, as mine does as well, her approach was purely conceptual, whereas mine demonstrates the sanctity of human chance and the charm, the reward of finding peace among man-made chaos amidst the beauty, the guiding force of Nature.

We two artists' outputs represented mind versus instinct: Claire's pieces produced solid reverence of the intellect, totally opposite to my work's intentionally letting-go of too much thinking. Perhaps due to our close familial relationship, we never discussed these fascinating differences of ours. As her son's wife, whom she alone called Big Cat, it was not my place to bring the subject up, I strongly felt.

△

Just as both of us created art with soul, we likewise took very seriously our responsibility as protectors of our children. One day Claire was driving just us two somewhere, her myopic vision laser-focused, riveted on the exact center of the paved road ahead. There were very few cars on this scantily traveled street near both our houses. Glancing neither left nor right, even past eighty-years-old she navigated her truck-sized Buick station wagon with mastery, charging ahead at a good clip. Her large thick glasses were set dead center on her wide-open face as she sat fully erect behind the wheel. I was a little nervous, wondering if she ever glanced at the rearview mirror, or if she was aware of what was happening on any other side of us but straight ahead. No matter, she wanted to talk; so, I tried to relax.

All business, Claire began: "I want to thank you, teZa, for marrying my Will. Because in the past he's made some strange, unfortunate choices about what kind of people to associate with."

Claire was above saying names, but I knew who she meant. Debby's family was not so different from my own in their being several rungs beneath Will's on the social ladder. But unlike myself, Debby had been uninterested, or incapable of participating with Will in the intellectual and spiritual areas. There was another person though, whom I knew Claire was alluding to in this discussion of ours.

We'd talked about him before, she and I. In private she always called him "that sea guy," preferring to never mention the name of Will's childhood friend whose presence lurked around her son like a vulture waiting for its corpse. As an adult, this guy Mason had acquired a shady reputation, although he'd never been brought to justice because his alleged crimes had all been committed out of the USA's jurisdiction, far out at sea. Either out of a misplaced sense of Christian charity, or his kindness-driven, nonetheless severe handicap of chronic people-pleasing, Will could never—and he tried, believe me—bring himself to abandon Mason, his pal since forever. They'd played together as boys, and as men, they'd worked together on Mason's tugboat. Mason was Elsbeth's now ex-husband, their divorce happening right after Elsbeth had urged Will to call me several springtimes before this day.

Will told me he couldn't deny the possible validity behind the rumors surrounding Mason's degenerate behavior. Yet whenever I asked why he didn't shun this guy whom I had met, and immediately received chilling vibes of an unnamed evil exuding from merely being in his presence, Will said, "Somebody has to keep talking to the motherfucker—to be there when he's ready to embrace the rest of the human race."

Claire and I never referred to Mason by name during our conversation that day. She spoke only about his ever-looming proximity to Will, "the unpopular guy's only friend," she presumed, when the sea guy wasn't out working his towing vessel as it plowed the world's oceans. I immediately assured her I understood.

"I promise he will never come around the kids on my watch, Claire."

Claire's stoic face glimmered a faint smile of relief.

"Thanks for that, teZa. Thanks for saving my grandchildren. I know you'll keep them from bad people," she said. "I can rest easy now, knowing you'll not be letting that dangerous man, who everyone says does terrible things to children, ever come around Jonny and Kara. Those things people say about him, well, I just get sick thinking about him around our grandkids."

It went unmentioned that day, the past sexual abuse allegations pointing to Mason's guilt that I'd found out first, through my long and intimate friendship with Elsbeth.

"You don't have to worry, Claire. I'm wise to Mason. He doesn't fool me. He's not welcome in our house now that I'm on duty. He's a sly one, but I'm hip to his wily ways."

Claire glanced over at me and for a moment I feared she'd crash the car.

"Especially Kara," she said, peering at me through her glasses' magnifying lenses, her eyes scarily off the road, searching mine.

Our eyes locked firmly. *Especially Kara.* Those two words shouted the nature of Mason's transgressions.

"Don't worry, Claire. I won't let him, or anyone untrustworthy, ever near the kids."

"Good." She thankfully turned her gaze back to tunnel-visioning ahead. "As for Debby," Claire made a clearing sound deep in her throat, "you and I both know she loves her kids and, crazy as everything she does may seem, that's all that matters. Her love for them."

"I totally agree," I hoarsely whispered, half glad Claire was speaking so directly; half regretting she felt the need to.

"It would be lots worse for them if she didn't care," she said, nodding her head like a dashboard granny doll.

She stated what I myself had said many times over, each time someone pressured me about why Will and I allowed Debby's being in the kids' lives.

"Not to worry, Claire. Will and I believe Debby's motherly love justify the adverse effects of her sphere of influence. No matter how bad she acts, the woman hasn't forsaken her kids; and we're so grateful for that. You have my word on both counts. I'll protect them from any bad people and do my best to help Jonny and Kara heal, to become whole and happy grownups. I give you my word, they're safe with me."

"Good." Claire's chest heaved with a huge sigh. "You don't know how relieved I am to hear you say that. I feel better already. I'm glad my son had sense enough to marry you."

For the rest of our short ride we chitchatted. She never glanced my way again or cracked a smile, but focused straight ahead.

PART TWO

lightkeepers

the sun and the stars are our compass

CHAPTER 13

the sun and the stars are our compass

A few months later, a phone call from New Hampshire relayed the sad news that Claire had collapsed from a heart attack while getting ready for a hike in the mountains with Phil. She was rushed to the hospital, where she gave last minute instructions to Phil about the sculpture she was working on. In another hour she had a next attack, this one fatal.

Phil was devastated. He'd lost his very own eighty-two-year-old angel. Although he was stoic at her funeral, as were Will and his brother and younger sister, the older sister, a psychoanalyst, was a sobbing mess. Jonny and Kara, seven and nine then, took their emotional cues directly from Will and me, as children do. Since we both believed in reincarnation, death for us is not as emotionally challenging as it is for some. "Grandma Claire will always be with us," we told our kids.

Back in Lackland, as our lives assumed the *new normal*, we went up to Grandpa's as often as we could. Otherwise, he claimed he wished to be alone, except for his loyal housekeeper's half-time presence. The kids and I spent hours playing board games while Phil and Will watched football every Sunday when we could visit. We shared as many meals as was practical for a family with two school-age kids.

Asked if he'd like us to temporarily move in with him, he said, "No thanks, I have other plans in mind." We didn't press for an explanation. Phil preferred complete quiet: no music, no TV; we knew that meant no loud children. Honoring his wishes, we left whenever the kids got too rowdy. During this time the old man bonded with our CBD, Bruno, who often sauntered up to the big house by himself and spent entire afternoons comforting Phil while Jonny was away at school.

Phil spent the next six months mostly in solitude, grieving, refusing to go anywhere. "I just want to think," he would tell Will when his son tried to cheer him up a little too often.

With Phil widowed, it was no longer a certainty that Will could honor the exact time schedule we'd set for getting our family out of Lackland. It was now three years into that five-year promise of his. I tried to keep any discouraging thoughts in the back of my mind, preferring to nurture the positive thought-seed of our leaving. Besides, our present-day activities were way too consuming to bother worrying about something looming so far in the future.

Claire was now relegated to being my Patron Saint of Slim instead of the demanding mother-in-law to be reckoned with. No longer was Lackland Claire's domain, with me as a closet yogini in this pre-mainstream-yoga time, as much a social misfit as an alien-in-hiding. No longer did I feel an obligation to dress and behave to reflect her eminently respected status in this company town, with its church oriented, cookie-cutter social scene. Now Will and I no longer had to figure ways of getting our kids out of going to the prissy Cotillion that Claire had founded, where they'd be subjected to the same mandatory torture training for how to behave, never useful anywhere but in royal palaces or State banquets, over-the-top utterly gracious manners, as Will and all his siblings had been subjected to as youngsters. Despite being sad about losing my arty, spiritual in-law, I could finally be my own woman in this town I was forced to live in … for a while longer.

△

Phil generously invited me to take over both of his beloved's now-empty studios. The one attached to the house was the largest work space I'd ever had, with spectacular high windows, paint-spattered wooden floors, and a lofty ceiling with marvelous light. At Claire's passing I'd already been back in full swing for a full year, making new pieces, preparing for exhibitions, sending work off to galleries and public spaces in bigger cities, connecting with interested venues of all sorts, selling to patrons and corporations. The other studio Phil let me use, the one called the Claire Mahal, where her assistant had done the messy finish work of filing, sanding, and polishing of her stainless-steel totems, I re-christened the teZ Mahal. Here I did no art, but set up a desk and began to write seriously. In that rickety old trailer's cramped back bedroom, a dark cave-like space big enough for only two people's mats to fit tightly side by side, Will and I did a very private yoga practice together—in the nude. Maybe that's why Will liked calling it *fun*-ga, not wishing to be reminded that the *yo* of yoga stood for the union of an oxen being *yoked*, a not-fun syllabic reminder that doing asanas is a demanding discipline.

Most times though, I practice yoga alone, wearing a bikini. "Yoginis wear bikinis," is one of my lifelong mottos. In that tiny back yoga room of the teZ Mahal that was heated up like a pizza oven, winter and summer, sweating became part of my feel-good therapy. The intense heat allowed deeper stretching, helping me release pent-up anxiety from the challenges of raising kids and coping with suburbia. Will agreed with me after he got into it: sweaty yoga was better than having a shrink. Our yoga time together became our *date time*: this silent (but for music), prayerful, primordial (naked, remember) way of doing meditative poses, which we did several times a week together, strengthened and detoxed our bodies, at the same time.

At last—a place all to myself—the teZ Mahal, my hideaway. A writing place where kids were not allowed, except by my invitation; where my husband couldn't bug me either, but could reach me anytime in those pre-cellular times, via the landline installed for an internet hookup. There, in Claire's former filing-filled, metal finishing space, I created *A Room of My Own* that would have made Virginia Woolf proud.

With this second, completely private studio, it was the right time to explore more fully being the writer I'd always been, as well as artist. Back at the bigger, airy studio attached to Phil's house that he was happy to let me use, Claire's main one, it was business as usual for me, making sculptures and paintings for upcoming shows. But writing—ah, here I was to find my life's challenge.

Up to this time I could never decide which to do: write or art. It was never easy to decide how to divide my creative juices, and some days in the past I would separate doing one at a time, because I didn't have space or mental freedom enough to explore both. Now, with a designated writing place, word-smithing became the fulfillment of the thought-seeds I'd planted long-ago. I've always been a lusty-for-making-everything kind of artist. Words, concepts, images, objects—they're all creative arting—any way I can find to express the weird and wonderful ideas constantly bubbling up, I want to pursue.

Located a short stroll from my art studio at Phil's house, or a two-minute bike ride from ours, at the teZ Mahal I either did yoga or wrote. It also became my private spot in which I could unfurl my infrequent freak-outs, when those fetal-positioned grips of the remnants of my inner turmoil leaked out, bubbling up from my soul's otherwise delicious stew. Those times became less and less with each passing year. Other times, I'd be seated at the funky kidney-shaped desktop I made for myself, with enough room to spread out pages of a manuscript plus accommodate computer and printer—my view looked out onto a postcard-perfect scene of Mr. Bull and his devoted cow-harem off in the distance. Whenever I took a moment to think out a phrase, a character's dialogue, a chapter's point, I'd watch the herd grazing under oak trees or drinking from the pond where, years before, Jonny and I saw Bruno fight for his life with the ferocious baby gator.

On one ocasion as I sat at my desk thinking, I observed a bald eagle descend and stand alone, perfectly still, under the shade of an oak. He would stare at the ground ahead of him for up to ten minutes at a time, testing my patience for bird-watching, while he was visually discovering the perfectly-shaped twig for his nearby nest.

Once he found it, by sight alone, the majestic eagle rushed headlong to snatch-up his selection in his beak and immediately took flight. One super-lucky day I looked up from my keyboard to see an endangered Florida panther taking his turn sitting casually under the oaks, the rare cat's honey-colored fur gleaming with wildness as he stared off into the distance from where he'd crept into the middle of the unfriendly suburban sprawl.

△

Things were going smoothly, sailing down Rio Blisso. By default, I was permanently stuck with the bum role of having to discipline Kara and Jonny, since Will didn't want "to make more grief in their lives," he'd say, but I knew that was just his lousy excuse. At times, his shortcomings really got to me. Then, I'd succumb to my former dark thinking. I'd indulged in short-lived escape fantasies, letting my imagination take flight after suffering one of the now-scarce bouts of Lesser-me's disquiet. I'd shake myself out of any pussified regrets I had, never sinking to loathe my role as wife or Angel Mom, or ever admitting it was altogether too much for me. I achieved this by allowing myself some comic relief, always humor! amidst the worst of any one day's events.

In satiric scenarios, I imagined speaking to a sympathetic judge in divorce court. "Judge," I would say to him, "I hate to say it, but Will is such a hopeless case when it comes to discipline that I'm forced to seek a divorce."

In real time, I'd laugh at how silly my playacting was, as my imaginary judge asked: "On what grounds, young lady?"

"Mental cruelty from not-caring," I'd lament, my lower lip quivering, my eyes welling with tears. "My man refuses to even pick up any of the stuff he throws everywhere, so how can he possibly teach his kids order and discipline? That shitty job is all left to me!"

My pretend courtroom drama always ended in both the judge and me laughing—at my one and only ludicrous charge, Will's slovenliness, in our otherwise loving, supportive marriage. Yet it helped me, relieving those feelings of resentment over Will's lax attitude, and allowed me to laugh instead of cry.

By the time I finished one of my remedial daydreamed divorce-court spoofs, I knew how ridiculous I was being. Divorce him because he's a slob? C'mon! *Here was a man with a golden heart*, I chastised myself. Who cares if he threw his underwear all over the place? Then I'd slap myself awake, ending another of my blow-off-steam, hilariously imagined, mental escapes.

And made another private appointment with Dr. C, with whose help I was slowly learning to get through my stubborn resistance, a workable solution of how to accept the unacceptable.

"You simply have to tolerate this about Will," she told me. "He's no disciplinarian. Neither of himself or his kids. And he never will be.

"You can't change another person," she sweetly but sternly reminded me of what I'd heard a katrillion times ... but never could believe. "People have to want to change, themselves. Psychologically, it's textbook: Will's slipshod way is his unconscious rebellion against his Neatnik Mom. Only he can do something about that, when he's good and ready."

I left Dr. C's office that day adding item three to my marital list of Things to be Accepted: suburbia, no nips-peeking, and now—expect no change from Will until he's interested in changing himself.

Even without support from Will in laying down the law—or him ever once using the non-rules that were my guiding saviors—the kids grew stronger and more independent each passing day. Who was I to talk anyway, about Will's behavior? Former outlaw-me still had to work hard censoring my salty sailor-speak, those expletive-heavy but oh-so-satisfying-feeling, loud rummy ho-ho-hos and gobs of neon-colored epithets shared by all sea-going comrades around the world's nose-twitching waterfront barrooms and smugglers' coves ... my old haunting grounds. Between Will's self-deprecatingly calling his own obsessive use of bad language, "Tourette's afflicted," trying to compensate for his lifelong addiction to the sensational bad-mouth rush of using explosive profanities; Debby's ain't's and the double negatives of the illiterate South that I even heard come out of the mouths of (horrors!) grammar school teachers—the kids had an overload of bad influences in the proper language and behavior department. What would it hurt me to put a muffler on? Besides putting on a tit harness, I made every effort to tone down my fondness for the f-word as soon as becoming Angel Mom. So why, I'd fume, couldn't Will pick up his lousy freakin' undies?

Acceptance.

Once again, breathing away the angst, I remembered to repeat: *So'hăm, So'hăm.*

Will and I agreed to monitor the kids' use of electronics. We encouraged their jumping on the trampoline, riding bikes, fishing in Grandpa's pond, hanging out under the shade of a tree, lying on the lawn watching the clouds go by above, noticing the billowing shapes shift. We allowed no screen-gaming that wasn't educational because our kids got plenty of that visiting their maxed-out game-friends and at anything-goes Debby's. We wanted to help Jonny and Kara discover their own personal, more healthy alternatives to the mega-overdose, consumer-and-digital world out there: to learn that life is more than a series of screens. We wanted them to love and respect Nature and enjoy their own rapturous physicality.

We gave them lots of alternatives that other kids seemed not to appreciate as much, those fixated on devices and chat rooms in this pre-social media era. Tragically, one grade school pal of Jonny's, after having a few back-and-forth visits between them, told him, "I don't want to be your friend. You don't have any games at your house." Even more heartbreaking, this same boy ended up as a drug user, and died of an overdose before reaching twenty-one. He'd been nurtured by a pill-popping mom who, too early in her son's life, substituted computers instead of parental hands-on. The mom's demise sadly echoed her son's a few short years after his.

I insisted on calling myself Angel Mom, because that's what I was: a yogi-artist suburban-mom. I offered all of my nurturing (to myself, my family, my art work) to the greater good of the entire world, and that's what angels are known for: guiding humans. My

Teacher stressed that the spiritual path meant offering whatever we do for the betterment of all beings, everywhere: the true meaning of selfless service, the practice of seva. I decided to spare no effort in the nurturing department. Neither my own family nor strangers would get anything less than the most I had to give. Each nutritious meal I prepared, each dish I washed, each floor I swept, each kid's mess I cleaned up, each painting, each essay: I offered up to the Source, to the unlimited possibilities we humans all share. By continuing to think I was performing household yoga when doing domestic duties, my life took on a luminescent kind of glory, shining my mind, expanding every part of myself. This new attitude transformed any duty I felt drudge-like to being a true fountain of bliss: everything from caring for the family's or my own needs, to making visionary art, or writing the explosion of stories that flowed out of me in the teZ Mahal. My heart felt like a warm balloon swelling my chest wide, freeing me from any sense of smallness, of restriction.

As the demon within me loosened its grip, I focused more on the Teacher's guidance: how to become friends with my own Better-me.

I did this by making sure I exercised every day, slept well, and ate mostly plant-based foods, challenging in a family used to meat, meat, mostly meat. Slowly, I got the rest of the crew on Rio Blisso used to my way of eating. "Cow-flap Spaghetti!" became our family's inside joke for how I accomplished this feat. That was a dish I'd invented that resembled a plate of bovine manure, but it was a delicious splat of brown-ish tomato sauce amid white noodles. Jonny liked to explain in detail to any shocked visitors who heard the phrase, for years after the event actually happened.

"When I was real small I hated vegetables," he'd say, "so teZ tried to get them in me without my knowing. She knew how I loved spaghetti, so she mixed some green leafy vegetables in with the red tomato sauce. Until one day she went too far—and the sauce turned a really gross dark greenish-brown color. When I asked why the plate looked like a newly splashed-out cow-flap we see all over Grandpa's pasture, Dad and teZ just looked at each other and grinned, but didn't say anything. After I got to like veggies, they told me what she'd done. How she'd gone a little overboard with the greens that one time. I didn't mind that it looked bad though, 'cause it tasted real good."

△

Our boat glided down Rio Blisso. The waters surrounding us always new, the landscape along the banks of the rushing river ever-changing, glorious to behold.

Even before all the daily chores were done our boat's crew, the four of us, relaxed and played games, opposite to the way I was raised. Will always took the lead as Big Giant, the kids squealing as he chased them in all directions while I kept our cruising boat's helm steady, our nose pointed in the right direction.

Admittedly, my favorite time of all was being alone with my co-captain, after the kids had gone to sleep or we had a kid-free weekend. Minus time and extra funds during those first years, we took mini honeymoons every single night, when we fell into each other's arms, thankfully alone and behind a locked door. The duties of child-rearing and money-making over, the day's many pulls gently put to rest for a short while, we melted and became one united pulsing sensation.

Then I was in heaven. Every problem gone. All the hard work worth it, for these precious hours of soulful satisfaction. To be held by this man who was my match, who filled all the empty spaces inside and outside me, and I for him, he said: we two were One. Our love felt like a gift, given not just to make us happier, but to fulfill something in each of us we'd never been able to tap before. I never knew that a love like this was possible, but here it was, growing larger inside me: a good and benevolent growth, roaring like a furnace, helping to burn out Lesser-me's inadequacies.

This love, this great adventure. I wanted to be nowhere else.

I was as drunk on loving Will as I was in love with Aum.

△

As co-captain of our ship I kept my focus on being the See-er, instead of fleeing from, denying, or overreacting to life's nonstop difficulties, like Lesser-me once tended to. The Teacher showed me how to stop mentally running away, how to be present, always. "Follow your breath," she said, over and over. But life is chaotic, so often I forgot and, losing my focus, drifted straight into the headwinds of life's often harsh, but in the end golden, and certainly infinite opportunities to experience Oneness. From the safe distance of the See-er state, on the outskirts of my ego, I could face any of life's tough, sudden catastrophes, and deciding to accept its handicaps, short or long term. In this super-aware state of being the See-er that I was finding easier with practice, I'd found a hidden gear within my consciousness—an overdrive, hyper-reality: Aum-ness. All I had to do was remember to be the See-er, and I was automatically one with Aum.

When I purposefully slipped into the See-er state of mind, I found my highest high, naturally attuned to the subtle rhythms of life. This mental focus, which gradually I got better at, being the witnessing See-er, enabled me to gradually feel more fulfilled in a long-lasting manner. And much steadier at the helm of our family's vessel.

Whatever life brought I found I could handle. When I remembered to be the See-er, I helped our boat stay centered in the flow, instead of careening sidewise in Rio Blisso's conflicting currents. After nearly a decade of having practiced the Teacher's method of meditative presence, applying awareness to all I did, I knew, from having tested it, that the See-er within is everyone's most trusted ally. Learning to remain in the See-er state became the source of my life's greatest joy. As I caught more glimpses of how wonderful this state made me feel, I became greedy to immerse myself even more in its supreme bliss.

Being the See-er required detachment from whatever drama or chaos erupted around me. Constant, silent repetition of *So'hăm, So'hăm* was my main meditation practice when kids came along; the mantra's comforting constancy helped me focus on staying in the core, the joyous, acceptance part of life's bigger picture. I was learning, during this period, to not allow my mind to be drawn into whatever madness was going on, either at our family's glowing hearth, or outside in the crazy world with its never-ending irrational evil lurking everywhere. Slowly, ever so gradually, I learned to detach from energy-sucking negativities.

With my trust in life restored, I decided, for the benefit of Better-me's sake, to perfect the spiritual skill of detaching from negatives in an area where I'd been most challenged. The BM.

Debby proved to be an excellent way for me to practice detachment. Our history had been, after all, an irritating splinter in my soul. Her proximity to, but strict exclusion from our family's intimate happenings, provided an opportunity for me to explore in depth the inner peace I so coveted, and wanted to get better at nurturing within myself.

When the kids reported, "Mama called you Big Foot again, teZa," I ordered myself to not react to this latest jab. Inwardly, I located that pinprick within and sent it rays of grace, silently repeating *So 'hăm, So 'hăm* to calm my inner upheaval from her latest insult. After repeating the mantra with several rounds of deep breathing, I could smile, and say to the kids without a trace of malice: "Oh, how interesting. Debby's got such funny names for things, just like we do, like our CBD and Cow-flap Spaghetti. Hmmm, isn't she a good storyteller? Let's tell some stories of our own as we get ready for bed."

Who, other than me, was going to civilize these unruly, half-trailer-trash kids, who hadn't known how to make a bed, wash a dish or speak without saying an ain't or two? When I first started mothering Jonny, he knew nothing of butt-wiping or face-washing. Thanks to Dr. C's suggestions, I stepped in, risking Debby's mistaking any reports from her son about my training him in the personal hygiene bathroom business. As soon as I taught him how to wipe properly, Jonny's underpants stopped having those brown tracks, one of the earliest outward signs of the impact household yoga was to have on our family.

Honestly, I detested it, the relentless job of disciplining kids. It requires personal discipline to be a discipliner of others, which I barely had, but in comparison to Will, I had it abundantly, thanks to practicing yoga and meditation since my youngest years. Other than eating well and the daily asana practice I benefitted from since my scoliosis-suffering teens, I'd only become acquainted with Better-me's need for self-awareness type of discipline from working with the Teacher for so long. No other adult in our house—meaning my darling, goofball man—was disciplined enough to dole out chores or consequences to the kids. So it fell to me, ironically, the former space-cadet, runaway rebel herself, to teach Will's offspring how not to be the feral, unconscious jerk as I'd been. What a joke.

Countless times Dr. C tried to impress upon Will that, to a child, discipline is not only Love, but a life necessity. Instead of expecting Will to take an interest in showing them some structure, or teach them how to organize, or have a balanced routine of some sort, Dr. C helped me realize that chore was on me, and me alone. Then she and I, the two of us together, designed that trio of non-rules, the guidelines she wisely recommended I enforce from the start, to help rein in our boat's rowdy kid-crew as we cruised down Rio Blisso.

How many times did Dr. C repeat it to us? *Discipline is Love.*

"Each of us gets out of life what we discipline ourselves to achieve," her words echoed with each new situation our boatload faced. "Focus on love, love, love. Then everything, no matter what it is, works out for the best," I could hear Dr. C's words echo in my heartbeat.

△

The roles for which Will and I were best suited were clear to me from the start. He was the kids' playtime Big Giant, and by far, best suited to be the family's main breadwinner, while I reluctantly accepted the role of being the kids' Behavior Cop—ironic indeed, for a recovering she-pirate. I preferred to focus on the mountains of love and heaps of rewards I dished out, rather than penalties, called consequences and discussed ahead of the fact, instead of after bad behavior happened, giving the kids their own choice about how they wanted to act. Surrendering to being our family's sole disciplinarian (I had no choice, really, and was forced to be the kid-cop) within the often-conflicting currents and tides of Rio Blisso's strong flow, was essential. I had to accept my role, and that meant the good parts of that responsibility along with the regrettable.

Nothing, no entreaties, no enticements, would transform Will into a kid-cop, even a once-in-a-while deputy kind. The sooner I accepted that, the happier I'd be. Just like the sooner I accepted that he was a slob, and quickly learned to throw all his things that were strewn about, in a hidden spot alongside his side of the bed, where no one but he ever saw them—I'd be free as a bird.

Although I knew I was an adequate breadwinner, for myself I mean—these were *his kids*. My wages as a single gal had never presented a problem. I'd owned my own businesses; I knew what prosperity felt like. However, our family's circumstances pointed to Will alone needing to be in charge of our financial burden. Will's business was thriving, he claimed, "only because of your partnership," which pleased me enormously. He and I considered ourselves part of a successful money-earning team besides being two-as-One lovers. "Before you came along, I couldn't earn much of anything, teZ," he told me repeatedly. "Your presence has allowed me to tap the best I am, in so many ways."

To keep peace among all of life's disparate influences, that's why I kept insisting we use the communication system he'd insisted on when Will and I first discussed becoming a blended boat crew: regular, democratically-run Family Meetings. Which ironically swiftly turned out to be the no-fun FMs.

△

To help with the constant of daily challenges and conflicts, I asked everyone to save their gripes and bring them up at our FMs. Sure, we had them, but begrudgingly. I had to do some heavy-duty beseeching to counter Will's stubborn unwillingness to do what he'd been the one to originally insist on doing.

After over a year of having them regularly, the kids themselves called a particularly memorable FM. It centered around Kara and Jonny wanting me to get rid of my indispensable Yo-pickup that I had driven since being a gardener in the Hamptons; the one I'd driven to

Florida loaded with all my belongings when I followed my heart's pull to know Will better. At this FM, Kara snidely called my trusty To*yo*ta, "the sorry car." Ouch! I'd used it for my garden business, hauling plants and tools and picking up bulky art materials, as well as hauling art stuff around. Listening to Kara's opening statement, I was being told, in effect, that my favorite vehicle had outgrown its usefulness. As a family car.

Okay, I admit I'd been fitting an illegal number of squirmy, slippery kids into the front seat meant for only two adults as I chauffeured our kids, and up to three more neighborhood chums, when it was my turn to drive them to the nearby elementary school. In my defense, on those mornings the Yo-truck's cab resembled a happy tin of laughing-kid sardines. Sure, I knew I was breaking the law. That's why I told the extra kids to duck and hide their heads when we approached the school's drop-off point. At least I didn't put them in the rear of the truck's bed, like some local yokels in the recent news did, who'd sadly lost (and lightly injured) a kid overboard. My ways weren't exactly kosher, but they were safe. I'd always insisted all kids had to ride up front with me.

Regardless of how earnestly I presented my case at the FM, my reliable red miniature pickup and I were overruled. Our democracy of four took a vote, the system that FMs were based on—equality for all—which Will had, since our first discussion of blending, demanded I follow "to raise my kids the democratic way, where everyone in the family has an equal voice." Besides sharing feelings, FMs were where we voted on tough issues by choosing, with our family's majority vote. Regrettably, my Yo-truck had to go.

Kara loudly proclaimed, "I hate being seen in it!" when questioned about her reasons. More details emerged. "In front of my friends," the eight-year-old explained, "whose parents drive nice BMWs and Mercedes."

Beemer-chauffeured friends? My trusty truck didn't stand a chance. Jonny took his sister's lead, as he always did. I tried objecting, stressing the Yo-truck's gas economy, its status as my artist-cum-naturalist ride, how fun it was for me to drive with its stick shift, not to mention its spaciousness to haul our collection bins to the far-off recycling center because Lackland was so barbarically unconscious, and hadn't yet any curbside recycling service—but no dice. Will stated he'd remain neutral, pissing me off no end. Which meant my vote got overruled by two pipsqueaks'. The Yo-truck was voted off to the car graveyard, "to make the kids feel better," Will said, sealing its fate. With my trusty artist set of wheels forced out of my life, the last vestige of my pre-family rebelliousness evaporated into thin air. I was so low after that FM's show of hands I wanted to cry.

I couldn't help feeling the Yo-truck's demise was a mockery of democracy. Back when we first started talking about merging our lives, Will had impressed upon me the importance of instilling in our kids the ability to make good choices. He told me, "We'll demonstrate that process by holding FMs where we'll discuss big and small issues, hard or easy, but mostly topics that are difficult to discuss any other time." Of course, I agreed. Who can stop what they're doing right then—when bad things happen—to sort out every single disagreeable aspect of life?

In our regular FMs, everyone expresses their feelings, flips them around like hot potatoes and then we vote on what to do, as the democratically-run, fun-loving family Will envisioned. Before we met he'd read about FMs and demanded I read the blasted book, then got me to agree to that parenting methodology—practically making me sign my name in blood to that effect.

Then—selective memory a convenience for all non-disciplinarians—Will quickly forgot these meetings were part of the well-known program he'd presented to me, back when he was an obsessed single parent. "This is the S.T.E.P. method I use to raise my kids (Systematic Training for Effective Parenting)," he stated.

Now, sick of being the only one of us two grownups to get FMs going, reminding my partner it was he himself who'd once insisted on using them, he finally acquiesced; a team-playing man to his core. We were still just getting the hang of this give-and-take thing: our co-captainship on Rio Blisso.

Fate would have it that the biggest casualty of our FMs—besides resolving the endless string of kid or parent conflicts—was sacrificing my Yo-truck for the sake of family peace.

△

FMs were also the safe place where we could discuss scary things going on in the world. And as the years passed, FMs were the safe, non-threatening place where we could plan the direction of our family's future. We knew that the older the kids got, the more disruptive our eventual move from Lackland would be for them. Like everything else, we carefully weighed that subject's pros and cons. All together, we made long-range family goals, so there wouldn't be any hard-to-swallow surprises.

I made sure the idea of relocating didn't add to the already burgeoning list of things stressing the kids out. By far the biggest family issue was Debby's nonstop alcohol-induced mishaps, the consistent stressor in the kids' shattered sense of security. At FMs we regularly discussed what we could do about their concerns, regarding damage control about her behavior's injurious impact on the kids. The four of us came to the conclusion that all any of us could do, was to accept that Debby kept choosing to make dumb choices. There was no stopping her drinking, doing scary things, yelling, and keeping too many messy animals. The one thing we could do for her as a family, we kept reminding ourselves, was to pray for her. We'd sit at our kitchen table and hold hands whenever we needed, FM or not, sending her the strength of our combined positive thought-seeds, sowing intention for her to eventually choose ways that would lead Debby to improved health and happiness.

FMs helped the kids from stressing too much about the BM.

△

At the end of every meeting, the cleared dinner table hurriedly emptied as kids and Will scattered like cockroaches in full sun. All three of them overwhelmed by so much feeling and talking. Talking and feeling. I'd remain in my seat alone, reflecting on this home of mine, so unlike the one in which I'd been raised. My father's alcoholism was the Tyrannosaurus Rex my mom, sister and I warily watched after eating silently, watching Dad's monster-within growl and snarl at the kitchen table. In my childhood home, no one ever talked about the discomfort the three of us females felt. I was never counseled how to allow, or accept any of those painful feelings I had, or how to provide some escape from them, outside the confines of my bruised soul. All I learned from my parents was how to bury hurts as deeply as I could, inside, so nobody would ever know how I really felt. Not even me.

Dr. C again came to my aid after Will tried to dismiss their importance, convincing him, no, *demanding* that he cooperate with me and hold regular FMs—to help the kids learn about choices, and how to deal with their deeply conflicting feelings. There at our kitchen table, we could easily talk about everything, including frightening news involving the changing world and frightening people around us: life's difficulties as well as its perks. One by one, we resolved our challenges as they arose.

Including Jonny's sadness over "Why can't Mom be part of our house in Lackland?" raised at an early FM. Sitting around the table, everyone spoke their mind about how they felt about Debby not being part of our family of four; or ever invited to sit with Will and me if she attended games, school plays, picnics, and other events involving the kids. Not that she'd ever come, but the kids wanted to know what would happen if she did.

"I'll speak last," I said. "I'd prefer to hear how you guys feel first."

"I don't see why she can't be with us," Jonny quietly said.

"Mama always says how bad Dad is," Kara forthrightly offered. "How he bought us from the judge. And Jonny, you know how teZa hates it when Mama calls her Monkey Arms. It makes Mama even madder when we talk about how much we like teZ. It would be weird, Jonny, to have Mama around Dad and teZ. She hates teZ too much."

As Jonny sulked, his usually bright open face shadowed in grays, it was Will's turn.

"Well, kids, life is difficult," he said, measuring his words. "This might not be an easy thing for you to understand, but maybe it's not best for our family, or for Debby either, to include her with the four of us."

When my turn came, I took a deep breath.

"Kids, honestly I can't take having Debby any closer than she is into my intimate heart-circle. It's tough enough she badmouths me so much, from what you tell me. Just like you guys insisted I had to get rid of the Yo-truck, which you know was hard for me 'cause I loved it so much, I think you might have to let go of having Debby join us in what we four do as a family."

"Don't forget Bruno," Jonny softly added.

"Sorry, the five of us, then," I said.

"Okay, it's time to vote," Will spoke.

He was taking a rare turn as chairperson, a task he didn't relish. Only Jonny voted in favor of including Debby. The majority ruled, just as the S.T.E.P. manual spelled out. After the FM, Jonny went out and jumped super-high and extra-fierce and for a really long time on the trampoline, his feet pounding against the springy material, getting out whatever soul scream he hadn't been able to articulate at the FM. Even though one of us usually didn't like the outcome, at least we talked the hard stuff out till it was over. Sharing pains and sorrows, as well as joys and triumphs, helped our family, as it does any family, to heal.

I came to accept that Debby had every right to be in her kids' lives—from her side of the road. Though I regarded her very proximity as a contagion, a deadly pathogen, or at the very least a BM-stink bomb, who was I to deny her legal right to be with her kids? Despite the countless times when she triggered revulsion in my gut, she was the woman who'd birthed my darling Angel Kids. I was truly in awe of her in that biological regard. And though I secretly loathed her and would have preferred never to see her or hear her barbed-wire voice, I resolved to outwardly act and speak with kindness to her, no matter what. By offering nods or waves of greeting as she picked up or delivered the kids, regardless of her visible, stonily silent animosity toward me. And whenever the kids quoted her degrading remarks, I worked hard to train myself not to think anything but compassionate, accepting thoughts about her.

"She is who she is," was my constant Debby-mantra, spoken in the spirit of *faking it 'til you make it*, like the actor, the See-er that I was in this most difficult of roles—forgiving the person who'd punched my heart's innermost valve the most fiercely.

By these conscious choices, weaving together my kid-raising performance art and practicing household yoga, I made bearable an otherwise impossible situation. Additionally, Dr. C's advice was incomparable; her wisdom being the glue holding together all the loose strands in this helter-skelter blended family of mine. Not only was I trying to neutralize the monster of darkness that Debby's lies had created—feeding fears into her kids' impressionable little minds of the sort the Brothers Grimm's evil stepmother-archetype, who she swore I really was—but I also attempted to make each moment I had with the kids as upbeat and enjoyable a love fest as possible.

I swore to Will, "If something we do isn't fun in the long run, it's probably not being done right."

Learning to nurture the kids was forcing me to nurture my higher Self, to become my own Angel Mom. This was a completely unexpected byproduct of taking on the challenge of raising another woman's kids.

CHAPTER 14

darkness in the light

How many times in my Caribbean sailing days, had I cruised far out to sea on a barebones sailboat? Enough that I was accustomed to being jolted awake upon the first shift of any unusual condition, whether a wind change, altered compass heading, or trouble among the crew. So naturally, I was the one to rush down the hall when Kara's screams signaled another of her frequent nightmares, back when our rocking ritual turned out to be beneficial to both of us. Simple healing love begun in action, each swing of our chair worth a million shrink sessions, rebirthing, or Reiki ones too.

On another note, Jonny and I did not instantly fall in love as Kara and I had from our first meeting, when she announced she'd seen me in her dream the night before. Jonny's and my relationship was fomented by that first year of our being full-time playmates, we two alone. The day Jonny let me pack a picnic basket and drive him far from our small neighborhood to seek an adventure in a new, unfamiliar-to-him, bigger place, was major. Previous attempts of mine to expand his territory had ended in his wailing for me to turn around, and drive him back home. Angel Boy's comfort zone was sticking close to the familiar: Bruno, Grandpa's pasture, his own yard.

We spent the entire day together, every day, during that year I took off from making art. Until Jonny started nursery school, our time was comprised of doing fun things together. We built forts and cardboard trains and pretended we were caboose-and-locomotives or rails, pioneers and Indians in tents. I wasn't quiet, like Jonny, but loved playing and wrestling. We bonded by accepting each other, interacting without needing to talk, the way playmates do. I didn't try to teach him anything. I let Jonny call the shots and make up the games we played together.

Once, he got it into his mind he wanted to be a swamp thing. Insistent, he only subsided when we went to Grandpa's pond to fill a bucket with green slimy mud crud, duckweed, algae and feathery wet-brown gunk. Then we returned home where he demanded, "Put it all over me, teZ."

"Are you sure, Jonny? This stuff stinks," I warned.

He nodded, in his sturdy, knee-high stance next to tall me in the driveway. His face beamed brightly as I covered him from head to foot with gooey vines and vile swampy stench. But as soon as he felt the slime slither down his chest and back, seeping into his drawers, his crotch and down the crack of his backside—his five-year-old self burst into hard tears, yelling for me to get it off! Laughing in spite of myself, I swept up my little guy and rushed him to the shower. After rinsing him off, I held him up close to the bathroom mirror for him to see how nice and clean everything was again, and right away he relaxed. Happiness restored, the next game chosen, and once again Jonny's wide-open, luminous face revealed his curiosity to know everything about his immediate surroundings.

Anything he wanted to do, whatever kind of at-home adventure beckoned him, I assisted his vision. Whatever intrigued him, we made, be it flimsy or substantial, a simple song or a full-blown diorama, we made together. One day we built a fortress of sheets and cushions; another we made white plaster casts of everything small we could find from outside the house. My favorite of Jonny's creations was how he used stiff black mud to make a mold of his two feet that he then connected to big seashells, with a bridge joining them out of strong sticks, a brilliant, complex composition we cast in white plaster that amazed me, so simple and conceptually, visually pleasing.

Jonny picked up the creative bug as any kid does when encouraged. Any idea he cooked up, we did. We played out pretend narratives based on whatever he invented. And then we had even more fun destroying what we'd made; jumping on it, tearing to pieces outlandish sets, on which we'd spent so much time making; and squeal with abandon as we smashed them, he and I exhilarated by the destruction as much as the creation of objects. Except for his inspired foot-and-shell sculpture—which I hung high up on our kitchen wall, and where it stayed safe for years as a witnessing trophy to this bonding time of ours, qualifying as sophisticated art in my humble opinion—nothing was so precious that it warranted forever-status. Each day held plenty of new discoveries for Jonny and me.

Before he consented to have fun with me, though, Jonny had been a morbidly sad kid, afraid of being left behind. When newly his Angel Mom, many a time, right out of the blue, I saw him stop in the middle of a room, stand perfectly still for a few beats, then begin to quietly weep. I knelt on the ground or floor next to him and put my big arms around this lad with such a heavy heart, holding him tightly to me as I let him shed tears, as he made short whiney whimpers like a dog missing its owner.

Being free to cry at any time, I promised myself, was a necessary part of this little guy's heart-mending. Jonny had to feel his sadness over losing Debby's closeness. I knew letting his tears flow would help wash away his pain, help release that bruised soul of his. I never tried to stop him and wouldn't let anyone else, whether a future nursery school teacher or occasional babysitter, stop his crying either.

"Tears show a person who they really are," I remembered the Teacher saying.

I didn't try to convince Jonny, when his tears gushed, that everything was okay, by telling him we were an everything's-fine, fake-happy family. I told him the truth as I hugged, "We're a family—through thick-or-thin, an all-of-us-together kind of family. I'm here for you, so cry anytime you want. Of course you miss Debby. That's natural, Jonny."

Jonny had to weep. Because the sad truth was, without Debby around, this little boy of hers ached through and through for his Mama. He revered her as his very own magical White Fairy Queen.

To his not-yet-formed mind, his Mama was perfect. And she wasn't here with him, anymore.

I wasn't going to interfere with Nature's way of processing human misery. All I knew was it felt natural for him to be sad, and the easier, softer way he could get his sorrow out, the better. I remembered how it was in my own younger life. How messed up I'd been, driven to drugs and alcohol because I hadn't been able to sort out, even feel, my childhood wounds. Sure enough, as each new wave of my little man's sadness flooded him, and his tears spontaneously gushed, when his broken heart came crashing on the narrow shore of his tiny new reality of no-Mama, the dark clouds of Jonny's heavy-duty trauma would ebb and flow. Until slowly, these suffocating moods, his sadness disappeared entirely. But at the beginning, when he cried, only when his tears dried would we carry on playing.

I told his teacher to let Jonny cry until he was done crying, which, she told me, he did every time he was awakened from the nap the kids took at the half-day of nursery school he attended the second year we spent together. Whenever he awoke on his own from a nap, he never cried.

▲

One thing always made Jonny smile, even after a real hard cry. It was a game we played whenever I made his bed. When I asked him to lie down on the bottom sheet.

"Ready?" I'd say, and Jonny would grin, knowing what came next. Flinging the top sheet high, I'd let the cloth burst open into a boy-sized parachute, catching the air like a blossoming bomb of love. Jonny would lie flat, perfectly still, expectant, anticipating the exciting updraft, ready to sense the thrilling descent of his treasure-cave sheet all around and up above him, like a womb. Enraptured with the change of the air pressure around him, the charged new sensation caused pure joy to radiate on Jonny's face as he watched the ballooning fabric slowly descend, until slowly, slowly, he felt the gossamer-light blend eventually alight, its gentle weight barely pressing on his face, his hands, his feet, the tops of his clothes—like a thousand butterfly wings landing on him, one by one, tenting him with gentle grace.

From under the sheet cover I heard him softly beg, "Do it again," and I would. Over and over, so happy to hear my Angel Son laugh, to see his too often, sad brown eyes fill with lively diamond sparkles, delighting with each new uplifting of the sheet, we'd play this game.

Before he started school, rain or shine, sleet or hail (rarely snow in Florida), Jonny patiently waited for Debby's arrival at the end of our driveway every other Friday afternoon, before they'd go pick up Kara at school in the big blue pickup. With a heavy heart, I watched this repetitive, heart-wrenching sight from an upstairs bedroom window. Jonny cutting such a sad, forlorn figure with our cartoony CBD-dachshund Bruno by his side. My Angel Boy waited and waited, sometimes tossing pebbles into the street, into rain puddles, never crying, never minding how badly he felt or how late his favorite person in the whole wide world was.

He never came back inside to wait, or get anything to eat or play with. Jonny would sit alone at the end of our cement driveway, the heels of his sneakers touching the street pavement, hyper alert, his perfectly round head turning every two seconds to watch far up the street, like a patiently hunting hawk, waiting, so he could catch the very instant when she finally, really, truly, was coming for him. Jonny's only desire was to see his White Goddess's big truck when it finally appeared as a dark speck turning onto the quiet street that led to our house. Jonny's sullen face then flashed into that of the happiest urchin ever alive! He jumped from his seat, up and down and cried out in pure joy as his mama pulled into our driveway with her dog-filled, beer-can-rattling Ford truck, papers flying off the dash, with tiny Bernice the Chihuahua tucked inside her no-bra blouse.

Three bubba-mongrel dogs barely hung onto the bed of the truck when she swerved into our place. When Will wasn't around I'd come downstairs and manage to squeak out my pretend-friendly Hello. Debby would scowl at me with slanted eyes and grumble something unintelligible. My phony smile might have looked more like a grimace, my determination to be kind quarreling with an intense desire to knock her out, or run away. I'm not proud to admit my personal agony in overcoming my aversion to this person. Perhaps my features were unable to repress my revulsion at her wanton beer-bloated ruination, perhaps my fake-greeting was mixed with leftover scorn, sickened by the thought of how my very own sweetheart could have been intimate for as long as he had with such a woman.

Working hard to release my negative judgment toward the person I secretly called the BM, I was being forced to become deeply acquainted with the lifesaving attribute the Teacher told us was the secret of happiness: getting along with others. In time, I chose to be the See-er with Debby. I forced myself to see the divinity within her soul, as densely camouflaged as it was for me. The hardest test of all, I found, was embracing the Teacher's favorite aphorism: "See God in each other." With the BM, Debby presented the biggest test of all, for me to follow this primary instruction of the Teacher's.

Wow, I thought—watching Debby's monstrous truck depart, roaring up our empty street, three or sometimes four dogs howling as they held on for dear life with the tips of their claws—where's God in her? But I kept trying to be the See-er because the Teacher said that our job, as spiritual seekers and as her students, was to see God everywhere and in everything.

△

Even though Will and I had vowed to never bad-mouth her in front of the kids, many of Debby's kid-centric acts proved to be, unanimously untrustworthy and unspeakably irritating. One by one, we had to stop her kid-relevant, dangerous or plain dumb habits. This is when Will got tough, demanding, threatening to report her to Children Services. It seemed the only discipline he could do was with his kids' bio-mom. The kids told us she was drinking soda now, not beer while driving, but that happened only after he threatened to turn her in to the authorities. Will and I included her in every prayer time we had with the kids. It was our way of trying to balance her crass insuf-ficiencies, teaching the kids to bless and protect their Mama each night, "along with Dad and teZ and Bruno, and the rest of the whole wide world," as we taught them how to include all in their love.

"Debby's just being Debby," was how Will put it, his way of accepting what to others, including myself at first, was simply unacceptable.

Whenever I felt reactive toward her, I sharply reminded myself, silently saying, *Hey, cut the crap and shape up, teZ! Kara and Jonny are half Debby's gene pool. Accept that. Without what I think is "bad," namely the BM's character, the "good" these incredible beings of light and love are—my Angel Kids—would never have existed.*

No matter what adversity happened around me—or how much hummin' in the dark or silent mantras I repeated, or if I forgot to see as a See-er, nothing ever changed the fact that, good and bad, all of it, together—I was now beginning to feel that everything is Aum. This strange individual named Debby was creepy to me for the main reason that she was so unknowable. But I didn't want to stick her in the "I'm so repulsed by your actions that I have to spit-on-the-ground," despicable-person category, of which there were no others left in that slot I'd worked hard to clear, and was relieved to have no other resentments presently. Now I was being forced to accept her as part of my Angel Children's past, present and future. And Will's past. And peripherally, my own present moments. Without accepting this, I knew, I would never be happy in my blended family. I tried to remember how to view her as the incurable *cancer* that I had to accept lived somewhere, not in the center part, within our family unit's sphere. That worked. Most times.

Truth is, Debby represented all the negatives I'd worked so hard to scour from my own previously lopsided existence. I too, had been pure ruination, before sobriety. Let her stew in her own juices, I said to myself whenever anger or revenge knocked me over, destroying my hard-earned peace of mind one more time. Despite coaching myself to detach, regardless of the endless rounds of calming *So 'hăm, So 'hăm* I repeated silently—Debby could not be erased from my life.

I had to accept who she'd once been to Will, and who she would forever be to our kids: their bio-mom.

It won't kill me, I assured Better-me, to accept that this vile person hates me. I can handle that. Maybe one day I'll be able to consider it a compliment in a perverse, reverse-psychology way; the same way I didn't care that Mason the child molester, detested me too. It took me speaking honestly only one time to Will's ill-reputed childhood friend, whom Claire had asked me to keep away from her grandkids, to sweep him out of the kids' lives forever. His loathing of me, ever since I privately told him he wasn't welcome around me, ever—telling him that I knew of his sexually depraved acts committed out at sea, out of bounds of legal repercussions—was because I dared to bar him from our family's door forever.

Acceptance of badly-behaved people takes way more practice than you'd think for a Better-me in training, a forgiveness-friendly smartass like myself. As I got better at detaching, from Mason and the BM, then from anybody and anything else that disturbed me—incendiary politics, religious intolerance, racism, the Earth's vandalism, ecological pollution—I got better. I changed. I became freer and less fearful.

Better-me was becoming stronger, surer, with each passing day of our journey.

△

Letting the kids figure out for themselves how our home was, as opposed to Debby's—to me, comparing mint tea to whiskey, or ephemeral mist to a murderous mudslide—Will and I focused on celebrating life and fostering its positive, productive gifts. We left Debby and other malcontents to worry over the negatives of the world. He and I made sure our main concern was to nurture ourselves and the kids, first and foremost. In that spirit, we figured, we could help others, as many as we could, through our propitious use of sowing thought-seeds and performing focused actions. We agreed that for the time being, putting the kids' happiness above our own was the healthiest approach for our multi-challenged blended family. Our needs, we decided, as individuals and as a couple would, for the time being, have to come second. We knew we'd have the rest of our lives ... for that.

"If these kids are going to continue healing," I said to anyone who asked, "I need to balance my needs as an artist with accepting I'm the main female who's guiding them. My role of Angel Mom has to supersede that of me being a groovy artist." Of course, Will agreed; as a filmmaker who'd been forced to become a successful businessman to support his family, he knew well the pining of a creative heart that knows the limitations of having to make sacrifices.

With each new demand of being our family's shaman, what felt ordinary became mystical, to my thinking. My heart grew so big that sometimes it felt as if it were going to explode inside my chest. My heart, the altar of Love, could have run marathons and entered thirty iron man races each year ... if that organ of mine were an athlete. Will's love had yanked me out of my flaccid half-life dream as a non-breeder. In my private thoughts each magic trick of Love we performed as a blended clan, kept me speechless and spellbound in my current role as Angel Mom, with nary a clue how things were going to turn out. Each day, as we travelled together down the currents of Rio Blisso, Better-me blossomed more fully. I felt such elation, ever more blessed and rewarded, as I learned to love wholly, unconditionally. As I surrendered ever more deeply to being Angel Mom.

In bed at night, I imagined this was how heaven ought to feel, being held so tightly by my other half. Will's loving me, me loving him, us loving the kids—this was the splendiferous eerily-real dream I was in. We slept intertwined, we two recharging—without either of us ever speaking of it, or noticing. No one had ever known my soul, so closely, so deeply as he. Will, my life partner who was practically my physical twin of the opposite gender. This is how I came to know that heaven and hell are right here and now, depending on what choices we make.

Paradise or Hades are not fairytale places or biblical insurance clauses we get to cash-in after dying. Ours was a bit of both, our get-down-and-dirty, accept-all love. Awakening in the middle of the night with Will's soft open lips engulfing mine, swallowing my pain, lessening my empty places, he totally satisfied me, healed my hurts, and he said I did the same for him. His sleeping-self squeezed me to his full body-length, our passions arising in perfect synch even as we half slept. And then—we'd awake in each other's deep embrace, joined as One.

We laughed and sang and played and prayed, did yoga and meditated together. I even went to my first football games when Jonny started playing at age eight. Serious or frivolous, everything was a cut-up to Will; everything a joke, except Jesus. Will was a sweet Groucho, a handsome Ape-Man, a born-again Charlie Chaplin—all rolled into one highly unpredictable hunk who made me swoon at his every sexy glance. Those sibilant Ss always put me in a molten butter state when he whispered softly in my ear, deep in the night.

CHAPTER 15

prepare for the unexpected

Not half a year had gone by after Claire's sudden passing when Phil, at age eighty-seven, shocked us all by getting himself hitched again, literally overnight. I suppose he'd been inspired by the successful second marriage of his younger brother who, just a year earlier, had lost his own irreplaceable wife at the same late stage of life. Everyone was stunned when Phil did the same thing. Everyone in his family tried to reassure ourselves that our patriarch's impulsive move would work out: ol' Phil still had spunk enough to reinvent himself and start life all over again. We all wished him the best despite our shock.

Instead of wallowing in sadness, going into hiding, or curling up to die, as some feared the fate of a man like him would be, who didn't know how to even boil water—he wed. Of all the many choices Phil had, being as successful, witty, and deeply spiritual as he was, a rare combo, he surprised everyone by his choice. We could only suppose he'd been swayed by her classic blond good looks, salon made, a dangerous criterion for wedlock, blaringly superficial and shocking us all. Neither a spiritual match, nor an intellectual, artistic, nor high culture aficionado, as his angel had been all combined; but he chose instead, an attractive bleached blonde, one with a more ample and well-exposed bosom than his voluptuous, but always modestly dressed Claire's.

Will and I met the dynamic, outspoken Dolores, introduced as an "old friend" of Phil's (whom oddly, nobody knew), just a week before the elderly couple's surprise elopement. Contrasting Claire's girlish figure, two women couldn't be much more unlike except in height and blondeness, and not even vaguely there afterwards, in outward appearance. Dolores was an amply put-together matron whose only exercise program was playing cards, unlike the natural beauty Phil's angel had had, thanks to years of hiking, tennis and golf, good thoughts, and Christ Consciousness meditation. Dolores' looks relied heavily on her careful, thick application of makeup and a teased short coif, dyed practically the same shade of blonde, and also like Claire's, epoxy-sprayed to the max, following the style of their generation.

The first thing Will and I noticed was the shocking contrast Dolores' pedantic approach presented to Phil's more than half-century, enlightened first marriage. A two-as-One kind, like ours, of expand-the-mind, build a sound economic foundation, dedicate time to a meditative approach to life type of marriage, where a couple puts kid-raising above all other responsibilities. Phil, having chosen his angel, had not just married a beautiful and intelligent woman, they both married the Divine to the mundane, as he and Claire had so assiduously, so successfully done in every possible way.

No problems, Will and I thought. "Dolores is a real spunky lady," he said. "Let's hope she'll make Dad happy. We have to accept his choice," my always-positive man said, as I rolled my eyes.

It soon became clear that Dolores was not any kind of angel, by any stretch of the imagination. After a couple of short visits to the newlyweds, we saw who she was. Waiting to unearth her sensitivity, asking her sweetly inquisitive, not-prying questions, back at home Will and I were speechless. We'd discovered Dolores to be not a meditative person but a chronically socializing, gossiping daily drinker, about as interested as a grub worm in anything *expanding* other than her waistline, approximately twice the size of Claire's. Everyone who loved Phil knew he'd acted uncharacteristically impetuously. Will and I looked at each other and could hear each other's loud *gulp*. We knew the old man had gotten himself in deep water, way over his head.

At our very first family meal with Dolores, now the official new step-grandma, she loudly declared to me before taking another swallow from her wine glass: "We're going to have to charge you rent for using that old trailer for your work, back there by the pasture. And of course, you'll have to move from this indoor studio space you've been using, dear. I plan on building a bar in there, to entertain guests."

My mouthful of water nearly shot across the table at this. Dolores looked blankly at her new husband and said, "It's only right for teZa to pay rent for that old place she's using out there, isn't it, Phil? Business is business."

I looked from Will to Phil and back again, both father and son mumbling as they chewed, acting as if they hadn't heard what Dolores said.

Phil stared at his plate, pushing his fork around Dolores' fare of overcooked gray broccoli, white rice and anemic chicken breast. I glanced over at Will and saw him wink at me as if to say, "Humor the old broad, please. Just do it." I decided to follow his lead, and not object, but wondered if Phil considered the teZ Mahal, Claire's old trailer that had become my writing studio since he invited me to use it, to be part of Dolores's domain.

As if to assure me, Phil finally cleared his throat. "Dolores is in charge of all things inside the house; I'm in charge of everything outside."

I suspected that Phil had married this pushy lady either because of her mound of saggy boobs bursting forth from every outfit she wore, or because he knew he'd probably starve if he didn't marry someone, anyone, soon. I was glad to see he was no longer locked in grief, as he'd been the previous months spent in solitary mourning for Claire. But I was concerned to see my father-in-law pour himself a second, then a third thimble-sized glass of wine, evidently determined to keep up with his tipsy geriatric bride.

In all the years he'd been married to his angel, Phil had been almost a teetotaler, only raising the occasional party toast or having a single beer with the guys, when watching Sunday sports on TV. Will told me once, "Because Mom leaned toward having that problem early on, Dad pretty much quit drinking so she'd never be tempted." I guess his policy of abstinence, which Claire adhered to mostly, didn't apply to Dolores.

At my next office visit, when our family doctor, the same old geezer who had treated Phil and Claire for all eternity, referred in unabated scorn to Dolores as *that socialite*—both Will and I began to seriously worry about his dad's bizarre choice of a new wife. Everyone tried to put on a happy face around him. But a serious crack had appeared in the makeshift facade of this dissonant new union.

Dolores had a stiff Scotch on the rocks at 5:00 o'clock sharp each afternoon. Phil joined her with a glass of watered-down wine that thereafter became "just one more." Whenever we came for dinner, Dolores was always argumentative and Phil already half in the bag, more taciturn and withdrawn than usual, stumbling his steps—forget about any dream analyzing. His drinking stunned us. It was a startling shift for a man who'd prided himself on faithfully adhering to personal discipline, all his life upholding rigid standards of physical health, mental and spiritual integrity, attributes just as important to Claire as himself.

We duly noticed there was virtually no affection between Phil and Dolores, not after the first months when they partied nearly nonstop, going out to celebratory dinners and clubhouse dancing, visiting other couples to play cards. Will and I started to seriously worry. Keeping our concerns to ourselves, hoping we were wrong, Will and I thought our fears might be because both of us missed Claire. But we knew it was more than nostalgia we felt. With such an unfavorable match as Phil's reckless choice, the prospect suddenly had grown dimmer of our ever leaving Lackland, even though the promised date of departure was now looming close on the horizon.

Both Will and I were eager to move away and live close to the sea, far from this town's heavy miasma of judgment. Both of us grew increasingly dismayed. Not wanting anything to prevent us from leaving, Will and I agreed to keep out of his father's affairs.

Each new day my happiness level was gauged by how well I accepted what I couldn't change. Accepting and detaching, in that order, became my saving graces. Besides detaching from Debby's dark cloud, I also had to detach from my own mother, whose critical comments, until I learned to detach better, invariably left me shattered and in tears.

Now I had to additionally detach from Phil's new wife.

Dolores, who didn't even try to earn Kara and Jonny's affection, preferring her own kin's company, treated her only son, daughter, and granddaughter to special treats and events, but for our kids and Phil's other grandkids, handed out only the expected, mandatory birthday and Christmas presents. No one knew the woman's age, and I sure wasn't going to ask. Her easily triggered ire soon taught anyone to keep silent, who tried to ask prying questions. All that Will and I knew about her was that Dolores and her husband (who'd passed away several years before) had been bridge-playing friends of Phil and Claire's. Nonetheless, in response to questions about her family's history Dolores made a grand show, soon taking down one of Claire's abstract art pieces from the wall where Phil had enjoyed it, and hung in its place an ornately framed, pale and nearly indecipherable, eight-foot-tall, tree-like pencil drawing, a mishmash diagram depicting, so she proudly said, Dolores' ancestry, more English aristocratic than other many-generational colonial Virginians, as she claimed to be. This massive family-tree of hers hung in the living room as if it were Amerigo Vespucci's authenticated, original map of the New World.

If Dolores had known (and I wasn't about to tell her, for fear of more wrath) that on my father's common-man side of my family, I was a well-documented descendent of the earliest Pilgrims, eligible (had I been interested) for D.A.R. membership—Dolores' elite status alone, she believed—she wouldn't have liked knowing that one bit.

At a family dinner, when I gently tried asking if she shared Phil's love of Spirit, Dolores's face momentarily went blank. She quickly caught herself and replied, as if insulted: "You don't seriously think I believe in ghosts, do you? Good heavens, no!"

As paradoxical as it seemed, Dolores appeared to amuse Phil, even if boozy interludes with his tabloid-loving new spouse now circumvented his working with others to interpret their dreams, not to mention superseding his own longtime meditation practice. Several times I attempted to revive our intimate talks about dreams, but I felt unwelcomed whenever Dolores was at home. She was always banging about in another part of the house, in one stage or another of organizing some kind of social function. For over a year she prepared for a two-hour-long afternoon fund-raising cocktail party, in honor of the then-Governor. Another one-time soiree took six months of pre-arrangements. Mounds of white and gold-edged invitations were strewn about in what had once been the play, music and poolroom hangout, central headquarters for gatherings of our clan when any of the other near-dozen grandkids came visiting. Now the oversized room served as Dolores' social-planning camp, guarded by Helmet-head, the nickname I secretly gave her so-called assistant, whose greatest talent appeared to be moving piles of papers.

Soon we limited our visits to a quick now-and-then Sunday dinner of overdone mush, and the much rarer invitation to one of the grandiose affairs Dolores regularly threw at her new showcase hacienda. In between she kept Phil rushing to so many gatherings that the old man became virtually inaccessible. We tried to honor his having chosen a wife with a demanding social agenda—with much more going on than the holiday three-events-a-night, plus weekly bridge games that he and Claire had enjoyed—sadly noting that Dolores now orchestrated a mint-julep Kentucky Derby, Santa's day rum punch, paid bartenders serving specialty mixed drinks at every single excuse for a festivity.

In his dotage, Grandpa had become a party animal.

No longer did we enjoy those quiet moments I'd cherished with Phil, when I could share with him a dream I'd recently had. I felt cheated of my connection with this sweet old gent who, until Dolores's jarring arrival, had been everyone's spiritual mentor and patriarch.

I tried to see the Divine within Dolores the same as I did in everyone and everything. The same as I'd been practicing being compassionate with Debby. How well I did, seeing God within either of these difficult people, depended on what happened any particular day. I kept trying though, is all I can say.

Will and I determined to remain neutral about Phil's unknowable, but to us insane reason for choosing such an unlikely spouse. Okay, the two geriatrics both really enjoyed partying and dancing together, we knew that much. After a while I stopped looking because there simply wasn't any rapport deeper than casual socializing between them, none I could detect in their presence. I suspected the seventyish sex bomb must have captivated nearly-ninety Phil. And my detective-self also highly suspected she'd done so unscrupulously, setting some kind of a seductive trap for this kind-hearted old man, who was more like my naively too-trusting Will than any of his other children.

△

Soon after Claire's passing, one day Phil had discreetly shared with Will—months before Dolores entered the picture—that what he needed most of all was the closeness of a beautiful woman. Something he'd "enjoyed with your mother right up to the end, son," Phil said to Will in a shaky voice, completely out of the blue, his face hidden behind his wide-spread newspaper. Saying this was out of character for his father, Will told me. "Dad was being uncharacteristically candid. He's never talked about intimacy between he and Mom before, ever. Maybe he was a little batso from loneliness."

Before Dolores, Will had been so determined to help his father through his grief, and more so after learning of his dad's craving the lovemaking he'd regularly enjoyed with his mother. At a business lunch soon after this disclosure, Will shared in confidence to an elderly friend of his father's that his dad missed the physical comfort he'd enjoyed with Claire "right up to the end."

"The community owes your dad!" the strait-laced Lackland businessman exclaimed after two martinis. "We're going to get Phil laid before sunset!" Will laughed as he assured the well-meaning old friend, "That isn't really necessary." But pretty soon after this event, along came Dolores.

Honestly, Will and I hoped things would work out between this inscrutable choice of a wife, even if that meant watching Phil drink, act strangely silly, then later get morosely sullen, mentioning less and less esoteric matters, no longer tossing out occasional metaphysical tidbits or Readers Digest lowbrow jokes to entertain his doting family.

As time crept by, his second marriage revealed itself to be more enigmatic than Dolores' tacky heritage that took the place of Claire's avant-garde art in Phil's living room. Will and his three siblings, coming from a family tradition that never spoke unkindly of anyone, privately agreed that—in marrying an alcoholic *floozy*, as one sister called Dolores, whose conversation amounted to celebrity tabloid gossip or which parties she'd been to lately were hits or duds—their dear dad, now noticeably growing more maudlin, more forgetful by the day, had done the dumbest thing of his thus-far admirable, and by all accounts, heretofore blessed, long and brilliant life.

All four of Will's sibs privately concurred that marrying Dolores was by far the most foolish thing their father had done: getting himself in a real pickle. Not unlike the rest of the human race—at least fifty percent of us modern adults making a mess of marriage and getting divorced, their father had unsuspectingly married an unsuitable person—he'd made a poor choice just as Will and I had done, and two of his sibs had too.

"I think Dad just expected every woman to be exactly like Mom," Will said when we were alone. "So naive. But in a way, this is a gift, Dad marrying so inappropriately."

"Oh yeah, how so, Will?" I asked.

"All his life Dad has appeared as absolutely perfect, to us. We kids always thought we were just fuck-ups compared to the great successes—business, and relationship wise—he's had. Here it is, nearly the end of his life, and he's finally showing us that he too, can make a mistake." Will sadly shook his head. "I never thought I'd ever see Dad make as terrible a mistake as this, though."

At the all-sibs gathering the next year, Phil's grown children privately agreed to make light of this increasingly regrettable situation. Will and his brother and sisters sat around our kitchen table, we five trying to cheer each other up. Each of the others said in their own way the same thing about their dad's obvious error.

"It's almost a relief to see that Dad is human enough to have made such a horrendous mistake," one softly added.

"Let's just hope she doesn't end up throwing him down the staircase," another sadly noted.

Theologians, as well as mystical Eastern teachers such as mine, say that what might appear as *bad* could actually be Universal Consciousness, Aum, presenting an opportunity to attain a *higher good*, if one could only know the whole picture, which of course, no one ever can. Hence the catch-22 of believing in a Higher Power. Every scripture claims that the God-force, Source, or *What's-Its-Name*, an often nameless energy is credited with being within all matter, having created all in existence, the dark as well as the light. Who's to say that one situation, or somebody who *appears to be bad*, can't end up serving the greater good in the long run? Certainly not me or my wide-minded Christian consort. This topic came up at the dinner table one evening when Kara and Jonny asked why we didn't go to Grandpa's so much anymore.

"Kids," Will said, "there are things in life we'll never be able to figure out. Judging others is not our job. Grandpa and Aunt Dolores are real busy. We're going to be happy for Grandpa, like he tells me he is whenever I ask. We're just not going to be spending as much time with him, or as often as we used to. It's too bad, but that's how it is."

Will and I glanced at each other, nodded, and began to enact our everyday way of explaining life's never-ending conundrums to the kids.

"It's like this," I said, ready for our favorite duet.

Will chimed in, "We keep working on our stuff, all of us trying to get it right, just like Grandpa is, just like teZ and I do."

"And both of you kids, too," I added.

"We keep trying to figure it out until *we think* we're getting close to what feels right," Will said.

I nodded my head. "And then, when we finally start to see the light at the end of the pitch-dark tunnel of life ... that's when ... that's when ...." Right here is when I always clutch my chest and shout out in alarm.

"Arrggghhh!" In unison, Will and I grab our hearts simultaneously and our foreheads immediately crash-land on the table, conveniently beside, not in, our dinner plates. The kids' eyes pop wide-open each time, even though they've seen this cornball act of ours a thousand times before.

Will's head lies perfectly still—for about three seconds—then it bobs up. He bursts out laughing, alive and well with a huge grin and the kids shout their jubilation once again, so happy to see their 'rents being so silly!

At this time in our little charade, both Will and I start cheerfully speaking in harmonic turns.

"Kids, life's *never* gonna be perfect—ever.

"We just keep trying to make it better until we croak, that's the way it is.

"If you give it your best, that's what counts, the *only thing* that counts.

"Keep trying to be happy. It's our jobs as humans."

Each and every time Will lifted his head off the kitchen table, he'd playfully speak the next line of our repeated dialogue: "Even if it takes us the rest of our lives, we'll never give up trying to get better. Right, teZ?"

"Right! Kids, your dad and I will never give up. And both of you too, will never give up trying to make yourself and our world a better place," my voice trumpets.

Will nods his head. "Never give up trying to be happy. If you're happy inside, it doesn't matter what's going on around you."

Many of our evening meals ended with another of our Americanized *Punch-And-Judy* kooky puppet shows, Will and I enacting basic life lessons, all four of us laughing till we fell off our chairs. The way Will landed dead, forehead crashing smack on time, his head barely missing his plate, with only a few drops of gravy and a few crumbs in his hair, cracked me up. I was this guy's biggest fan. I loved how he could make something great out of something pretty awful. How he'd hang an old sock from his reading glasses—all for a giggle as well as another kid-lesson. I never thought my own dinnertime performances, way more subdued, were as convincing or memorable as his.

Will's message of not ever expecting perfection made me think of another brilliant nugget of truth, one commonly spoken by the Teacher. Whenever I heard it, this simple truism helped me accept things as they are, instead of worrying or getting angry about how they should be.

"Things are not what they appear to be," the Teacher often said, and would relate another entertaining parable as an example: the rope that resembles a snake on a dark road; the stranger knocking at the door who turns out to be God; the bully who's only a frightened child inside; and on and on.

I smile recalling this favorite phrase spoken so frequently by her. It took me a while to figure out what it meant, it wasn't obvious when I began my studies. *Things are not what they appear to be.* But when I began to live more from Better-me's perspective, when I began to be the See-er, I discovered a whole other *world* beneath (more accurately, *above*) the one we think is here before us. And that is: the invisible, spiritual realm of our existence. Only when I began to sense the spiritual in the mundane did I know that my Teacher's statement was absolutely true and not just an aphorism to make people feel good or keep them interested in the teachings. An interconnection exists between everything, all the time. After a decade of vigilantly meditating and doing japa repetition, stilling my busy mind in other words, I finally could feel the Truth in this statement.

The outside appearance of our physical world is just the tip of the proverbial iceberg, I knew this now. "Things are not what they appear to be" was no longer some glib saying, making everything more bearable if you buy into some philosophical opinion.

The spiritual domain of everyday life was now as real to me as the healthy breakfast, lunch, and dinner meals I put before my family each day.

Traveling down Rio Blisso, I often marveled at my great good fortune of having chosen to take this journey with my blended family. Every day, as I comforted the kids about the next thing, I remembered that life is what we make of it. Reminding the kids that life is unpredictable, imperfect, that there are no blacks or whites in any situation, Will and I gave them basic spiritual tools with which to ease life's many burdens. We were giving them mind-calming tools they'd need for what inevitably lies ahead, for every single person on the planet.

Even though Aunt Dolores, as she wanted to be called by Will's grandkids, was more like a black-widow spider who'd forcibly made her unwanted nest in our own backyard, Will and I would keep trying, and we showed the kids how too, to see the best in her. Even though none of us could understand Phil's incongruous, suspicious union.

Whether dealing with Debby or Dolores, I chose not to pay any attention to the unseemly traits of either. Certainly, there's bad as well as good, equally, around us all the time. We get to choose what we concentrate on. My job as an artist focuses on documenting my own spiritual awakening. And I get to renew myself, continuously, through my connection with Aum's God-energy. By repeating silently *So'hăm, So'hăm*, by choosing to be the See-er; by believing in the power of planting positive thought-seeds; this is how I choose to live my life and practice the craft of being useful to others.

That's why I minimized both Dolores' and the BM's influence, downplaying any involvement with both women. That's why I seldom spoke the BM's name aloud, and when I did, I always called her Debby except when Will and I were alone.

△

I suppose it was inevitable that Jonny would awaken one day to who and what Debby really was: not his glorious White Goddess, that's for sure. I just prayed his already fragile psyche wouldn't be further damaged, as Kara's so evidently had been, by their mother's deficits. The day of reckoning had arrived for my sweet little fellow, his heart so pure, so generous and hopeful. Will and I both had sworn to never tell either him or Kara, not until their twenties, about the grotesque things that Debby had done in the past: the continuing mess she made of her life, the dangers she presented to everyone, including herself. That's why we made a point to never criticize her actions in our kids' presence.

We both repeatedly said to them, "She loves both you kids, with all her heart, soul, and might." Will called her "your mom" and I never contradicted him.

Despite our efforts, we couldn't protect them hearing inevitably from others about Debby's bad choices.

One day, Jonny acted strangely after coming back from his weekend spent with Debby. He was unusually reserved upon arriving that night.

"Anything wrong, Jonny?" I said.

"It's nothing … It's just …."

Then he stopped. I asked another question, my method of communicating with the quiet boy. Will always marveled how I was the only one Jonny ever talked to. I reminded Will that was probably because I asked questions while he tended to lecture.

"What's going on?" I prodded now. "Come on, you can tell me. You won't be in trouble, I promise."

"It's not me," Jonny squeaked out. "It's that creepy boat of David's."

David was Debby's on-again, off-again boyfriend, the one with the son who'd rubbed himself against Jonny in Debby's backyard pool sometime earlier.

Jonny nervously said, "The front of David's big pontoon dips way underwater when too many people get on. Everyone's drinking beer and being real loud. I told Mom I was scared but she laughed and called me a sissy. Then David drove us all down the Peace River with water all over our feet. It felt like we were sinking the whole time." I could tell Jonny was shaken.

The following afternoon I escorted him to Dr. C's office and waited for him, as I always did when he or Kara had their talking or SandPlay sessions. Later, when he reappeared in the waiting room, he didn't stop to hail me as he always did, but rushed right past, his head bent low, not looking at anything but the ground. I hastily said goodbye to Dr. C, who shrugged her shoulders, and found Jonny waiting by our locked car with his back turned.

"Whoa, hold up there, Ninja," I said, using my favorite nickname for him. "What's going on?" I turned him around and saw Jonny's face, crunched up with hurt.

"C'mon, what's wrong?" I urged.

No answer.

"Okay, let's go home."

Driving for a few minutes, I looked over at the passenger seat and saw the wet cheeks of my Angel Boy, his narrow shoulders trembling. The poor guy was broken up, his heart wrung out, turned inside out.

"Oh Jonny, I'm sorry you feel so bad. Do you want to talk about it?"

His head shook violently, just once. Saying nothing he sat there with a crestfallen gaze fixed on the truck floor. I knew how he was, the quiet weeping, the no-words sadness. A bliss-shredding moment for both of us.

"Jonny, I think we should go right back to Dr. C's and let her talk to you some more."

"No!" he shouted, turning to look straight at me, his strong reaction alarming me. Gulping words in between short breaths, he said, "I hate Dr. C! What she said about Mom is so mean—she said—she's a—an unfit mother she says—that's why Mom—didn't get—custody—of us—not like Mom— says that Dad—bought us—from the judge."

In that instant, I could have strangled both Dr. C and Debby. One for having such a big mouth and telling our seven-year-old such intensely traumatic, potentially harmful information no young child needs to hear, especially without conferring beforehand with Will or myself. The other murder would have been for the bio-mom not being a Better-Debby, always choosing to act like such an ass. Instead of acting on my anger though, I put on a voice as soothing as I could for my shivering Angel Boy.

"Well Jonny, Dad and I have always tried to accept Debby as she is. She doesn't mean to hurt others, we're certain. She just can't help herself. I'm sure whatever Dr. C told you, she figured was for your own good. I can't say I agree with her timing though."

As we drove, Jonny's body frightfully rigid, his squeaky, whimpering sounds not diminishing by the time we reached home, twenty minutes later, I made up my mind. The awful revelation, whatever he'd heard, had cut him deeply. I couldn't begin to think right-or-wrong, from a mental health point of view, for Dr. C to have given him information that we'd told her, on many instances, his dad and I had decided wasn't necessary for him to know, not for many years to come. We didn't think it would be constructive to tell Kara or Jonny the truth about what Debby had done: calling the authorities, making false reports, accusing Will and me—separately and at long-spaced-out times—of molesting both kids, or any of her numerous, crazy-paranoid, psychic-vampire shenanigans arising near daily.

"When we get home," I gently said, "I'm going to call Dr. C and tell her you need to return to see her tomorrow. We have to resolve things that only she can make right. Okay, Jonny? Dr. C has to help you to understand this better." He kept quiet this time.

That night Jonny was more subdued than usual. He didn't want to do anything except hang out in his room and play with Bruno and his pet hamster, Hammie.

The next day I took him out of school at mid-afternoon. When we arrived at her office, I had already told Dr. C on the phone that Jonny needed more help, to better process what she'd revealed to him the day before. Jonny spent the full hour-long session alone with her.

As I browsed magazines in the waiting room, I questioned for the first time how I'd blindly trusted Dr. C from the moment I first met her. Usually I welcomed any input she offered to the daunting challenges of our family, mine especially, of taking care of other people's children. At last, my Angel Boy came out from the inner chamber of Dr. C's temple-of-feelings—with his frown wiped entirely clear. I breathed freely for the first time since the afternoon before.

Jonny walked out with his head high, brow smooth and that freaked-out, deer-in-headlights look banished. He wasn't exactly beaming, but his features were no longer twisted by yesterday's sad shades of grief. His face had been transformed from the expression he wore when he went in, of a pitiful little fellow whose fantasy-mama had been rudely exposed as a fake. Now Jonny's face was lighter, less burdened, his sudden fear replaced with a smattering of understanding, of ease. I felt intensely grateful to our trusted, wise Dr. C.

On the way home, he and I did our usual slow-mo word-swap.

"You feel better now, Jonny?"

"Yeah."

"Did Dr. C clear up whatever got you feeling so bad yesterday?"

"Yeah."

"What did she say to make you feel better?"

He took a big breath. "She told me Mom doesn't mean to be the way she is. It's just the way she is. Dr. C says I'm old enough now, I have to know the truth about Mom's choices, so I can grow up to be strong and healthy, and make better choices and become a happy adult, she says. It's not my fault, she says."

I let his words sink in, like the balm they were.

Then I said, "Dr. C thinks it's best for a kid your age to know the truth, I guess." I was still questioning the need of such early revelations; but what was done, was done.

"That's what Dr. C says. Now I have to remember that Mom is a good person but she makes bad choices. Like a lot of people do."

"That sounds about right," I said. "What else did Dr. C say?"

"She doesn't think Mom makes such good choices when she does stuff that scares me, so I need to tell Mom when she does it. 'Cause if Mom never knows how scared I get, she'll keep doing those same dumb things over and over."

"I'm sad to hear she scares you, Jonny," I said, acting as if I'd never known this fact before.

"Yeah, me too. Her truck broke down again, I didn't tell you. We had to spend another whole night in the creepy woods, all three of us sleeping in the cab of her stupid dumb truck. With all the scary sounds and big wild things moving around outside all night, I was so scared. And Mom snores so loud, Kara and me couldn't sleep a wink."

"Again? You never told me."

"Sorry. Forgot."

By the time we got home, Jonny was once again wearing his usual wide beamy face with the Cheshire cat smile.

△

The phone rang at our house. I answered. In her customary non-greeting, Debby growled "Kara there?" Her gunshot manner always jolted me no matter how many times she spoke to me this way. I kept thinking the BM was joking around, but she wasn't; Debby was just plain rude. Each time I'd go find Kara, she'd skip to the phone and lightheartedly answer, "Hi Mama," always cheered to hear her mother's gruff voice. Then—after their brief Hello exchange, and listening for less than a minute—Kara would visually morph into a green-eyed shouting devil girl.

"NO! I'm NOT going to do that!" she'd yell at the top of her lungs. For the rest of their conversation, daughter screamed at mother. I can only surmise what Debby was demanding on the other end.

The first time I witnessed this disheartening mother-daughter duel I rushed back into the room and demanded Kara to stop. "Be more respectful to Debby," I whispered, and Kara immediately did Number 2, *Listen and do*, by lowering her voice. But, as time wore on, Dr. C helped me understand that wasn't necessarily the best thing for me to do, admonish my charge in the middle of a brouhaha with her bio-mom. Besides, it was impossible get Kara to stop yelling back at Debby for less than a single pacifying sentence. One day in a private session, I discussed having to witness this with Dr. C.

"You have to accept Kara's shouting at Debby," she told me. "Believe me, she needs to do it. Yelling is her only survival mechanism with such a dysfunctional mother. Unfortunately, you have to let her. If you stop her she has no other defense, no psychological protection from her mother's negative influence. Let the child scream, teZa. Kara won't have any chance of ever healing and acquiring a healthy psyche if you don't."

I rebelled at this, challenging Dr. C's opinion.

"But Kara is learning it's okay to be a bitch," I protested. "It's terrible, the way those two go at it on the phone."

"No one wants to allow a young girl to develop such a bad habit as screaming at adults," Dr. C said. "But believe me: this is Kara's only coping mechanism right now; it's life-saving to her future. Just cope with it somehow. That's your job as stepmom."

"I guess I see your point," I said, feeling powerless. Acceptance, I heard the whisper deep within. I tried resisting; but Dr. C's point of view was, well, psychologically sound.

"Otherwise," the doc explained, "Kara has no power to deal with her mother's skewed view of the world."

"A skewed worldview. God, Carolyn, that's so sad to hear."

"Let Kara yell and scream at Debby all she wants," Dr. C urged. "And trust that she'll develop other coping skills as she emotionally matures."

I kept trying, but it was hard. Listening to this sweet angelic girl of mine shapeshift into a screaming banshee in front of my eyes, made me wince and recoil. But eventually, I learned to detach, walk away, shut the door, take deep breaths, and accept Kara's need to yell at her irrational mother.

"Let it go," Dr. C advised. "Pick your battles, kiddo. This one's not that big a deal. Compared to the crazy stuff your family has to face."

It hurt so much each time, hearing the soul-bruising Kara was subjected to, having to scream and act-out every time she spoke with the BM. It took quite a while to finally manage letting it go.

prepare for the unexpected

CHAPTER 16

snafu

Phil's home-hearth was growing colder, his fun side less familiar to us with each passing season. No one, not any of his relatives or close friends wished to intrude on the old man's privacy. Aside from our Sunday dinner ritual, no invitations to visit were forthcoming from the icy Aunt Dolores either. Every time Will offered his father discreet help escaping this unfortunate union of his, it was rejected.

"Dad, if you want to get out of this bad deal, just say the word. It's plain to all of us that you're miserable," Will often privately whispered.

"Naw," the old man steadily replied. "She's kind of cute. A real sports-model. I like having her around. Even though she can be a real pain," he said as he snorted a deep-rumble, reaching for his breast pocket's handy white handkerchief to wipe his forehead.

▲

Years before, right after Phil's impulsive marriage, I'd been talking long distance to Louise, my trusted clairvoyant advisor, about the direction my own life was heading. She'd accurately, psychically forecasted Will's spring equinox entrance into my life. This time Louise was just as sure when she said, without any provocation: "There's something not right brewing in your father-in-law's house."

"Really?" I hadn't even asked Louise about Dolores or Phil. So it surprised me she'd brought the subject of in-laws up. The session was supposed to be *about me*.

"My guides clearly tell me the darkness of abuse surrounds your husband's father," Louise said. "I can't tell you exactly what it is, but something's wrong. Keep your senses alert, be on the lookout."

When I told Will what Louise said, he didn't shrug it off as some kind of occult foolery. Thoughtfully he said, "I honor that Louise got it dead-right about you and me. Doesn't appear to be anything going on with dad and Dolores, other than he married a lush. Still, we'd better keep our eyes and ears open."

Having been raised in a home that respected Edgar Cayce's teachings, Will was accustomed to people sensing the extraordinary in so-called every day, ordinary occurrences. He held as sacred his parents' path, which included meditation as silent communion with God, paranormal explorations, and belief in a soul's infinite number of reincarnations (until enlightenment is reached) instead of a one-way ticket to heaven or hell like other orthodox Christians such as he believed. Will had so absorbed his parent's mystical approach to spirituality, I often had to remind myself, that he was led in his youth to join other A.R.E.-ers as they dove under the Bahamian waves looking for Atlantis, and drilled into the Sphinx's guarding paw, never uncovering a shard of antediluvian secrets in either location. Again, it's the trying that counts most.

Will and I placed Louise's direct warning in the back of our busy-with-kids life, after agreeing to be watchful for the slightest sign of trouble. Having been subjected to Dolores' ridiculous demand that I pay rent for continuing to use the teZ Mahal (which we conveniently ignored), both Will and I were keenly aware that greedy Dolores might be a wee bit more than the solely society-minded matron she wanted others to think she was.

A penny-wise man who'd never spent an extra dime, ever, Phil somehow had landed himself a high-maintenance big spender. I shuddered now remembering the time, back when Will had asked his mother why his parents didn't get the falling-down pasture fence replaced to keep the cattle in and the house grounds separate. Ever-honest Claire replied in her cleverest, best Tallulah-voice, "We don't get new this and new that. Your father and I get to enjoy life more by saving whenever we can, of what we've worked so hard for all this time."

I winced when I saw the acres of needlessly, newly-seeded lawn, new landscaped plantings, new indoor paint jobs and furnishings that Dolores insisted on for the next, barely hour-long event for some nationally known Florida politician, sure to arrive with his many-car-length entourage, impressive bodyguards, a parade of them coming and going, after each tens-of-thousands-of-dollars' worth of preparation for each new calendar turn.

Will ended our discussion of Louise's sternly warning me, saying, "Maybe that psychic of yours wasn't talking about Dolores slapping Dad around or poisoning him, but another kind of abuse. We better keep a closer eye on what she's doing with Dad's money."

stormy seas

CHAPTER 17

journey within the Journey

Preparing an exhibit for shipment, I stood back and admired the pieces I'd just made—paintings of daily life depicted as sacred ritual; sculptures of reconstructed creatures composed of other organic critters' discarded parts—my work of the past three months. Right then and there, I decided: after this exhibition in Santa Fe, I would stop making objects. I was tired of schlepping around wall-size paintings, too-bulky or so-fragile works of pricey, elitist art. They're just things, and I was ready to change the direction my art was heading.

Admit it, I was thinking. Since inheriting the teZ Mahal, I've come to love writing way more than making art. Art has become nothing more than just more *stuff* to me; just what the world doesn't need, more space-fillers. I've changed. My heart simply isn't into making art anymore. Something about stringing words together really challenges me in a way art-making never did. Especially since the injury.

Some months before my final, and totally private day of reconciliation, I'd freakily lost the use of both my hands. Making art was stopped for me, by my physical incapacitation. Both my hands had suffered a severe injury. My body made this decision long before my resisting mind could grasp the life-altering fact that I had to change.

The major thumb tendons in both my hands had gotten so stressed, so grievously injured when I twisted two extremely hard metal wires together, that my hands were now absolutely useless. My thumbs hung like dead weights at the ends of my arms. To drive, I had to grasp the wheel with my fingers, not including thumbs, which is a trick you don't want to try in traffic. I couldn't hold a pencil. I couldn't play the piano. On that totally non-aware art-making day of mine, obsessed with the piece before me in the studio, I hadn't used the proper tool for the task at hand. Now—sighing sadly, ready to regrettably admit that without the use of my hands I had to take a sabbatical from art-making—I was forced to surrender to what the Universe had been trying to tell me, for ages before. This would be the last shipment of art I'd be making, fulfilling my exhibiting obligations, which I'd obsessed so much over that I caused this injury myself.

Now, the writer side of my dual nature, my artist-writer one, would have a chance to bloom.

What excites me most about the creative process of storytelling, I continued thinking once this hard decision was finalized, is how word-narratives have the ability to sustain the magic far beyond what I've sought to create with paintings, drawings, sculptures. I want to mesmerize my audience—with settings, images and whacky people, with action-energy, and I knew this was possible to do with writing intriguing, character-driven stories and books, much more than making object-art. Just more *stuff* for people to fill houses and over-crowded museums with. Instead of making precious one-of-a-kind objects that get hidden away as someone's guarded possession, my published writings could be disseminated to untold readers. Art, with its elitism and snobbery among the world's aesthetes, had not as much vitality as universally appealing writing does, I contemplated. The Fine Ah-art world of collectors, clients, and critics is much more rarefied than the literary one, which includes practically everyone who likes to hear a good story.

My art is changing, I smiled to myself. *I was changing*. Change is the only constant other than Aum, and knowing that, finally, is the real Art of Living. I felt like congratulating myself for, at last, coming to this realization.

My lifelong identification as a person dedicated to ever more soul-clearing work, the only avid pursuit I've ever undertaken, once I discovered Aum within me, was now enmeshed with caretaking of a family as much as growing spiritually. Every day my gut reaffirmed that my most important role of all, even more than spiritual-artist or rogue-yogini, was as Chief Nurturing Female aboard our boat on Rio Blisso. My duties included—along with expanding my own consciousness—being life partner to Will, and together, guiding to maturity our boat's cargo of two deserving kids. Seeing myself like this, as far as I was concerned, made our family's traveling the ins and outs of Rio Blisso, The Greatest Show on Earth; and being Angel Mom the most spectacular part I could ever play in this cosmic theater.

△

I'd never known what being true to my own Self really meant until becoming Angel Mom. Being a Self-caring person had come unnaturally at first, but by now I'd learned how to be more genuine, transforming my crippling old fears into its antithesis—steady wisdom and unfathomable courage—so I could nurture others as well as myself. I felt this was how I was finally learning to become fully human. "A person who is awakening to their own Better-me," I remembered the Teacher saying, "has the same power within themselves as that of the entire Universe. Just as each acorn contains the same power within a fully-grown oak. Each and every person in the family of humanity is a separate microcosm of the infinitely expansive macrocosm. Aum: we are One," she'd said time after time.

I used to think that I had a long way to go, to feel really human. I used to think I must be an alien, forcibly transported to this planet as a human implant, and hidden within my biological family of origin. That was the only way I could understand my extreme sense of once feeling so out of synch with the general population of Earth. But when I first heard the Teacher say these strange things, "we are One, we all have God within," I didn't feel so far-fetched or out-there anymore. Now, after years of absorbing her teachings, I knew what she meant.

A happy life was to follow one's own heart, purely, simply. That was all there was to it.

So each new day I started as soon as my eyelids opened, silently repeating *So'hăm, So'hăm*, resolving to be the best wife and Angel Mom, the best Spirit artist and writer, the best human I could.

This commitment of mine increased after I'd discovered for myself that the Teacher spoke the truth. When she said that each of us has as much power as we need to get through any of the difficulties life delivers, I found that hard to believe. But in time, I discovered everything she shared, was truthful. Within my own being I was discovering, more with each passing day, that *I am*—I am my own best teacher—I am One with all that is.

"G - U - R - U: *Gee, you are you*" the Teacher laughingly told the yogic joke everyone's heard, meaning how each person's inner power is their own best teacher. "Your innermost nature is: *I am That*. Being the See-er. Seeing Aum in All. Learn to trust your inner Self, your Better-me," she reminded us time and again, her words as transparent as clear glass.

"You are only truly human," the Teacher insisted, "when you accept your own divinity within. Let Better-me be your guide, your own Better-me, not me. I'm just a meditation teacher."

△

At the same time, I was realizing it was absolutely essential to my being Angel Mom to have as much fun as possible. By fun I don't mean fleeting, let's indulge in flash-happy perks, like too much ice cream or a screaming Tilt-a-Whirl ride. In our home, we laughed way more than moped. Our joy promoted acceptance and shunned bellyaching. "No whining," could have been non-rule Number 4. I was lucky because my comedy king, Will, helped make everything—domestic, social, cultural, religious or spiritual—entertaining as well as wholesome.

My tendency to over-seriousness got neatly counter-balanced by his cosmic-clown foolishness.

He and I seized each moment as a no-strings-attached gift. Neither anticipating the future nor regretting the past, we shored up each other's commitment to be devoted fans of the great *Here and Now*. Consciously, we relished each new moment as it arrived. Each new NOW, each magic moment before us, where the breath resides, is where Aum beams brightest; but of course, Will didn't call it by that name.

△

We took the kids trail-hiking in New Hampshire. Bruno, whose legs were way too short to climb mountains, had accompanied us. We couldn't leave him where we were lodging, so the only solution was to bring our midget CBD up the mountain. Determined to enjoy our outing that summer day, we weren't going to leave our shivering-with-fright gator-dog in the car either. I gladly hoisted Bruno's muscular little body around my neck like a tight-fitting living collar, and securely held onto his front and back paws. I wore him like a lady from the 1940s wore a fox stole around her squarely-padded shoulders, only my dog-fur's stubby head and bright eyes were alive.

Soon he was half asleep, half condescendingly aware of being royalty in our family, carried aloft by his humble servant, Angel Mom. Bruno settled comfortably in, a hot-blooded scarf atop the shawl I wore that breezy day around my neck and shoulders. I proceeded to climb, carefully balancing my load as I negotiated the increasingly difficult path. The steps grew longer between each bigger gap. Sleepy-eyed Prince Bruno remained regally at ease on his human palanquin, oblivious to my struggle as the boulder-strewn hike worsened. I laughed at how funny a pair we must have seemed—a toiling long-legged woman with a stubby-limbed wiener-dog hoisted on her shoulders, the two of us, shepherdess and her pampered, half-legged brown lamb-ikins.

As our family continued climbing the steep alpine trail of Mount Washington, the kids were entertained by the sleepy-dog accessory that dangled from my on-high. They called him floppy-eared shoulder-candy, everybody having fun. Approaching the end of the hour-long trail, puffing and panting, I lagged way behind as the others raced to the top. The kids had long before reached the summit with Will following their footsteps. I was exhausted, but Bruno, contented canine that he was, was having the time of his life, heavy-lidded like an opium addict, his neck and head wobbling, never making the slightest peep. Bruno could have spent the rest of his life being my live-in scarf, no problem. Will returned to ask if he could spell me. I said, "I'm cool," actually enjoying the warm closeness of Bruno's thirteen pounds on my neck.

After finally reaching the top of the mountain, everyone famished, we were as surprised as relieved to see Mount Washington's seasonally off-putting snowy peak. The mountain had another surprise at its crest, one we were sorely in need of. An excellent restaurant, open throughout the summer season. As we walked through the door I sucked my breath in, seeing the sign, "No Dogs Allowed." But I was hungry and I was Mrs. Funsie, not to be daunted by posted rules. Turning my back, I quickly shifted nearly comatose Bruno from my shoulders to my chest, and wrapped him completely up in my wooly shawl. The complacently obnoxious pooch was now a perfect replica of a swaddled infant, held close to my bosom like a newborn. Being a fake bambino was not a stretch for this spoiled always-held CBD. I knew as soon as he got horizontal he'd become even more catatonic than before. Bruno lay perfectly motionless, cradled on his back in my lap for the duration of our family's entire lunch.

Every once in a while, the fake-swaddling's head cover started to slip off, and a long black wet snout popped out from my shawl. A red tongue quick-licked the black nose before I could replace my baby's veil. When our college-age waiter saw this he winked at me, smiling conspiratorially. All the servers there were outdoorsy, anything-goes young people. No one but the insurance-haunted manager cared about rules, I knew, and he or she was nowhere to be seen.

After the meal, the kids and I had to use the restroom. Jonny, real young then, came with Kara and me to the Ladies. Naturally *Baby Bruno* went with us, still tightly held in the crook of my arm. Inside was another mom who happened to have her *real* infant bundled in a traveling arm-swing. As Kara and Jonny went bug-eyed, flummoxed by how forward a fun person such as I could be, I sidled right up to the baby's cradle, looked in and said in the feigned-affectation of a challenging, competing tone, loud enough for all to hear, speaking directly to the hip-looking (I quickly noted with relief) thirty-something other mom: "My baby's *way* cuter than yours!"

The other granola-looking mom stood frozen, a look of being momentarily distraught on her face at this other, brazen hussy-mom accosting her. But I quickly flipped back my wrap's heavy covering to reveal an ugly doggy baby with the longest-ever, shiny black snout, as Bruno flashed his famous white toothy smile, happily snorting in attention-getting mode, rapidly flicking his bright-red and wet tongue, licking the air, slurping as much joy as he could get inside him. Everyone instantly roared, including the kids and the immensely relieved young mother.

△

Our challenge was how to joyfully be true to our many wildly disparate differences.

Acceptance was the only way.

Will's born-again, retrograde conservatism; my longstanding anti-politics and anti-organized anything, for starters. How could we traverse our religious-spiritual divide without confusing the kids? As agreed, I dutifully accompanied Will and the kids to the only congregation I could abide, a New Thought Christian church. After a few years of regular attendance though, Will turned to me one day and said: "teZ, you act more Christ-like than any Christian woman I've ever met. As far as I'm concerned you're off the hook: you don't have to go to church with the kids and me anymore if you don't want to."

You bet I opted to stay home. When Will took Kara and Jonny to services, I was relieved and used my free, quiet Sunday mornings to chant and meditate, listen or read talks by the Teacher; study other inspiring scripture, even Bible verses.

We taught our kids to pray, to direct their thought-seeds so they had access to spiritual assistance, no matter where they happened to be or what was going on. Our family held hands and bowed our heads, saying blessings over our food and those who brought it to us, before breakfast, lunch and dinner, even in public. Prayer makes everything more special, more delicious. Each night when we put them to bed, the grownup in charge prayed aloud after reading to each of the kids separately. Will directed his prayer to "Jesus' Holy Name," while I addressed The Mystery as "Great Spirit of the Universe" for the kids' benefit. I only said *Aum* or repeated *So'ham* to myself, silently.

We taught the kids that, whether silent or aloud—called either prayer or intention—our thoughts are seeds we plant, which either produce loving or fear-filled fruits. What our minds linger on in each present moment, even fleetingly, we become. We taught them: "The best thought to have is to know deeply that God is pure Love, and you are One with God, always. You can send your own God-energy that's within you, to whomever or whatever you wish, whenever you want."

I told them about the visual thought-seeds I did, little rituals of protection I use each time I board an airplane or get in a car or bicycle and travel down a dangerous road. I envision putting a brilliant white Light, an invisible shield, around myself whenever I swim in the sea. By that simple act I imagine a trusty barrier between myself and any threat, like unseen sharks, stinging jellyfish, deadly riptide currents.

△

Kara was interested in every single thing I did. If I was chanting at home, she'd sit beside me, swaying rhythmically to the sound, humming the tune, copying my crossed-leg position. She helped me find heart-shaped rocks, an odd-shaped fungi, gnarled roots or other natural objects I collected and placed on windowsills and shelves around the house and gardens. Since Lackland was, well, lacking in spiritual fodder, each month I drove to a nearby city to join other yogis in communally performing a ritual of devotion. Kara always asked if she could come along. At each of these gatherings she sat right up close to me, joined in singing sacred mantras that stilled a busy mind before meditating. She enjoyed being with her Angel Mom and then shared every trip, new tune or ceremony we did with her friends back home. She'd sweetly tell me. "I love all the stuff you do, teZ."

As she approached puberty, Kara asked increasingly pointed questions about my spiritual experiences. She appeared to be genuinely interested in meditation and the other yogic practices I did. Even today, I never speak of my inner experiences unless asked, because they are ... inner things and quite indescribable. But Kara wanted to know what it was like, to sit doing nothing for so long, as meditation appears to the uninitiated. Will never objected to Kara coming with me to my group chants. I was happy to explain my spiritual life when my Angel Daughter asked, and later when Angel Son Jonny also showed an interest, about the time his voice began to change.

▲

If the spiritual urge to know Oneness, following the awakened *Kundalini* energy within, isn't nurtured at the onset of adolescence, it falls dormant again, waiting to be aroused at some other time in life, usually after some spiritual crisis like a loved one's re-joining the Oneness (aka *dying*), when we wish to be with them a bit longer ... so that's an opportune time to allow ourselves to wonder about the spiritual realm of things.

In our blended family, Will's religious view of heaven and hell pretty much answered all the kids' earliest questions. But when puberty's angst started to rage, particularly in Kara, the time when all teens' hormones and endocrine systems start to flood their still-forming brains, turmoil starts to run the show.

In Eastern philosophy, puberty is the time in a person's life when their hunger-to-know-Spirit (called the Kundalini, *awakened* Shakti, *spiritual energy*, in Sanskrit) becomes as real, as strong as every adolescent's sexual urges, which happens to awaken simultaneously. If a teen isn't encouraged then—to become aware of Aum in whatever path or manner their family honors Life's Great Mystery— any kid can easily be led astray. Without guidance, usually all that awakened energy gets funneled directly into sex. Every teenager who has one, ought to consider themselves lucky to have some special adult who can nurture the spiritual urge within their own being when these dual urges arise—spiritual and sexual.

The connection between these two energies is why so many spiritual and religious leaders often, too often, go astray. It's so easy, and natural, to mix up the sexual with the spiritual. If a teen isn't nurtured and given spiritual direction at the initial awakening of their seeking, the Kundalini energy goes "back to sleep" and becomes, as it always was and for some, shall forever remain—dormant. So many things are interconnected. Take, for instance, how this process of Kundalini-awakening is written about in the earliest yogic scriptures, the Vedas, as well as the Yoga sutras and other ancient holy texts that, scholars say, predate Christ's birth.

"The unawakened Kundalini energy lies curled like a serpent at the base of every person's spine," the Teacher explained, "just as Jesus said, 'the kingdom of God is within you.' All humans in their early teens experience the yearning to know Spirit, an all-consuming desire to know *who and what they are*. But if *It* is not nurtured, it goes back asleep, perhaps to be awakened later; but for some, alas, not until the moment of one's own death."

△

I heard a disturbance one day in Jonny's bedroom. When I peeked in, Kara and he were kneeling on the floor, staring at the motionless body of his hamster. "Hammie's dead!" Jonny cried, staring in disbelief at his favorite critter (besides Bruno) who lay completely still on the soft-carpeted floor. "He's dead, teZ!" wailed Kara.

I instinctively realized that Hammie must have taken a nose-dive off Jonny's bed onto the floor and probably was just knocked out. But I decided to take advantage of the situation. I knelt down on the rug and joined my wailing, grieving kids in a circle around Hammie. Inconsolable tears streamed down both their cheeks. Jonny and Kara howled and moaned like professional mourners as they knelt on either side of lifeless Hammie. Where I knelt, we made a perfect triangle around Hammie's lifeless form.

"Kids, let's not waste one more minute being sad," my sure-ness rang out. "Let's send our healing energy right into Hammie and maybe we can save him. Remember that pressure point I squeezed on

Dad's hand the other night? How right away it cured the awful headache he had? Let's use our combined God-energy, the invisible power we all have inside, and send it into Hammie. Maybe that's all he needs—our loving, healing thought-seeds sent his way—and he might come back to life. Let's do it right now, okay?"

The kids perked up at this new game and immediately stopped their sniffling. I demonstrated extending my hands with my palms facing the hamster's still form. Jonny and Kara eagerly copied me.

"This is how we can use the power of prayer," I soothed, "by focusing our thoughts. Close your eyes and envision a perfectly healthy Hammie in your mind. See him running around, happy and well. Let's send those healing thoughts right into his body, healing what's been broken. There's no time for fear or sadness now; that only sucks-out our God-energy. Our thoughts are like invisible rays of light; they can't be clouded with misery and darkness."

Silently, eyes closed, four small and two extra-large hands outstretched toward Hammie, the three of us centered our thought-seeds on helping this helpless creature instead of bemoaning his loss. Within seconds of our combined efforts—Poof! Hammie awoke with a start, rolled over and shook his teeny head as if coming out of a dip in a pool. The last of his stupor evaporated and he scampered into Jonny's waiting hands.

Of course, he'd just been knocked out. Of course, he hadn't arisen from the dead. Hammie was no rodent Lazarus. But his faux ending provided a great chance to demonstrate to the kids how, at any time whatsoever, they can choose not to waste their own powerful inner energies by becoming overly emotional, which only blocks spiritual influences. Jonny and Kara both opted to do something other than be sad, after I showed them how.

In this moment of crisis, after I presented the choice, they reined in their unchecked emotions that had started going off on the uncontrollably unhappy ride of shock and despair that most people think is normal. A choice that always ends in depression, anxiety, prolonged grief, or paralyzing fear. Thanks to Hammie's timely accident they were learning, firsthand, to focus their mind's thought-seeds on the positive. The kids got to watch a real-life miracle of their own making. Well, I helped a little.

Hammie ran in deliriously exultant circles and we all laughed, overjoyed to see the transformation before us.

Then Kara looked up at me.

"Do you love God more than me, teZ?"

"Or me?" Jonny chimed in.

I chuckled, glad the kids were curious about my relationship with the Almighty.

"I love you both, the same as I love Great Spirit. Because God is part of us all. Spirit is part of both of you ... and Dad and Grandpa Phil ... and Debby ... and Aunt Dolores, too ... everyone, everywhere, in fact. I'm serious about this: everything is God. In our house, your dad and I believe we're all part of God. Everything that exists is One with God, you see: like a separate cup of water, or a handful, is the same and part of the big wide river it came from; or drop of water from a vast ocean; or a single raindrop has the same God-energy within it as the entirety of the never-ending torrential rainfall from which it came. That's why it's so important to remember our Number 1 non-rule."

As they sat on the floor focusing on their revived pet's unrestrained exuberance, Kara and Jonny sang out in unison the most important non-rule of all: "See God in All!" as they giggled and played with a fully recovered Hammie. Quietly, I left the room.

△

Not long after Hammie's resurrection, another opportunity arose for me to demonstrate to Jonny the value of using his own powerfully positive thought-seeds. It happened at the beginning of his first year in grade school. He was having a horrible time with Mrs. Wolff, an overbearing, all-serious no-fun teacher. She'd already bawled out my sensitive boy twice before, for his coloring slightly outside the heavy black border of the day's lesson page, unfairly singling Jonny out in front of his peers.

My Angel Boy told me afterward, "Mrs. Wolff came up real close to my face and said, real mean and loud: 'Thumbs down for coloring outside the lines, Jonny.'" Then he looked down at his shoes and softly added, "I felt real bad."

Hearing this and seeing his torn-up face, I burned in outrage. As an artist, getting reamed out for unlimited joyousness, instead of dead serious crayon-coloring, was tantamount to child abuse. That very next evening happened to be the first parent-teacher conference of the school year. As soon as I got there, I privately approached Mrs. Wolff, forcing a pleasant look onto my face.

"I hear you don't approve of Ninja, I mean, Jonny, coloring outside the lines in your class. That's our son's nickname at home."

"First of all," the woman straightened her spine and answered with the distinct tone of going all reprimanding on me. "I refuse to call any child by such an odious name. It's the name of mass-murdering terrorists, which is what Ninjas are in Japan."

Brother, I thought, as if I didn't know that. And so, every kid in America—who loved the nuclear-blasted Ninja Turtles, just arriving in the collective consciousness from the New York sewers at that time—were *all wrong* according to this propriety-Nazi, I shivered.

"Secondly," she continued, looking around anxiously for rescue by another parent, "all children Jonny's age must color inside the lines by this time, period. In or out of my class."

Stiff-necked Mrs. Wolff's attempt at dismissing me didn't work. "I don't agree," I said.

"I am a professional educator," she said, in a demeanor that felt to me like condescension. "Believe me, coloring outside the lines is substandard for Jonny's age group."

I refused to argue with this control freak. I made up my mind right then to pull Jonny from Mrs. Rigid's class. We'd change schools if necessary, I thought, knowing Will would unquestionably agree with me. But then, as soon as I took my seat—Mrs. Wolff was asking our group for quiet. She had an announcement.

"Regrettably, I'm going to be leaving my position here, teaching your son or daughter, but happily to take a position working with Special Ed kids at …" and she mentioned another school in Lackland. Working with these particular kids, she explained, was more suited to her specialist's graduate degree. Then she mentioned she'd be leaving in just a few more days.

"But please, don't tell your children about my plans," she advised. "I'm more skilled than you to handle any grief your child might experience over my unfortunate need to leave them so soon."

Clamping my lips tightly together, I hastened out of the classroom to stop myself from loudly shouting, *Hooray!*

The next morning at breakfast, I said to our sweetheart boy: "Why don't we try another experiment, like we did with Hammie? Let's send out our combined thought-seeds this morning, and pray that ol' thumbs-down Mrs. Wolff gets taken away somewhere else, where she's really needed more. What do you say?"

Jonny's eyes popped with wonder. "We can do that?"

"Sure, we can," I nodded. "We can ask God for anything we want, Jonny. Great Spirit wants the best for us, always. It never hurts to put in special requests, even for what seems impossible. So, let's close our eyes and visualize Mrs. Wolff going away to some other place. Ready?"

I wanted to make the whole God-thing an amazingly wondrous, offbeat fairytale that was as much fun as it was comforting—for my kids' sake as well as Better-me's. Our prayers were similar to made-up bedtime stories, about angels rescuing us, God's energy visualized as swords of saving-us-from-danger Light, helping everyone as other heroes do in a kid's world of knights on white shining horses, rescuing damsels from fire-breathing dragons, or secret wardrobes opening onto other less painful, more magical worlds. Why couldn't God use magic, too, as part of His Holy Armor? The power of thought-seeds is so real, so strong, I knew how from experience, so imparting how to use our own God-energy within, to en-Lighten life was my pleasure, my gift to the kids. Conveying this information was as much a part of my nurturing role as providing meals and gently reminding the kids to use the non-rules, when they forgot.

Sure enough, that afternoon when I picked him up from school, Jonny's face was aflame like a campfire on a moonless night.

Journey within the Journey

"My prayer got answered, teZ! She's going away forever, yay!" he shouted. "Mrs. Wolff told us about it, just now, when she dismissed us, and said for us not to cry, but I'm so happy. I didn't want to hurt her feelings, so didn't say anything." He was out of breath with all that excitement coming out.

"That's wonderful," I said, "on both counts: our prayer working and your being kind to Mrs. Wolff." I beamed back at him thinking how big this kid's heart was, unlike how my Lesser-me's had been once, remembering how I chose to be Better-me, and how it now felt as natural as breathing air.

"Next time you want something really special, Ninja," I said, "don't forget to ask help from that unlimited source of powerful energy we all have inside. Some people call the God-energy *Good-Orderly-Direction*, Jonny. Exercising our free will, making good choices is one of God's peculiar ways of helping us here on planet Earth. That means, basically, if something's meant to be, God will make it happen. Even if something doesn't feel right at the time, God's in charge. That's why life is called a magical mystery tour, because we don't know what's going to happen. Even though yes, bad things do sometimes happen, life can be so much fun, if we relax, and learn to make good choices. That's why some people prefer to think "Good-Orderly-Direction," because that's pretty much what the God-thing's about. We just have to never let ourselves get down when we're being tested by the hard stuff. We have to remember: we have a hand in creating our own life's miracles."

△

After so many years of practicing mind-centering techniques under the Teacher's tutelage, I was seriously only beginning to grasp what I was sharing with Jonny just then. That I needed to accept *what is*.

Not to crave happiness, or success, or any-*thing*; to not think I *know* anything either. I was beginning to understand what she meant when the Teacher often quoted the koan-like Vedic sutra: "Those who know, don't know; and those who don't know, know."

245

Things that I used to think I needed in order to be happy: to live outside Lackland, to have acknowledgement by my peers in the art and literary worlds, to execute challenging yogic postures, enjoy good friends, become bi- or trilingual overnight—all this, attained while still performing my seva, household yoga—were becoming less and less important to me with each new day. Seeking outer adventures, waiting for *thy kingdom come*—none of it really mattered anymore. I was cherishing staying in each moment before me, focusing on my mantra, and having no more inner demons tormenting me. No longer was I addicted to the next Big Thrill, as Lesser-me had been—once upon a time.

That old obsession of mine, to constantly change, had gradually changed itself. It all began on the very day, years before, when I sat down as a newly sober woman and wrote out my simple wish list. In which I asked the Universe for what I needed in order to feel complete: to see Aum everywhere and in everything; have a spiritual-sexy-fun soul mate; and after finding him, together we'd raise two kids. When I wrote that blue-sky-thinking list, I never imagined all three could ever possibly come true.

My present life was the most astounding magic trick of all time, enough to convince me to trust Aum forevermore.

As we cruised down Rio Blisso, each day I allowed Love to take over a little more, as the only, and the true pilot of our family's boat. Before, I'd always thought it was just Will and me who were our vessel's equal but interdependent co-pilots. Now I was learning otherwise.

Whatever God is called by others doesn't matter. Love, Nature, Jesus, Spirit, the Almighty Driver of the Bus, good ol' HP—I still prefer to call the Source of All, Aum. Whichever of its countless names one uses, the Divine Power is ordinary down-to-earth stuff. I really like the remarkable answer my Thai Buddhist friend gave me when I asked what *God* meant to her:

"Simple. Make good choices," Jeab replied right away with a big grin. "Have good life."

Most people *want* to believe in *something* supernatural, that desire is as natural as can be. The Force within All can't be seen, and it's impossible to clearly define. All we can do, like my Buddhist friend said, is call upon this energy, direct it by using our intention or, in certain instances, simply watch it make things unfold by themselves without feeling the need to ask its intervention. All these options are choices.

▲

Like the time when my super-alert sidekick angel saved us four from being killed on South Carolina Interstate 77. I was doing around 65 mph, towing our heavy boat behind our SUV, when a rear wheel suddenly flew off. Flew off! The car, completely out of control! The bare-metal rear axle tore a long, knife-edge deep hole as the car kept trying to spin out of control.

It was my guardian angel, named Better-me, not I, who bolted my two hands onto that steering wheel as the Source took over and fought—way beyond my or any human's normal strength—the opposing forces of our vehicle and the two-ton boat our car was towing. The spin tried to jackknife the boat on its trailer and kill all four of us, with cars high-speed zooming and swerving all around us like projectile bombs.

In surreal stop-action, while my angel wrestled the wheel, I watched in the rearview mirror as the escaped, bolt-shredded tire slow-mo bounced ... bounced ... bounced behind our careening-sidewise car that was back-and-forth with the combined momentum of tons of car-and-boat-trailer steel forcefully trying to yank the wheel out of my hands; the tire coming along as fast as we were in the rear mirror, catching up and passing us, then kept bouncing on ahead, the hard-rubber bomb becoming more dangerous, its bouncing increasing in height and intensity as cars zoomed out of the way in every direction, the tire's next landing unpredictable with each consecutively higher bounce.

I held onto the rebellious wheel, my arms firmly unyielding, while the kids screamed and Will held them close to him in the back flat-bed of our car where they'd all been curled up napping when the tire flew off. Oddly, I felt only peace. Time stopped still. I looked at the commotion all around me, but from outside myself, seeing hunks of swaying, speeding metal and a hurtling black tire: knowing my job was to obey, and hold on. It wasn't me who did the ordering. It was my silent, so-strong angel I call Noname who held the wheel—not me. It felt as if all five of us were in some surreal magical enactment. Called Survival.

Yes, I knew—it wasn't me at the wheel. I don't have that kind of strength nor rock-steady fearlessness. It was my very own Angel, my Higher Self, all-knowing, invisible and Aum-blessed Better-me at its life-or-death, miracle-best.

After that near escape our family was shaken and badly car-shy for weeks. I was convinced more than ever that my cruise down this at times joyous, at times dangerous Rio Blisso, was a joint effort between my family and splendorous Aum, plus its legion of protecting guardians. After the wheel-flying-off incident, I solemnly declared Aum our boat's official captain. Without a doubt, Aum was and is, ultimately, in charge of everything, including our ride on Rio Blisso, way more than Will or me. How we handle each variously blended challenge influences every aspect along this journey of ours. My angel Noname, whom I knew had held onto the wheel that day, is my personal and direct connection to Aum. I'm glad he was there to help out, as he is upon every other occasion when I let him.

In my ship's log for the day of the highway accident, I documented this truth. "God's in charge of even the bad stuff," I wrote. "I surrender. I'm accepting Aum as our boat's true captain."

That day, Will and I became Aum's two first-mates, no longer perceiving ourselves as our boat's co-captains. Aum was now our ship's one and only navigator, the go-to Font of Wisdom we sought and listened to, and would henceforth blindly rely on in emergencies.

I considered this not a demotion for us, but a reality check.

CHAPTER 18

stormy seas

One late night a call came for Will from the sheriff of the one-bar town Debby lived in, seeing as he was her only family the law knew about, from their long-ago divorce disturbances. A neighbor had found her alone, unconscious and bloody, sprawled on the floor of her house. Debby was rushed by helicopter to the hospital in Tampa, and was still in a coma, the sheriff said. This happened on Christmas Eve. At eight and ten, Kara and Jonny were jumpy-excited about Santa's gifts arriving the next day.

I urged them, "Now's the time to really put your God-healing energy to work. Let's pray hard for Debby."

Will and I and the kids prayed as a family, talking to an invisible rescue-squad that's waiting to be called upon, anytime.

She was due to have picked them up that very day. Every year she had them for the entire two-week school holiday. The kids were looking forward to playing, country style, dirty and rough, with their no-chores mom and her circus of docile animals. They were deeply confused, stunned to silence by Debby's life suddenly in an unknown, precarious condition. Kara had been looking forward to getting all dolled-up, cowgirl style, then riding Debby's swayback horse in the Arcadia holiday parade, as she did every year at Christmastime. Jonny would have tried to shoot a turkey or deer with his bow and arrow right from Debby's front porch, and fish his little heart out in the slimy pond, if the gator didn't get his hook first.

We rushed to the hospital where Will took the kids into Debby's darkened room. From the hallway where I stood, not wanting to disrupt the patient in any way, even if she was unconscious, I could see the kids stand shock-still, staring down at the motionless ballooned body with tubes all around that I presumed must have been Debby. Standing on either side of this blob of strange misshapenness lying in the bed, they stared at the grossly swollen person who, Will reassured them, "This *is* your mother," even though she bore no resemblance at all. Except for the stringy bleached-blond hair matted on the pillow. There was no differentiation on this person's smooth basketball of a face, from the swollen cheeks to where eyes and nose were supposed to be; everything was one big blob of puffy flesh. Staring at the horror-show mask, unable to see their wise-cracking, truck-driver-tough mom in this helpless, unnaturally bloated stranger's face, Kara and Jonny were too stupefied to even cry. We rushed the kids outside the room to help them understand.

Outside in the hall I gave the kids a game to play with while the doctors whispered to Will and me at a safe distance. He said there was nothing to do for her but wait.

"Something unknown to us, must have happened," the white-coated physician explained, "that sent her either into sepsis, or perhaps she's contracted encephalitis; we're not sure which of these yet." He told us Debby's condition couldn't be ascertained until she regained consciousness, when she could tell the doctors exactly what had happened.

We said Sure when the doctor asked if he could question the kids. In a small shy voice, Jonny replied when asked if either of them knew what might have happened. "Mom told me she got bit by a black widow spider a week ago. She said her arm turned black and she could only hold the steering wheel with her good arm."

Kara nodded her head, offering additional insight.

"I told Mama to go to the doctor's three days ago," she said, "but she wouldn't listen, she just yelled at me. When she called last time, she said something really weird happened. She says it happened once before, how she woke up in the middle of the night in a pool of blood, so she didn't think it was that strange. Mama told me there must have been a robber in there, in the house, who clobbered her. That's what she figured, she said, because in the morning, day before yesterday, she couldn't figure out why she was out of bed like that, on the floor, or where all that blood came from. She told me she didn't have any cuts anywhere, and wasn't sore. So it had to be a robber, Mama said."

The doctor nodded, jotting notes on his clipboard. He looked up at Will. "We'll treat her for a spider bite and see if she responds."

Long before that Christmas vacation, Will and I had made plans for a romantic getaway during these two weeks, on our favorite Mexican beach. It was to have been the honeymoon we never got, a much-needed break, an extended time off from all-consuming kid duties. Now, the kids were with us. Acceptance. There was no time for disappointment. When any crisis appears, like this grave one here, we have to accept life's twisting our plans, and act fast. Shifting gears, we vowed to make this holiday season as pleasant as we could, under such dire circumstances.

The next morning, Christmas morning, right after opening presents, we rushed back to the hospital. By the doctors' reckoning it was Debby's third day in a coma, and sadly, there was no one but us to visit her. All day she hovered close to death, tubes sticking out everywhere from her bloated body. When the kids got bored, Will sent them out to me in the hall, where they played board games I'd brought. He alone remained, reading a book, sitting beside his ex's bedside. He didn't feel right, he said, leaving her alone like that, not my kind, forgiving man.

I always stayed out in the hall believing, as did he, that consciousness exists even when a person is in a coma. I knew it would upset Debby if she sensed I was in her room, that close to her, even in her grim state. Occasionally I peered in through the doorway, which Will left ajar so he could feel more connected to the kids and me. All of us, coping with comatose Debby the best we could.

The kids' subdued shock gradually wore off during the day, as they grew accustomed to seeing their frozen Mama stuck in total paralysis, most parts of her body unrecognizable, her fingers and toes like broken bits of toothpicks stuck on a Humpty-Dumpty swollen egg-shaped torso. Her chin wasn't there; her country gal, decent-enough looks were so stretched she looked like an engorged tick; her features were like a badly pixilated photo, in today's terms. She lay unresponsive to meds and the fluids being administered in double amounts through tubes suspended around her bedside, machines beeping, their multi-colors mocking Christmas cheery decorations outside. Unresponsive to the kids' every attempt to communicate with her, they kept touching her, shouting at her, until we told them to knock it off. Growing restless, they'd come in to see her every ten minutes, hold her lifeless hand, and stand like mute, sad sentries beside her stillness under the sheets. Then Kara would shove or start a squabble with Jonny, who loudly defended himself, and a normal kids' tussle broke out right over their mother's morbid form. At which point, many times over, Will shooed them out of Debby's room, into the corridor with me.

Everyone, out of sorts. Our Christmas in hell. The games I brought helped, but not much. I stood by Debby's door and observed my too-kind man sitting stiffly on a straight back chair, moved now to a far corner of the room. Hands folded on top of his head, not reading, not watching any screen—just staring at close-to-death Debby—keeping his disapproving feelings toward her in check. Will's selfless magnanimity, a sight I'll never forget.

On the stark white bed, eyes like veiled swollen beets, body stiff as a board, intubated air hose down her throat; every part of her looked painful, as if overnight she'd gained a hundred pounds in fluids. Incomprehensible, I knew, for the kids to see their much-loved Mama like this, so helpless.

Doctors came and went. They told Will that if Debby didn't come out of the coma soon, she'd suffer permanent brain damage. No one else visited all that day or night, no friends, neighbors; nobody came to see her. Her sisters called to say they'd be arriving from Arkansas the next day, or the next.

We spent all Christmas day in the hospital so Will and the kids could give Debby, aware or not, some semblance of solace, having people around who cared enough to be with her. I didn't begrudge my man doing this. On the contrary, I was proud of Will's compassion, his canyon-wide ability to give, teaching his kids to love and care, no matter what. This woman who lay so near death had given Will far more headaches than she'd ever given me, with those ugly false accusations of hers.

The kids, over their shock now, wandered in and out of Debby's room, barely glancing at the blonde matted head, heaped on the bed. A mockery of the person who was the ever-joking, never-serious, always mad-as-a-hornet Queen of Their Universe they called Mama. Such a harrowing sight might be emblazoned on our kids' memories forever, but I dearly hoped not.

△

Four days later, after her relatives finally arrived, Debby miraculously awoke. By the time Will and the kids arrived to visit that day, Debby was pacing the hospital room, trying to yank out her IVs, yelling that she wanted to get the hell out of there and why the hell couldn't she? Yelling how pissed she was that Will had been watching a football game when he was sitting with her.

"Which I heard!" she bellowed in a hoarseness that sounded not like hers. "Which really wanted me to wake up so I could kill you!" she screamed at him.

Will said the doctors were absolutely flabbergasted at her instantaneous recovery. He wasn't. The neurologist, the more seasoned one, declared his patient to have no discernible brain damage. Our family's thought-seeds at work again, Will and I figured.

If there was any good arising from this ordeal, it was the brain specialist saying to Debby that she couldn't drink anymore because of the anticonvulsant drugs she'd have to be on for the rest of her life. When she was released from the hospital a few days later, Debby would no longer be riding around the back roads with an open beer can on her lap, nor use any other kind of intoxicants, doctor's orders. Was being forced to clean-up worth what she'd put her kids through? One would hope so, and that healthy changes in lifestyle could be less stressful. Will and I were glad she didn't die. The kids needed her. They'd suffered enough already. Yet in future years … she would be almost-dying on a regular basis, forever wrestling with the bottle. Until … the sad day when her final bout with self-destruction would arrive. But not before the kids had become healthy and reasonably happy adults, on their own.

CHAPTER 19

devil mom

Carl Jung claimed that every person's search for their individual truth includes accepting the existence of their Dark side, the so-called Shadow, as well as the Light-filled one. Admitting the things I'm about to relate is not fun, but my story as Angel Mom would be incomplete if I didn't.

When Jonny was six, he needed to test me as all kids do with their in-charge adults. Kids are notoriously pushing parents' buttons, sending them right to the teetering edge of madness, seeing exactly how much they can get away with. I knew that from my friends with kids as well as all the dang parenting books I'd read and movies I'd seen.

In our house was an antique Steinway, an upright with real ivory keys and a unique resonance associated with its coveted name, which had been Grandma Claire's wedding gift to us. On it was an invisible sign: "No Sticky Fingers!" which I'd made perfectly clear on many occasions. Kids were not allowed to bring food or balls or wheels or projectiles of any sort into the living room where it stood regally and stately, our memory of the inimitable Claire.

One day while I was sitting at the keys tapping out a tune, Jonny, then a kindergartner walked into the room, slyly smiling at me. I saw that his mouth was covered with the messy remains of his Oreo and milk snack I'd just given him. Thinking he'd come to get me, I got up, ready to go outside to play with him on that glorious fall day.

Before I could say anything, silently, stealthily, looking at me the whole time from the corner of his eye, Jonny snuck directly beneath me and leaned over on the piano bench, twisting sideways so he could look right up into my downcast eyes. As our gazes locked I wondered what mischief he was up to. Before realizing that though, Jonny bent his body over the bench, looking up at me all the while—and in one smooth side-to-side motion of defiance he rubbed his cruddy cookie-covered mouth back and forth, right into Grandma Claire's classy mustard-colored velvet piano seat cover.

Reflexes taking charge, my unthinking arm swung high like the *Who*'s guitarist, in a trance. My hand smacked hard on the seat of the boy's bent-over bottom—as loud as a booming rifle cracks.

Alarming myself as much as Jonny.

Both of us jumped. He burst into tears and so did I. I dropped to my knees and hugged him hard to my chest. Shocked, he clung to me in confusion. No one hit anybody in our Number 3 non-rule home. We stayed together in a tight embrace until both of us calmed. I whispered my apology for unintentionally striking him. Jonny apologized for intentionally messing up Grandma's bench.

The other dark stain on Angel Mom's scoreboard happened soon afterwards. I was working in the spacious studio I'd inherited after Claire's passing, hell-bent on the creative steamroller. The last thing I wanted was to be distracted, especially by kids. Kara and Jonny had been given strict orders that their dad was on-duty if they needed anything that day. Painting with my hands at the stage I was at, which I often do, brushes often not providing a needed effect, I was spreading an already-prepared tub of quick-drying acrylic paint of a hard-to-match bishop's purple, working at breakneck speed. Totally lost in the mesmerizing process of birthing this piece before me, I was listening to its inner rhythm—when suddenly in burst both kids, roaring and screaming.

"Kara did it!" Jonny bawled; Kara yelled, "He made me!"

Disregarding every request and non-rule in every manner possible—starting with my earlier demand for them to seek Will's help while I worked—both kids had run down the long driveway from our house and made the mistake of barging into my studio, hitting, shoving, screaming names at each other. Kara already received many warnings, had already had multiple stars taken off her side of the non-rule chart for breaking every one of the three, but still she couldn't stop bullying her little brother. Given that my hard-to-match paint was drying faster by the second, I had no mind for any patient reminders. Hence, the phantom guitarist struck again.

Fragmented haze surrounds bad moments. I recall nothing: neither ordering Kara to stop, nor for her to drop her shorts, nor to bend over, which in retrospect, I knew I had to have done. The next thing I knew, an arm ripped through the air—in *Who*-Pete Townshend style—delivering a man-size, paint-smeared hand-print smack on Kara's bare buns. A foreign voice, maybe mine, shouted "Get out of here!"

Returning to my tub of paint, I didn't notice her tripping as she pulled up her shorts; didn't hear her racing back down Grandpa's driveway shrieking bloody murder; didn't notice Jonny trailing right behind her, terrified of me more than mad at his sister. I was absorbed. Determined to claim *my* time, *my* space, *my* need to make art right at that moment. Nothing else mattered. Finishing the quickly-drying layer of the quickly setting pigment, I eliminated all thoughts of kids and quarrels from my mind to focus on the creating process.

When this frenzied work session calmly came to a conclusion, having just enough purple paint to accomplish the effect that pleased me—I stuck my tools in a tub of water and went straight home. I found Kara had locked herself in the bathroom, loudly sobbing, miserably arguing with herself. Will had been busy making a complicated business deal on the phone, it turned out, and waved at me, oblivious to the drama taking place on his watch. I rushed by the glass-doors of his enclosed office when I saw him talking, wearing his headset.

I knocked lightly on the kids' bathroom door. "Kara, I feel bad, too. I'm sorry I hit you."

No response.

"I'm sorry," I said through the door. "Sorry that you chose to act so pushy with your brother after we've given you so many warnings. You knew some kind of consequence was going to happen if you chose to do it again. We've talked about this so many times. So now you got what you deserved. We warned you about this at the last FM—what might happen if you didn't stop being so mean to your brother."

"Go away, I hate you!" she screamed. "Mama's right. You're way too big and fat and scary and ugly and mean to be anything but a witch. Your big stupid purple hand is all over my butt. I can't get it off. It's going to be there forever! You're a lousy stepmom and I'll hate you forever for this!"

I walked away sad, frustrated, resentfully remembering Dr. C's words: Discipline is Love to any child. Angry with Will that I had to be the one to always be the kid-cop.

▲

Later, Will said to me in private: "We both know she had it coming, teZ. I'm sorry it was you who had to dish it out to her. She needed that. She's been way too mean to Jonny for too long."

His words were no consolation. If I could have taken back both times, hitting Jonny at the piano bench and Kara in Claire's old studio, I would have. I think. A stepparent, any parent, ought not to lash out; no, I believe not, under any circumstance, especially with such emotionally fragile kids. If I'd had more control over myself, if I weren't so damn serious—in love with Claire's fancy piano, protective of my own right to make art in peace—I might have chosen differently. The kids were emotionally frail, I knew that. More than any kids I'd ever met. Both Jonny and Kara were blown out of skin-thin glass. Whenever I think of these two incidents, I vacillate between feeling regretful and justified. My jury is still out.

However, from that awful day, when the imprint of my purple hand branded her lily-white backside, Kara began to pull away from me. I can still hear her from behind the bathroom door, screaming at me as she scrubbed, "It's not coming off! You've ruined me, with that creepy psycho hand of yours!"

Down the drain—along with scrubbed-off paint morsels Kara persisted rubbing off—went the deeply trusting, blind admiration we'd had for one another since day one. No matter how I tried to repair the rift, whatever I said or did after this event only further alienated Kara. Neither Will's interventions, conciliatory sessions with Dr. C, nor countless FMs to discuss feelings, non-rules, rewards, forgiveness and, okay, the necessity of consequences—none of it could alter the fact that my Angel Daughter no longer thought of me as her Angel Mom.

Now I was just mean old wart-nosed, hurtful Big Foot to her, just like her mama always said I was. We would have no more chants together, no more swaying in the car as she and I listened to Miles Davis bebop or Bob Marley's irie reggae. Kara was no longer interested in anything about me.

CHAPTER 20

the main blows out

Along Rio Blisso the closeness between Will and I kept multiplying, surprising us both as our love deepened to trust of the highest magnitude. In addition to our spiritual and sexual magnetism, we now enjoyed a profoundly enigmatic male-female, yin-yang intimacy we never thought humanly possible, being the stuff of not-yet-written stories, until this one.

Happily, Jonny's heart was opening wider to include me; but sadly, as Kara's teens drew closer, hers shut more tightly against me with every effort I made to reach out to her. Her distancing began in small unspoken ways. Rolled or averted eyes to whatever I offered; limp and perfunctory responses to hugs or my attempts at talking with her. She avoided doing anything alone with me, and only did when Will forced her to. By the time she reached fourteen, her loathing had grown so foul, it was like a stink in our house, alongside the BM's that wafted in with Kara's careful mimicking. I grew so frustrated that I had to share my concerns with Will and Dr. C on an as-needed basis, depending on how terrible Kara was any particular week.

Will always said the same thing: "Thanks for bringing it up, teZ. You're right. We have to face it: ever since the hand-thing, everything has gone downhill between you two. Sometimes it seems like Kara's a jerk, yeah, but sometimes it seems like you have it out for her, teZ. It seems like you're too hard on her a lot of the time. Let's hope Dr. C can sort it out."

Whenever anyone points out something about myself, I give it good honest scrutiny. Here, I had to admit that Will might be right. Maybe I was too bitchy. Kara's constant disrespect had begun to wear me down. She tested my ability to stay detached and compassionate toward her negative attitude about me. With every terse word or slant-eyed diss of hers, I felt a stab in my soft spots. I'd come to the place in our relationship where I couldn't do anything with her except protect my heart from the barbs.

Sure, I knew that Kara's and my falling-out was a common occurrence between teens and their 'rents, especially in blended families where the temptation to create a wedge between parents is hard to resist for any stepkid. Dr. C helped me with this—to realize this, intellectually at least—and not take Kara's rejection personally.

"She has to withdraw, to forge her own ego-identify," Dr. C comforted me.

But all the shrinking in the world didn't ease this drop-kick feeling in my heart. My no-strings love toward Kara had become strained and tattered, anything but unconditional. I was a sore mess of an Angel Mom. Our every interaction grew to be a burdensome chore for me. When it came to Kara, the truth was that parenting her no longer felt like a selfless offering, but a bummer, a nuisance byproduct of my adoring Will.

She hadn't said one nice word to me since the purple handprint. All I could do, and kept trying to do, was accept Kara's new, seemingly intractable rotten attitude toward me. I tried to keep my aching over Kara mostly from Will. He carried around enough guilt already, over the kids, big-time over-compensating, as if he'd done them wrong by taking them away from Debby. Each new heart-owie Kara gave me, I recorded and talked over with Dr. C, alone. I desperately needed help. I prayed. And hoped that Better-me was strong enough to grow out of this common step-family glitch I'd fallen into, being labelled something I wasn't. I tried to do it without my man's solacing me, figuring I was strong enough. Besides, Will was engrossed in a creative project that took all his attention.

Both of us were working on Will's next feature film—he, writing, producing, and directing; I made the props and costumes and acted. I played the part of a magical woods creature in his eco-fable about the threatened Wild of Florida. Will slaved over the script, editing till late at night, getting up before dawn, then making breakfast for the kids, and spending the majority of the work day scrambling on the phone with his demanding job. Without my help, the feature film he made would have taken years more than it did.

Life went on, though not so blissfully as before. The currents along Rio Blisso were becoming more intense, crisscrossing at unpredictable angles, disrupting the up-to-now enjoyable ride of our family's cruise. My hurt over Kara's change of heart was compounded by having to stand impotently on the sidelines and witness Dolores' increasingly deplorable, harsh treatment of our patriarch Phil. Increasing my distress further was that I saw every last chance of ever escaping Lackland's trying unimaginativeness—people unbelievably still staring at me, whispering "that occultist yoga person, she has to be a lesbian painting all those nude blue women like that"—grow slimmer with each yearly flip of the calendar.

To help replenish our coffers, decimated by Will's intricately complex endeavor I was helping on, his second feature-length film—a project I loved, and in which I was an equal partner—I started scouting for real estate deals in Sarasota, two hours away. Sarasota properties were more desirable and therefore profitable, and the tenants way more hip than the Land of Lack. When we crunched the numbers, Will agreed that this idea of mine was an excellent plan. The kids were old enough now to fend for themselves, except for rides to activities. Will was able to fill in for me during days-long absences, when I'd stay overnight in Sarasota to renovate our investment properties. We started with one then expanded into several, buying the worst houses in the best neighborhood, the historic district. This was a formula that we figured would offer not only a fast track to our financial stability, but afford me the freedom I craved—an escape hatch from suburbia with its ever-unpleasant teenage Kara.

I could get away from the house, away from thorny Kara, away from the unsettling Dolores-Phil debacle. My writing was portable thanks to a laptop. With my first cell phone clipped to my leather work-apron, I took leave from the home front right after Will wrapped up filming his movie. He'd keep busy editing it for the next year while I created our real estate and rental business. I felt fulfilled as an artist, transforming crumbling houses into the upscale Sarasota properties we rented to yuppie professionals.

Xeriscape landscaping with terraced levels of coral stone became my next expressive medium. I placed mountaintop-sized timber bamboos and ground-covering vibrant native plants as easily as I'd sloshed paint around a canvas. I returned home each weekend and for any special events; but during the week I enjoyed my solitude, working hard in Sarasota. Will was happy to run the Lackland show because soon enough, I had tripled our income through these property investments. He cooked for the kids and paid others to help with the heavier aspects of household yoga, just as I had.

Back in Lackland, from Grandpa's inner circle of friends we kept hearing reports of Dolores' public displays of verbal disrespect toward the ever-more feeble-minded Phil. We were crushed to hear of her pushing him around in stores and restaurants. I wanted to confront the old bitty, but Will requested me to stay out of it, saying, "I keep asking Dad if he wants me to help and he keeps insisting everything's okay."

We heard how she'd leave Phil alone and confused to sit by himself at parties, stranding him again at a social auction. With each report of Dolores' next incivility inflicted on our patriarch, Will and I winced as the evidence piled up that our favorite old man was being cruelly mistreated, but always behind our backs. Will and I discussed these snippets we'd received of Dolores' publicly displayed mean-spiritedness. When I suggested we talk to her about our knowing of her bad treatment of Phil, Will wanted to stuff it into the same category as he had about Kara's disrespectful behavior toward me—to put a lid on it.

"Stop being such a behavior cop," he admonished me. "Just let people be who they are, for crying out loud. It must be people gossiping. Dad keeps saying everything's fine. Let it go."

But the disturbing reports kept coming. Friends who belonged to the same social club as Phil and Dolores began calling Will with ugly things they'd seen and heard. I decided I had to do something. Without Will's knowing, I contacted the leader of Dolores' parish.

I addressed the Episcopal priest point blank on the phone, no longer having any patience for excusing bullies of any kind after suffering Kara's tyranny. "Aren't you supposed to be the shepherd of your flock?" I asked the collared man I'd never met.

The taken-aback pastor murmured that he was, so I said, "Well, one of your sheep needs looking into." Then I presented the sad facts to him about the abuse we'd heard about. At the end of my brief call the stammering clergy promised to go to the elder couple's home soon, unannounced, "to observe their dynamic together," he said. A few days later he called me back.

"Everything seems fine to me," Father Jones proudly reported. "Dolores and Phil invited me in for a cup of tea. I stayed an hour. Nothing's wrong in that good Christian home, I can assure you of that."

I sighed, knowing how obsequious Dolores acted with strangers in social situations.

Meanwhile, the five-year deadline for our getting out of Lackland had come and gone. "No matter," I said, letting Will know I was letting him off the hook. "I know we have to stay in Lackland to watch over Phil. I'll just keep using Sarasota as a getaway. It's perfect. I get some distance from both Kara and Lackland. It's obvious something's not right with Phil and Dolores, even though the good Father thinks I'm a crank caller."

Worse reports came of Dolores' mistreatment, humiliating Phil in public. Whenever Will spoke to his father in private, Phil, constantly in a daze now, smiled and said, "Isn't Dolores a looker? Nah, everything's fine between us, son. You're just a worrier, Will."

Soon enough, the day of reckoning came that Will and I had both anticipated, and feared.

Thinking she was alone, Will caught Dolores loudly berating Phil when the couple were taking a stroll down their property's thickly shaded lane. "You need to give *me* your power of attorney so I can pay *my* bills!" Will heard her shouting.

As soon as Will made his presence known, approaching them from behind the other side of the lane's tall shrubs where he'd been taking an innocent walk of his own, he interrupted Dolores' finger-wagging rebuke that centered on her accessing Phil's legacy.

Will demanded, "What's going on?" and didn't believe Dolores' quick-shift, smiley-lame excuse, whatever it was.

Will came straight home and called his siblings, relating the verbal aggression he'd overheard, his stepmom's violent barrage clearly meant to intimidate Phil. In relating the appalling encounter, Will was blowing the cavalry horn! Here, finally, was proof—up close, not just rumors—of Dolores mentally assaulting Phil. Her phony front as a caring wife, finally exposed as a sham, after we'd seen clues for the last couple years of the five-year marriage. When notified, all three of Will's siblings immediately agreed: by pushing around their father, Dolores was, in truth, attacking the entire family.

The bugle call resulted in the wagon train swiftly circling around Phil, protecting him from any more onslaughts.

▲

As the other siblings made their way to Lackland, the next morning Will went straight to Dolores and demanded to see his dad's accounting books. Somehow, she'd managed to finagle them away from Will, the trustee, just days earlier. Given that Will was his father's signatory for any financial transactions, there was absolutely no reason for Dolores to be involved with Phil's complicated finances. Will had complied with Dolores' inappropriate request out of his naively blind trust. Which he now realized was really another way of saying his *blind stupidity*.

It took a two-minute glance for Will to uncover proof of an extortion trail that everyone in the family, each of us so busy with our own lives, had suspected but truthfully, wanted to avoid like a plague. Every one of Phil and Claire's grown kids all had hoped for the best. Nobody wanted to face the fact that their beloved paterfamilias had been hoodwinked out of so much cash, even though a "Red Alert" had been signaling for years. The family tried to give the old guy his privacy, per his repeated response to everyone's entreaties to help him out of his obviously uncomfortable marriage. Dolores' blatant improprieties amounted to substantial money gifts for herself and her two grown children, now exposed by recent black-and-white entries she'd boldly made in the hand-entered financial records Will had gullibly lent her; her audacious money-grubbing screaming, "Abuse of Privilege!"

Before Will caught Dolores yelling at Phil, our family's denial of Dolores' controlling ways, slyly done right in front of our eyes, had grown as ripe, as deep, as stinky as the veins in a well-aged blue cheese. Our group denial—as human a characteristic as breathing—now came to an end. The malignancy of Dolores' actions forced us, all of Phil's family, to take swift action to save the dignity, if not the old man's very life.

△

I for one wouldn't have put it past Dolores to *accidentally* push the now weak and weary deal old soul, a whisper of his former manly strength, down the steep flight of stairs in their house, following her being outed as a money-grubbing crone. She was that wickedly shifty, to my detective-savvy inner See-er.

Will's youngest sister, Sally, who lived a couple hours away, must have suspected the same thing because she quickly showed up at Phil and Dolores' door, and camped out until the other two far-away siblings also showed up.

During the next twenty-four hours Sally learned that the elderly couple's pattern, which the good Christian pastor I'd called had failed to detect, had degenerated into Dolores' retreating to *her* side of the gigantic house all day long. She only spent time with Phil on *his* side when the five o'clock cocktail hour arrived. Then, an uncomfortably silent dinner of fetched takeout was followed by Dolores, highball in hand, retreating to her own TV in her own huge social-planning room (formerly the grandkids' playroom), while Phil sat alone and abandoned, but with Sally that first night, in front of the living room fireplace in an entirely different part of the spacious house.

The next morning, Will and Sally and the other two sibs, who'd arrived by noon, made the phone call to a divorce lawyer. The official rescue was on. Phil, at ninety-two, had entirely lost his sense of reasoning, Sally had determined. His family had to bring him out of this living hell, she told the lawyer.

Will and I tried not to beat ourselves up for not having paid enough attention to Will's plight.

Okay, for the past years my man and I had been preoccupied, raising kids, getting Will's next feature made while I commuted hours away to do property renovations in Sarasota. Phil and Dolores had even been extras in one of the scenes of Will's movie, which was in its final editing stage. Will was exhausted from not enough sleep, editing the movie in his scant spare time. What energy he had leftover went to our teenagers' active schedules of back-and-forthings. But we sure weren't the only ones in Phil's family who hadn't been able to admit that the old man's marriage had fallen into such dangerous decline.

Will's siblings, all professionals, and me too, we'd all been so caught-up in our busy, distracted lives, centered on our own needs, our children, our projects, to notice how very badly Phil had needed our assistance all along. Louise's warning had been right at the very moment she gave it.

We had to wait only several days for the emergency appointment Phil's lawyer made with the local judge. During that interval, his brother and two sisters, and Will and I took shifts sitting with Phil, to protect him 24/7 from Dolores. Each of Phil's children approached her and politely asked Dolores to leave the house. But she refused, ranting, raving, fuming, insisting there was no problem, retreating to her side of the house, making loud noises in the background, confronting us saying, "You interfering kids!" glass in hand, demanding *we leave*, with her equally sinister sidekick, Helmet-head at her side.

Repeatedly, Dolores was asked to do the decent thing and leave the old man with us, leave the family home, but she refused.

We suggested she move to that newly purchased, completely furnished, fancy house she'd bought for herself, in addition to the one she'd bought for her daughter with Phil's funds, clandestinely arranged just as all the other substantial money gifts were that she'd made to her children, by forcing Phil to sign papers without his knowing what they were. The capability of his knowing, sadly, was no longer his.

"I'll do no such thing!" she fumed. "Phil and I are happy, aren't we Phil? What are your nosy children fussing about? Why can't they leave us alone! Phil, answer me!"

But the old man was caught in the net of a brain fog of what was real and what wasn't. All he could do was hold his weary head as it sunk heavily into his hands, gazing blurry-eyed at his ever-burning fireplace.

Again, Dolores was caught bullying the old man, this time whispering, trying to convince Phil we were meddling in their "happy marriage." After that, we didn't dare leave Phil alone with the unscrupulous woman for even one second. We all knew Phil was incapable of realizing what was happening. When his older adult son asked, "What do you want us to do, Dad?" Phil laughed in a childish manner, shrugged his shoulders, and gazed off at bright white clouds passing outside the window, or at far-distant Mr. Bull with his satisfied cow gals, happy in their pasture.

Things had gotten too tough on Planet Real for this noble gentleman to figure out anymore. His mind had drifted far, far away. He sat quietly, blankly, not in any noticeable distress. Just peacefully gazing into the blaze that burned in his fireplace.

The court date arrived. Our troop of five protectors, four sibs and me, took our family's chief—trembling and confused—to the courthouse where, in private chambers, the female judge right away asked Phil, "Sir, do you want to be divorced?"

Phil looked toward his kids for direction. Will, his siblings and I vigorously nodded. Phil replied, "I guess so," in a flat tone. We weren't sure if he even recognized Dolores—sitting on the opposite side of the table, flanked by her genuinely startled son and cloned daughter—because he spoke nothing more.

With that one question, the judge then granted Phil an "incontestable divorce decree due to extreme circumstances."

Within minutes after having heard the evidence, seen the secretly absconded accounts, and heard Dolores admit the unauthorized financial transactions in question were indeed hers, the judge granted this rarely used legal move that was invoked only in cases of incompetency. Dolores—seated between her blank-faced daughter and shell-shocked son—howled and huffed at the judge's hasty decree, infuriated that the judgment happened so fast, even though her lawyer tried to contest.

Then, right in front of the judge Dolores looked at her now-ex and loudly declared: "Don't worry, my darling. We'll get remarried like we planned, just as soon as this mess with your nosey children is over. After I get the proper paper drawn."

It was unbearable to watch the old man's blank, dazed face. This had to be one of Phil's worst moments, ever. But I doubt he knew that.

Surrounded by the shield of his children, Phil not comprehending anything, he was quickly shuffled out of the courthouse. At home, in his favorite spot beside the roaring fire, Phil asked repeatedly what was going on and, "Where's Dolores?" Each time, his kids and his faithful decades-loyal secretary told Phil that he was now a divorced man. Later, Will clarified things for him when Phil, disoriented with the sudden change, again asked what was happening.

"Dad, you divorced Dolores. She's not a team player." Despite Phil's in-and-out awareness, Will hoped he still might have his funny bone intact.

The Main Blows Out

Phil thought for a moment. "Well, I'll never marry her again," he declared dryly.

A full-time caretaker moved into Phil's house that very afternoon, bringing her suitcases in as Dolores' possessions were being carted out. The judge's Court Order allowed Dolores to return to the house for two short hours, refusing her entrance forevermore after that. Helmet-head arrived with Dolores to grab anything important. When Dolores left, as required, her assistant finished resentfully packing over the next week. After that, it was to be the last time we'd ever see Dolores or Helmet-head, cussing under her breath that her "good friend and employer didn't deserve this."

Realizing fully how fragile the old man was, Will and I promised each other we'd stay in Lackland for as long as he needed us. Now there were three generations traveling Rio Blisso together in our family boat. After Aum, Phil held our crew's next highest position: that of our revered tribal Chief elder, his only onboard duty being honored guest on our family's voyage. We wanted Phil to be as pampered and respected as a nonagenarian can be.

△

Now when we frequently visited him, one of the several hired women companions, not nurses, were always there to care for Phil, as we chatted and munched raisins and walnuts with our boat's latest addition. Best of all, suddenly free in many ways, Phil began to sing old ditties at the oddest times, day or night. After the shock of Dolores' abrupt absence quickly abated, Phil surprised us all by singing from what turned out to be an impressive repertoire of drinking songs he'd mysteriously unearthed from his long-buried youthful folly No one had heard anything like this from him before, ever. With joy resounding once more in his heart, the old man sang as he sat sunken and immobile in his easy chair, his weary head held like a heavy stone in his one hand:

Bacchus must now his power resign
I am the only God of Wine

His eyes shut, Phil searched his memory, one skeletal hand on his brow:

> *La la la la ... the wretch should be*
> *In competition set with me,*

A moment's silence as he fished in the depths ... 'til the words were found and snagged:

> *Who can drink ten times more than he!*

Phil opened his rheumy eyes, remembering, smiling, softly humming the tune to himself. After quickly greeting us, he'd stare at the fire before him—oblivious to Will or Jonny, Kara or myself perching quietly around him—with nothing to say.

"How you doing," Will or I would ask.

"Oh, still in the ring, I guess," Phil's faithful reply.

Another remnant of Phil's youthful drinking days was his solitary tattoo. The official U.S. Cavalry insignia of two crossed swords, emblazoned on the inside of his withered right forearm. He'd proudly gotten it when war broke out, even though he didn't serve in either World Wars because the government required that his family's tanning factory in New England, stay open. The Armed Forces needed boots, now, didn't they? When Will reached his early twenties, back in Vietnam wartime, he'd gotten the same crossed-swords tattoo in the same place as his dad's. Jonny, a young teenager now, wanted his own tat as a sign of solidarity with Grandpa and his dad, soon after the ongoing "War against Terror" had been declared following September 11th in 2001.

I took a picture of my three guys sporting their identical tats. Three generations spanning four wars—nearly an entire century—grinning proudly, showing off their similar inky signs of virility for men who'd never faced combat. Tribal art; wise-guy smiles for the camera, mugging, joking, more masculine family traits. Their tats, male bonding more than by mere blood. A permanent body mark, as good a primordial connection as some folks get in our derailed, de-ritualized modern times.

As I snapped the photo of my three guys that day, Phil's voice burst out in another ditty.

> *Make a new world, ye powers divine*
> *Stocked with nothing else but wine.*

Let wine its only product be,
Let wine be earth, and air, and sea
And let that wine be all for me.

We laughed. If the old man had to be stuck in a one-gear state of mind, singing drinking songs from his youth's carefree days was a whole lot better than what he'd been stuck in before, with the socialite.

▲

During the time of Phil's marriage unraveling, Jonny was developing his athletic skills. From age twelve he'd attended special kicking camps, and practiced for hours on Grandpa's flat lawn. Jonny's goal was to play college football and with luck—get picked for the pros, his American hero's dream.

I continued renovating Sarasota houses, through which I brought as much cash in one year, as if I'd been holding down a steady job ever since marrying, eight years previously.

When I came home on weekends the kids laughed, telling me how much they enjoyed their dad's reenactments of the baby meals he used to make for them, before I came along. First, he'd put a dollop of yogurt on their plates; then, one olive apiece, followed by a single cracker with a chunk of cheese on top; then a slice or two of cucumber or tomato. On and on the mini-servings came, bite by bite, until both teens were full and aching from laughter over how ridiculous their dad was.

Kara and Will had no problem communicating. He could hold long conversations with her, but I had to learn to keep quiet around her because, no matter what I said or how nice I tried saying it, it pissed her off. There was nothing left for me to do but practice detachment, along with many silent rounds of *So'hăm, So'hăm*. I asked Aum to help me be strong enough, kind enough, forgiving enough to be a positive role model for her, to not let my feeling under-appreciated get in the way of nurturing this family of mine. I loved Kara; our estrangement tore me up. So I went out of my way to help her, never expecting any thanks or recognition.

Whenever I spoke to Will of my challenges with Kara, he dismissed my concerns. "You're too hard on her, teZ. Lighten up."

It felt as if a rotten fungus had permanently gotten stuck to the inside ribs of our boat, our otherwise gloriously proud and beautiful sailboat that took us, caressed us down Rio Blisso's intricate labyrinth.

Nothing I did seemed to soften the stench of separation between my Angel Daughter and me. Despite the sunshine of Love I shone directly on this moldy growth of ill feelings, regardless of the many talks we had at FMs about Kara's and my schism, talks with Dr. C, or conferences with Will … things stayed tense between us. Only me praying to "let go let God" and repeating the mantra helped quell the pain of alienation I felt from the darling girl I once knew.

CHAPTER 21

rite of passage

At the very start of our voyage on Rio Blisso, Will and I had made a vow. Both of us were concerned how our modern world has lost many cultural and a good deal of religious and spiritual rituals, events that in earlier times signaled important milestones of life. Such as the passage of a child's entry into puberty. To mark our kids' transition, as a "Hello to Adulthood," we planned years beforehand, to make a celebration of that event, by taking each of them on a separate, significant journey: a coming-of-age trip—Kara with me and Jonny with Will. Unlike the occasional misdirected father who takes his son to a brothel, or a misguided mother taking her daughter to a gynecologist for birth control, as Debby did with Kara (not discovered by us until years later), we wanted ours to be actual physical trips, which we saved for in advance. We wanted this sacred Vision Quest to be life-altering, monumental and memorable, attuned to each kid's interests.

Even though things were far from friendly between Kara and me, Will and I took seriously all the promises we'd made to each other. Will trusted me to guide his daughter into womanhood, so I stayed determined to make this trip, Kara's rite of passage, the best I could—even if it killed me.

I painstakingly organized things as if she and I were still best friends, even though we barely spoke two words to each other without hurt erupting from both sides, tainting whatever we did. When it came to me, Kara's words and body language switched from sweet to poisonous. Her ability to inflict wounds my way was, by now, well-practiced, her aim straight for my heart. No consequence dished out by Will or me could break this habit of rudeness she'd acquired. I remembered to respond (I was the adult after all), and tried not to react like she did, as a hurt child. Dr. C's words echoed in my head: "She needs to emotionally separate from you in order to become a healthy woman." Knowing that Kara's rage was teenage angst fueled by hormones, that didn't assuage my hurt feelings. As the time for the trip drew nearer, I swore to myself to keep cool, and cut her all the slack she needed during our time together.

Despite the prospect of our being alone for two whole weeks, at fourteen Kara appeared eager to take the journey that we 'rents had promised her for ages. I'd planned and timed every detail, trying not to let any projection of mine take over, that the antagonistic were-wolf-teen and I might not make it. Instead of dreading the trip, my intention was to show Kara what style of womanhood mine really was. By introducing her to people and places that held meaning for me, I also hoped to reignite that flame of loving Spirit that had burned so brightly within her as a child.

I remembered the Teacher saying how sexual energy arises at puberty, coinciding exactly with the awakening of a young person's desire to know the Unknowable, the Great Mystery of Life. My only goal, I reminded myself as I planned for months, was for Kara to reflect one day about how this trip was the spiritual quest she and I once shared.

▲

We began our trip in high spirits, both of us excited to be out on the road. Yet right after landing at the airport in Manchester, New Hampshire, Kara turned her back on me and hugged the door of our rented car's passenger side in silence, remaining in this defensive position all the way to our first stop, an hour away. Something I said must have pissed her off because she chose not to even look my way or speak. When I asked what was wrong, she mumbled, "Nothing." Perhaps it was my having insisted we share the music on the radio, half the time her favorites, half mine. This was pre-iPod, and her Walkman had been left behind, on the blink. I left her alone to sulk during the early autumnal green, gold, and red-glinted drive to the home of my old friend, Gail.

As we came up the driveway on the shady hill, we saw my friend's wooded fairy home. Surrounded by a thick stand of trees and a meadow of goldenrod, dotted white with Queen Anne's lace, the gnome-ish house stood flanked by a huge vegetable garden. Flowering and fruiting vines grew everywhere. Off to the side, several big sheds added to the aggregate mix. After greeting my dear pal with lingering hugs and direct-gaze smiles, we went in to see her hobbit house, filled with her family's hand-hewn charm. I also noted the dwelling of my friend—with whom as young bohemians I'd shared the thrill of making art together and cultivating the most free, most fun of communal lifestyles—had none of the modern conveniences, such as television or dishwasher (but they did have a computer) I'd come to rely on.

Gail and I remarked on the scant changes in each other's appearance since we'd last seen each other. She so short and me so tall. "Nothing's changed," I laughed, closely examining the slightly older but still beautiful face of my friend. "Except for our sexy gray hair and a few attractive wrinkles." Gail had a mischievous grin for this.

We both chuckled. We'd been half-baked, wild alternative-types, LSD-tripping freaky artists back in the sixties of Boston. I wanted Kara to know this extraordinary person, my pal Gail, whom I admired not only as a talented clay artist, always following her creative impulses, but also for her shunning superfluous materialism and living simply: my preferred style too. Gail and her conservationist husband were flourishing in their self-sufficiency—growing or making everything they could, living frugally, buying as little as possible. My kind of people.

Unlike me, Gail had supported herself solely from her dynamic art since her early twenties, with no additional income other than teaching clay workshops and assisting other ceramicists to organize shows. In contrast, I had either a business or some other paying job to support my obsessive addiction to making weird, unsellable art. Gail and Fred, married forever, put up a storeroom full of edible goodies each season, gleaned from the impressive harvest of their garden's abundant vegetables, sweet berries, tart rhubarb, and savory stalks from a hearty old asparagus patch. They canned, preserved, and dried so they could feast all winter long on the bounty of their summer labors. I admired the couple's basic survival skills—chopping wood, raising poultry, mending fences, and performing other farmyard chores—as much as I appreciated my friend's stunning artistic efforts.

Gail's studio was a short walk from the house. Here, two walls of bright windows looked out on a collage of purple asters among other end-of-summer wildflower hues. A twice-yearly mowed meadow lay just before the dark wall of dense trees that surrounded the couple's five acres. Inside her sunlit studio were shelves of clay works in varying stages of completion—from thrown, everyday-sized bowls, pitchers and cups for household use, to gargantuan hotel-lobby-sized vases, urns and sculpted forms. Gail showed us sketches of a commissioned tiled mosaic in progress—muted vine, leaf, and blossom patterns highlighted with scrumptious metallic glazes of mineral tones. The masterful aesthetics of her studio work delighted me.

Kara was uncharacteristically quiet, witnessing my friend's simpler, country lifestyle, a creative approach that included art-making equally with self-reliance, decidedly different from our suburban routine back in Lackland. Gail's one grown child had left home to pursue a sculptor's career in a far away city that supported a thriving art scene.

For the rest of that day and the next, the three of us played with clay and drew, and talked, helped with the ongoing harvest of the overflowing garden, and picked nearby berries. In the late afternoon, we prepared a wholesome, delicious meal right from the garden in Gail's aromatic wood-and-tile kitchen, then washed dishes by hand afterwards.

Kara was so peaceful. She was visibly moved by the powerful atmosphere of a life devoted to making art. When she spoke with

Gail, there was no feigned interest. She hung onto my friend's every word. However, whenever I spoke, Kara hunched over as if her stomach hurt, and she'd either hustle away from me or roll her eyes. As soon as our car pulled away from Gail's enchanting cabin in the woods, Kara again retreated into herself right next to me, hugging the passenger door, acting annoyed, sick, hurting.

Every one of my attempts to joke around with her, to make things lighter, elicited no response. I decided to keep mum and let her play her alternative-rock music on the radio; I couldn't take her sulking. All I could do was accept Kara for who she was. As I drove I silently repeated *So 'hăm, So 'hăm* a million times, renewing my vow to focus on the positive for the rest of this long trip ahead of us.

△

We pulled into the woods-lined lane that led to the homestead of Luna, another old friend who, like me, called herself a Spirit Warrior and consciousness activist. Whereas my Teacher was an East Indian meditation master whose spiritual lineage was linked to millennial-old scripture, my pal Luna followed a more Nature-based path as apprentice to a Native American shaman, a Navajo woman who also held a degree in modern western psychology. Using spiritual tools from Western and Eastern traditions, both Luna and I honored our traditions by using ritual to acknowledge each step of growth along the path to our own soul's fulfillment. Luna, her long black hair streaked with silver since the last time I'd seen her, her ardent eyes of coal alight as she spoke of her passion for performing Native ceremony, knew as I did, modern people's need to enact rituals. Simply because by marking special moments, ritual lightens the burden of life's complications.

Specializing in women's empowerment, especially since her own serious health problems had set in, sharing ritual was Luna's joy. What we'd been carefully planning for months now, would not be Luna's first leading of an initiation-into-womanhood ceremony.

Luna had asked me to bring along some artifacts from Kara's childhood. I told Kara to "Expect the unexpected" and nothing more. Arriving at noon, I greeted my friend's businessman husband before

Luna led the three of us into the thick woods adjacent to their spread of many more acres than Gail's, with only a small patch of lawn and a flower garden close to the ordinary looking house.

△

Luna instructed us to help her cut down some supple birch saplings. In a clearing in the nearby field, the three of us bent our harvest from the woods, to form an interwoven leafy arch of an adult's height, and staked it to the ground. As the afternoon wore on, we placed within the woven pine and oak lengths, other tree limbs, branches and leaves and finally, stuck in the personal mementos Luna had asked Kara to bring. She'd chosen a handful of paper sketches of her comic snails that she'd drawn in childhood. Those whimsical crayon and painted renditions of shelled creatures, the oft-repeated theme of her laughter-sprinkled childhood—such ridiculous curlicue beings with alien antennae, having amusing personalities within such small hard cases—symbolized to me the lighthearted, yet guarded young girl I had instantly fallen in love with so many years before.

My friend and I had long planned for Kara's sacred ceremony to correspond with this particular date in the calendar. The next day was to be the most sacred lunar time of the year, a "women's moon," Luna called it, when its fullness would rise highest in the night sky. "Tomorrow night," she explained to Kara, "we set fire to your arch, representing the portal, the entry to your womanhood, when you'll say goodbye to your girlhood." She explained how Kara would pass through the saplings' lighted flames, "signifying the end of your formative years," and emerge on the other side, ready to embark on the spiritual journey of womanhood. "Which is all females' sacred duty," Luna declared.

After dinner, we spent the rest of that evening making tiny bundles to be used during the ritual. The three of us sat at Luna's kitchen table, placing pinches of tobacco in matchbook-sized, cut pieces of soft deer hide. "Add a special intention or prayer into each one as you make it," Luna instructed as we carefully, tightly bound the soft bundles with red thread. Each finished bundle was the size of a tightly swathed peanut shell, mimicking a miniature papoose.

The next morning, we put the finishing touches on Kara's ceremonial arch, sticking in bits of dried stuff, all organic materials Luna had collected: a dropped feather, a few field stones, autumn flowers, shafts of grains, anything natural or decorative Luna had on hand, to burn in honor of the feminine, creative, fertile force, the creative energy of Nature.

"All that aids and empowers Kara's passage from girl to woman," Luna affirmed in her light-hearted ringleader fashion. "Each of us will offer the prayer bundles we've made together, one by one, to the sacred fire we'll tend. We'll whoop and holler and dance in our circle tonight. Once risen high in the sky, tonight's auspicious full moon will illuminate our spirits."

The night before, when we sat around the kitchen table watching our tall stack of bundles grow, making enough, it seemed, to include prayers for all the world's pains and sorrows, Luna and I reminisced, as two close gal-pals do, telling stories old and new. Luna asked Kara about her dreams and yearnings. I kept quiet and listened. How curious to hear Kara so willingly reveal her private thoughts to my soul sister, things my daughter stopped sharing with me long before. Several times throughout that evening, Luna reminded Kara she was being welcomed into the sacred circle of grown women, the caregivers. The fire-tenders.

"Our role as women," Luna told Kara as I sat silently, "is to be the fire-tenders. Our main job in the human family, our duty in our own family and the family of all humankind, is to lead by example, as we nurture and guide, and heal ... leading others in spiritual matters as we make ourselves whole. Most importantly though, is for us women to teach others to uphold the sanctity of all life."

Kara became silent. Perhaps she was uncertain about this *women-are-powerful* talk that Luna and I engaged in as easily, as naturally as other women exchanged recipes, or shared tips about where they got those great shoes.

rite of passage

Rite of Passage

All that morning and afternoon we prepared for the ceremony that we'd begin at sundown. Talking softly and seldom; sharing small quiet meals, taking a long and mellow, whispering walk together. After dusk fell we changed into the long skirts that Luna had asked us to bring: "To better capture with our bodies the power arising up from the core of Mother Earth."

It was time to light the transformation arch.

But it turned out the saplings we'd cut to create the sacred arch were far too green and didn't light up in the memorable blaze Luna had hoped for. "Next time I'll build the damn thing a couple weeks ahead of time," she laughed. "So it'll be dry and take off like a freakin' rocket ship."

None of us was disappointed that Kara's arch only had a few seconds of flame—then nothing but smoke. Kara's snail drawings supplied the main source of the puny pyrotechnics. Like people, rituals can be affected by circumstances and malfunction, forcing alternate solutions. So out came Luna's lighter fluid.

Kara, not accustomed to wearing an exotically long, wide skirt, was more than keen to participate. She was all sparkly-eyed and curious about my friend's Native artifacts and devices, happy to see her snail drawings set on fire, sacrificed to the fire like honored lambs, then fizzled to smoking cinders and ash. Kara remained the good sport she always was with others. Despite the lackluster show, Kara didn't act shy or skeptical about the ending of her childhood's dramatic enactment. With Luna's and my intention, the ritual signified Kara's right then, that moment, having entered into wonder-filled, unstoppably spiritual womanhood.

△

Our long skirts were doing their jobs. I felt the power of Gaia, the Earth Mother Herself, come right up between my legs, come deeper inside me, enter my heart, then—oh!—I felt Her, the Divine Mother's energy burst out through the top of my head, connecting my fibers of energy with the other two females there. Our threesome now connected with everything, the earth, the moon, our galaxy, the entire cosmos, as our energy extended forever outward from our innermost beings into the boundless infinity.

Following Luna's lead, the three of us sang, chanted, screamed sounds Luna said were Native American words as we stomped on the ground and circled the fire, each lost in our own magical experience. In sober rapture, under the clear night sky, the gloriously full-lunar beacon, we spun in elation, making circles, howling like she-wolves, frolicking like three crazy ladies.

Totally charmed by the deepness, the strangeness, the serious fun of the ceremony, Kara began to toss, separately, reverentially, each of her prayer bundles into the flames. Under Luna's direction, Kara declared a word or two, or a phrase, about the purpose of each bundle she was throwing, requesting the fire's blessing.

Luna said, "Imagine the old, gone; the new arising from the flames."

Some of the bundles' meanings Kara kept private as she fed more and more to the fire, like a new mother feeding her child. She was told to imagine each bundle bore a certain significance to her being included into Luna's and my sacred sisterhood.

The three of us watched as the hissing flames claimed each prayerful intention. The sky above us filled with smoke released as each tobacco bundle was consumed, signifying all that this tender young girl-woman wished to accomplish in her now, jump-started womanhood.

When Kara grew weary of throwing her bundles into the fire, Luna and I tossed the remaining few bundles into the flames, adding such things as *wisdom*, *sacrifice*, and *healing* to Kara's litany of already *asked-fors*. The flames blessed each and every virtue and request of the newly initiated, awakened fire-tender Kara now was.

△

The next morning, I left my pal's feeling high. Doing ceremony always awakens us, even more. I felt more in touch with the unseen sacred power of everyday life, that to us metaphysicians who work with spiritual energy is as real as blood is to physicians.

When I asked if she felt any different, Kara replied, perfectly earnest, "Yes. I am now a woman."

I didn't hide my pleased smile. I sighed relief, feeling rewarded for having honored the sacred pact I'd made with Will many years before, when Kara was an open-hearted young girl who'd been as close to me back then as I relaxed, and allowed myself to feel to her now.

But—soon after we pulled away from Luna's house—Kara retreated from me once again. Damn! Undeterred, I focused on breathing deeply, consciously renewing my decision to let her be, not to point out that her behavior was making this trip—a supposed once-in-a-lifetime spectacular event—a big fucking drag for both of us.

So'hăm, So'hăm.

CHAPTER 22

lightkeeper

Our next stop: the Teacher's secluded, traditional yogic ashram in Vermont, where I'd been going to study meditation techniques since long before marrying Will. This would be the most important place and person, of all: the axis around which the entire trip revolved from the moment I'd begun planning our Girl-to-Woman trip. More than anything, I wanted to introduce Kara to the Mother of my Heart, my meditation teacher.

My own mother, yes, she was of my body and blood, and I resemble her more than either of us were comfortable admitting. But Mom never knew the real me. She only saw her "baby" when she looked at me, and it pissed her off I wasn't her cookie-cutter self.

From the moment I met my spiritual role model—on a date curiously close to Kara's own birth—the Teacher kept urging me through the next, and the next portal, to seek deeper understanding. The gates of knowledge she threw wide open before me. Even though I didn't have a one-on-one personal rapport with the *Great Being* that many of her students proclaimed this meditation teacher, born in India, to be—who'd guided tens of thousands of seekers for decades—she'd arrived in my life just when I was ready to unconditionally love myself. She introduced me to the Better-me part of myself.

I'd met the Teacher during the early days of my commitment to no longer abuse booze or chemicals. As soon as I saw a photo of the Teacher, I was instantaneously transported, enchanted by her. Becoming her student was no leap of faith for me. I got knocked out, literally, from being in her silent presence at our first encounter.

Turns out, that was a common occurrence for seekers like myself to have, around Great Beings. Now I wanted to share with my daughter the profound knowledge I'd been given by this pure Being's clear teachings, derived from ancient scriptures and her own Teacher's spiritual guidance, who had learned from his own Teacher a generation ago, and on and on, going back hundreds, thousands of generations of this same sacred relationship I had currently with mine: when a seeker surrenders to a true, ego-less Teacher.

When I met my Teacher, guided by her imparted wisdom, I recognized how to root out my own anger and sadness that was stuck deep within my psyche, my soul. From the first moment I saw and heard her, the Teacher demonstrated *believability* to me. She spoke the language I needed to hear, in a way I could understand the Truth I'd been seeking. My first act as student of the Teacher, was to forgive myself, and then my parents, for the shortcomings we had. I did this as soon as I realized forgiveness and acceptance were key to Self-realization.

△

So here we were, full circle. Kara and I, waiting to register in the vestibule of the ashram, my Teacher's home, where I was bringing my Angel Daughter, who no doubt thought me as incapable of knowing her as I believed the same about my own mother. In my mid-thirties when I met the Teacher, I only then realized how important it is for any person who wishes to know inner peace, to forgive—for every perceived slight or misdeed—even an un-forgiveable evil. Doing the meditative work the Teacher taught, I was led to the unseen world that resides right alongside our everyday one. And soon, my rusted-shut heart was spontaneously pried opened, by learning to forgive, then love myself.

Ever since Kara, so many years before, saw the Teacher standing next to me in the dream she'd had the night before we met, I'd longed for my Angel Girl to meet her, this luminous, enlightened person, not at all a *normal* woman *to me*. From the way she always affected me since I'd first met her fourteen years earlier, she was indeed, a Great Being. She changed the direction of my life. I longed to share with my daughter the inner bliss the Teacher showed me that is every human's birthright.

Gifted teachers have been guiding seekers since we humans learned to walk upright. From the beginning of humankind, according to cave paintings and rock carvings' records of our earliest quests, every individual desires a mainline connection to the Divine—sooner or later.

△

In her first talk after we arrived at the ashram, while Kara was off at an ashram meeting for a teens orientation, the Teacher greeted the hushed, expectant crowd around her.

"The real triumph," she said, "about being born homo sapiens—people think that means we know so much and are so wise—but really it's our chance to evolve into *homo spiritus*." She laughed uproariously. "Homo spiritus," the Teacher said, catching her breath, "are we who have chosen to live from a higher, spiritual point of reference; we have chosen to be at One with our Better-me."

I too chuckled. I owed her so much, this Teacher who had shown me how to focus on my mind's powerful ability, once it was cleared of the junk that used to disturb it. I'd tried everything to find peace and happiness myself, on my own. But I was lucky. I'm one of those who found a perfect teacher, despite having resisted instruction for far too long.

When the student's ready …

Thus … my Teacher appeared … when I put down chemically altering my natural mind. Instantaneously, by being in her mere presence, this Teacher awakened my Kundalini energy, which had been lying patiently, awaiting its time to be activated behind that rusted-shut, old garden-gate heart of mine since my early teens. Just as I'd seen Kara's heart had closed to me.

Now I wanted to give Kara, as the ultimate welcome-to-womanhood experience (given by my own Teacher)—the meditative approach to life—my preferred avenue of connecting to our inner, spiritual nature. The Teacher's skill could help Kara to recognize the sacred in everyday life. I knew this much.

Every one of us several thousand seekers who were gathered at the ashram in the beautiful New England countryside on this glorious day, were there because we wanted to experience inner peace, or deepen our already existing connection to Aum. Yet it was clear to me that some of the rebellious teens, found in every crowd—their smiles askew, sporting combed-out punkish hairdos, emptied for now of their ear and nose studs, chewed-off fingernails with remnants of black nail polish, snarky faces made behind parents' backs about all this Hindu-*schmindu* guru crap—were there only because they'd been forced to come.

Earlier, as we left Luna's, I'd seen Kara's back hunch up again against the passenger door. And in that position she remained until we drove through the ashram's open gates. Her one ritualized glance into spiritual womanhood the night before at Luna's, done and over.

As she and I brought our suitcases to the spotlessly minimal two-person bedroom, I wondered if Kara would end up being one of those rebel teens I'd noticed on our way in. I hated to admit it, but I knew she sadly pretty much already was. Just like I'd been too, rejecting their 'rents just to spite them.

As soon as she could, the very next hour in fact, Kara magnetically glommed on to this small group of teens, whom I came to call the *wolf pack*. Not allowed to be punked-out now because of the ashram dress code, that didn't stop them from roaming the serenely tidy grounds like hungry howlers on the prey, doing whatever they wanted, knowing full well the retreat's demanding guidelines applied to everyone.

The spiritualizing of Kara started off badly, I'm afraid. She failed to report in with me at the certain times of day as we'd prearranged, per ashram family policy. By day two of our five-day visit, she was off with the wolf pack all day, only checking in with me at mealtimes, and only because it was mandatory for teens to eat with their guardians.

She promised she'd do better. But I never knew where Kara actually was. I'd see her off in the distance, roaming the manicured hills with her all-guy pack, her homeys. At least she'd be safe on the ashram's hundred-acre park-like grounds, I figured. Here at this spiritual sanctuary, I had to trust that Kara would gain whatever experiences she needed. We get what we need in life, I knew that. Kara was creating her own special memories—her version of her soul's spiritual awakening—by resisting it, I duly noted.

On the third day of our stay Kara surprised me, stating she was excited to participate in the required teen workshop. *Expand Your Consciousness* (the announcement read) *by Befriending Your Better-me*. She wanted to chant and meditate with every teen in residence, up to the twenty-one-year-olds. None of the rogue pack was exempt from this mandatory gathering. For an entire morning, every young adult was shown easy ways to go through the invisible portal within, to meet and befriend their inner self, their Better-me.

As we prepared for sleep that night, I noticed a change in Kara. She was less touchy about things that usually ticked her off. Odd, I thought, how unusually calm she was, with a mysteriously serene look that made her naturally beautiful face even more aglow. The next morning, she shared with me her dream of the night before, something she hadn't done in ages. There was wonder in her voice as she sleepily, un-self-consciously related the details.

As she spoke, it clearly struck me that this dream of hers described a spiritual awakening: a sudden and shocking and—as real as can-be—connection to a "power within me that blows my mind," she said in genuine amazement. From her bed, she spoke as if still in that dream, our eyes meeting for what seemed the first time since the purple-paint handprint incident. I sat straight up in my bed, listening closely, looking over at Kara's notably intensified radiance.

"In my dream I was sitting face-to-face, talking quietly to the Teacher," she said. "She was telling me things I'd never heard before, but it was like I knew them already, everything she said."

After relaying a few more dreamt interactions she'd had with the Teacher, Kara went still, quietly remembering, reflecting.

"How'd the dream feel to you?" I softly asked, noting how much like the old Phil I sounded.

"Good," she said. "Real good."

Then she said she couldn't remember anything else about it. Her stillness spoke far more than words could.

I asked, "Do you want me to tell you my impression of what you've just shared?"

"Sure," Kara said. "I know dreams are a big deal to you and Dad, and Grandpa."

I laughed. "Well, not the crazy nonsensical ones. Only dreams that seem to convey a message interest us."

"Do you think the one I told you is like that?"

"I do," I said. She'd told me enough to say this with assurance.

"Like what kind of message, do you think?" she asked, perking up.

"What do you think it might be, Kara? Do you think the Teacher was saying something specifically to you or—"

"Oh," she said, pumped by her remembering, "she definitely was! But I don't know what. I've never felt that way, not in a dream or awake. The Teacher made everything ... simple things, seem greater, bigger, more intense, somehow. I can't explain."

"You don't have to, sweetie," I said, glad to have her confidence back, if only for a few precious moments.

Kara looked at me and smiled. I knew what this dream was. She'd been introduced by her own dream state to the upward-heading, tsunami-like power of expanded consciousness, her Better-me.

She and I were having the longest talk we'd had since ... well, a long time. She lying, me sitting up in our own beds across from each other, chatting, felt heavenly. Then Kara remembered something else.

"I saw a gate, with a light behind it," she said, recalling more, her eyes closed, as if seeing the vision before her. "The Teacher was there on the other side, smiling at me as I walked through, and toward her, into a brighter Light."

I did not speak anymore. This precious moment was too special to ruin with words.

Later, we went to breakfast and ate quietly together, whispering, as ashram guidelines called for during meals. I was happy for Kara, because her dream clearly said to me that the part of herself she'd hidden away, her Big Heart as the Teacher called the place where Better-me resides, wanted so badly to be unlocked. At the table she spoke softly, not disrespectfully or loudly arguing like our trip's previous days. She'd returned to her old joking-around self with me. My laughing heart felt as if I'd crossed a barren desert and had just been handed a mouthful of refreshing water to drink, by my kind and helpful daughter.

Then—as unexpectedly as she'd opened up to me that morning, that very special morning—Kara rushed to finish eating, jumped up and waved to her pack that was exiting the cafeteria.

"Cutting-edge yoga brats, we call ourselves," she laughed loudly as she ran to join them.

The last day of our stay I'd planned to be the zenith of our entire celebratory Girl-to-Woman trip. We would attend an afternoon-long session at which the Teacher would give her students from around the globe, a special, final dharma talk. We'd start the afternoon by combining our thousands-strong voices in an opening chant; and we'd end, after hearing the Teacher's always perfectly attuned insights, with a meditation as deep as an ocean trench, as high as the clear blue sky. I'd been to many of these annual extravaganzas. I knew exactly how the Teacher would arrive in the crammed hall after everyone had been comfortably seated and settled in. Then, after the opening chant, she'd deliver the anticipated, transporting message for which we'd all come so far to hear.

After the Teacher's daytime talk, there'd be more evening chants, more meditations, celebrations and rituals. Bliss goes on endlessly in ashrams of Great Beings.

In the hall, you could slice the anticipation with a knife.

Everyone was quietly assigned a spot in the meditation hall; first come, best place. The custom was for each student to bring a cushion or blanket to accommodate their own level of comfort for sitting on the hard marble floor.

Finally, my Angel Daughter would get to meet my revered Teacher! My vision, my hope, was for the Teacher's and Kara's eyes to make direct contact—traditionally considered the surest way of awakening a seeker's heart, *a look* second only to having *the touch*, like I'd had been blessed to have. In this way, I hoped that Kara's Better-me would be awakened, and her Kundalini awakened, as mine had when the Teacher ritually pressed my third eye, the same year of Kara's birth. I dared to dream such an up-close, energetic initiation might occur between their two sets of eyes. Determined to make this happen—if such a thing were possible—I set out to get Kara seated as close to the Teacher's expected line of sight, unobstructed by others.

And—because I was familiar with the setup of this annual event I'd often attended—I knew exactly where to get us properly seated in order to make that hoped-for glance happen.

I motioned Kara to follow me. "Gather your cushion and blanket," I whispered.

Stealthily, I shepherded her to first one, then quickly, another empty space, finding the best two seats I could that were close enough to the side aisle, where I knew the revered meditation master would soon enter the hall. I knew the Teacher liked to enter sauntering down this particular side aisle. It looked out onto the hilly Vermont countryside, where she could see the rushing brook outside the floor-to-ceiling glass window wall.

Just as we were claiming our seats and spreading our blanket on the floor, a stern-looking, dark-haired hall monitor approached. Her face appeared stormy, her ankle-length silk dress swishy. She completely caught me off-guard.

"I've been watching you," her voice and eyes all steely. "And if you move one more time I'm going to ask you to leave the hall," she hissed.

I spun and stood face to face with her. "Oh, please, don't do that! I'm doing this for my daughter, here" indicating Kara. I implored the unsmiling, overdressed woman. "She's never met the Teacher. Please, I know it's terrible to change seats. I've never done this in all the years I've been coming here. You recognize me; I know you. I promise we won't move again. Kara *really needs* to see the Teacher up close. I'm sorry because I know it looks bad, but it's not. It's good, trust me: the Teacher would approve."

The monitor's black eyes narrowed, sizing me up. Her rouged face turned a shade darker. "We'll see," she said. Abruptly turning, she stalked away. I don't think she recognized me.

▲

And perfect timing, too, because at that exact moment, bending over to arrange my pillow, I heard a preternatural hush came over the excited crowd, a signal the Teacher had just appeared. Suddenly the rustle of people stopped all around us. Now standing, I turned around, and glimpsed the familiar sheen of white silk robes as she glided down the aisle, nodding to people, receiving, sending tangible but unseen transmissions of the energy that emanates from a person with a fully realized consciousness. In the Teacher's mere presence, I always feel my mind precisely attune to her frequency, the exchange of invisible energy is that strong between us.

Unaware of anything happening, Kara was bent over fussing with her pile of cushions. Her back was to me and to the approaching wave of power, the Teacher unseen by her. With both hands, I bent over and gently grabbed Kara's shoulders. Wordlessly, I twirled my charge to face the other way, putting her in front of me. At that precise instant, I saw the Teacher, now less than six feet away, looking right at Kara and me, with full recognition on her captivating face.

As if the Teacher had waited for me to guide Kara to that precise spot, my hoped-for encounter happened. My audacious moves, and now, we two—standing amid a sea of seated seekers—captured the Teacher's attention.

An intimate, time-stilling contact—that seemed to last for all eternity—happened with impeccable attunement to Aum.

I gently held Kara in front of me, my hands on her thin shoulders, her small back leaning against my chest as if a strong wind was blowing into her. We stood in our spot amid that huge sitting, pulsating, humming throng. The next moments hung in the air—for lifetimes. To me, the Teacher appeared to stand motionless for countless frozen eons. Her dark eyes looked deeply into mine, then— she shifted her penetrating focus directly onto Kara's go-green eyes. She gave my Angel Girl a nod. I saw her acknowledging gaze linger ... in blissful recognition. Then she looked again at me and nodded, her expression conveying how she knew full well the reason the two of us were standing there, alone, among thousands of other blissed-out beings happily seated on their cushions.

Without a word, the orb of Light glided past us in a whoosh of diamond-glow brilliance.

△

Kara now had the same kind of direct contact with this energy-transmitter as I'd had, fourteen years earlier. What I'd received, back then, because I was finally ready for it, was a radio beacon finely attuned to Grace that constantly emits from this Teacher. It was her inherited role, from her Teacher's sacred initiation, to spread this awakening power to all who sought it. Her glance penetrated me like a sword, slicing through my lifelong denial, my arrogance, my fear. *That* had been my precise moment of awakening. I'd experienced a wave of bliss that words can never describe, back when I first met the Teacher. Sustaining it became my daily task, as all seekers know: to experience true contentment takes work. Now I was watching my daughter receive this same great boon; having the same choice as I have with each new day.

My long-planned mission was accomplished! In that precious instant—my purpose for bringing Kara here, as the highlight of our Girl-to-Woman trip, to this authentic meditation center located in a nowhere-town in upstate Vermont—I felt my spiritual role as Angel Mom to Kara had been fulfilled, a *fait accompli*.

I sat down on my pillow, took a deep breath, and relaxed, utterly satisfied. Looking over at Kara, I saw how fascinated, serenely dazzled she was. My daughter's eyes followed the Teacher's every move; up the aisle, into her seat, watching her acknowledge everyone with small bows and nods, glancing in all directions. With the most intrigued look on her face I'd ever seen, Kara remained unmoving, silently absorbing the Teacher's presence. Smiling in wordless, indescribable joy.

By the end of the opening chant, Kara had straightened her crooked back. She listened intently to the Teacher's velvety voice as she gave her dharma talk. Everyone's attention turned inward, listening to explicit instructions on how to still the mind; doing short focusing exercises together; discovering more about the inner Source and how to elevate one's consciousness: deepening our connection to Better-me.

▲

"The whole world," our Teacher began, "is affected by each and every choice we make. Each person is a perfect microcosm of the entire Universe. We are all connected to one another, and to all in existence by pure, untainted consciousness. Within each of us is that same spiritual power contained in, for example, every small seed of the most gigantic tree. Every single drop of water—from the most insignificant cloudy mud puddle to the most stupendous crystalline waterfall—has the same power within it; the same power of the combined deep oceans resides in a single drop of water. We must remember this as we go about our days, working our jobs, raising our families, talking on our cell-phones, making choices, taking on life's next challenges.

"Never forget that you—every one of us here today, and those not here as well, and all of Nature—are connected. To best experience this is why we meditate. This is why we honor God within, to recognize that our human consciousness is Divine: to cultivate our Better-me. To make this world a better place to live in. This is why we are here today."

Hours later we left the hall in a trance-like contentment, but it seemed we'd been there for only minutes. My Angel Girl and I had quieted our busy minds—together—following the Teacher's instructions to a deeper meditative state than we could get to on our own. It was astounding, seeing Kara as interested as I was, a feat I hardly imagined possible could ever come true, yet ... it was really happening. I'd successfully navigated each hurdle, every obstacle as it arose on this deep, oh-so-blue deep-water section of Rio Blisso we were cruising upon.

At that moment I felt, more than ever, certain that it was my destiny to have been this girl's Angel Mom. If for no other reason than to introduce her to the Teacher, whose path had helped me make sense of The Mystery, the meaning of Life It-self. She, who'd unlocked my own shut-down heart, had now touched my daughter's as well. Whether or not Kara would even remember what had happened here, didn't matter. What did matter was how the Teacher's awakening glance would resound in her heart forever. Even if Kara never opened and walked through the portal of divine awareness again, to follow the energy and explore what had just happened to her.

△

The next day Kara was polite and reserved as we drove the long concrete ribbon that stretched west-to-east across the breadth of New York state. Finally, we reached Niagara Falls, where my older sister Lizzy lived. For the grand finale of her coming-of-age journey, I wanted Kara to experience the thundering celebration of Earth's overpowering magnificence. I took her to where water met earth and sky, a place where animals, plants, and humans and all creatures coexist in perfect harmony. This special place, where Nature converges so forcefully, is where ancient and oftentimes warring Native American tribes came together to enjoy its bounty, always respectfully guarding its peaceful sanctity. Here, at least in earlier times, First Nation people congregating in our country's northeast agreed to put aside their conflicts. Likewise, all power spots must be revered by all peoples: political, cultural, and religious, enemies and friends alike.

Niagara Falls, its overwhelming power always stuns me.

I sensed the oxygenated air, the aerated intensity of tons of water dispersing, before I heard the roar. Coming closer, I could taste the difference in the mist surrounding this sacred spot, its old forests of pines and oaks overwhelming both Kara and me with its dizzying beauty and vastly different visceral sensuality. The noise! The feel of water in the air! The smell of stringent pine opening my nostrils.

As we approached the falls, the thunderous roar resonated a deep drumbeat in every cell of my body—a unique, holy sensation I also experienced when I rafted through the deep gorges of the Grand Canyon, or sailed a star-guided course far out on the empty ocean, or dove the psychedelic-pizazz underwater cliffs of the Red Sea—meeting Nature head-on like this. Visiting Niagara is hearing-seeing-feeling Truth manifested on earth. Places such as these, where Nature rules supreme, humbles me, weakens my knees, reminds me that no matter how much we humans try messing around with being stewards of our planet, our highest duty is to protect Nature, she who sustains and teaches us, our true Mother, the Earth itself.

Nature, the best, most trusted Teacher of all.

The first glance of gigantic, far-reaching Niagara Falls brought a flood of remembrance to my soul.

For my dazed daughter's benefit, I paraphrased, out loud, some of my favorite words. The words of early Native American leaders are right up there with *So 'hăm, So 'hăm*.

"Chief Seattle warned the European invaders back in 1854," I shared with Kara this early teacher of mine. "'The Earth does not belong to man, man belongs to the Earth. Whatever man does to the web of life, he does to himself.'"

She didn't respond. Maybe the words got lost in the roar of the falls before us.

The Teacher's message had been remarkably similar, so I used her words next, speaking aloud again.

"Just like the Teacher said yesterday: 'We're all connected: Nature includes all of earth's people.'" I spoke against the rush of the falls' watery wind surrounding us. "Just imagine, Kara! We're all One consciousness: the water, us. This is why I brought you here, Kara, to help us both remember. To feel the water's, the earth's power."

Kara paid no attention. She shrugged, then turned and walked away.

On her own, I let her absorb the sensual display of Niagara's mighty roar. Silently, I continued to implore and honor Nature, all the ancient Ones, all humankind's gods and goddesses: Gaia, Shakti, Pachamama, Mother-Father-God, all the protecting Unseens that bestow grace upon we flesh-and-blood mortals. I called upon guardians, known and unknown, from everywhere, past-present-future—this was my silent prayer:

Please help my dear Angel Daughter retain an open heart and mind. Let her choose to stay awakened.

△

From a distance, I watched Kara's back hunch-up in her regular shut-down mode. Staying far from me, I witnessed her resume her familiar closed-clam, withdrawn snail-shell demeanor.

After all I'd shared with her—it seemed nothing, absolutely nothing!—had changed since we left Lackland, ten days earlier. Aside from experiencing a few heightened moments, Kara didn't appear to be any different now, not at all. Not transformed by Luna's two-day ritual ceremony; not by Gail's artistic, anti-materialistic lifestyle; not by the majesty of Niagara's breathtaking beauty. Even after that personal encounter with the Teacher I'd somehow orchestrated. Kara's teenage angst seemed to have won out over every transcendent experience I'd attempted to lay out before her.

To my sister Lizzy and her family, Kara was her usual sweet self, expressing interest in everything they shared. But to me—once more, her heart-door slammed shut.

After we returned home, I would discover that every picture on the rolls of film I'd taken of Kara at Niagara showed her in a bright yellow *Maid of the Mist* rain slicker, scowling, hunched over, arms crossed, directing all her loathing right at me behind the camera. Better-me knew—even as I snapped each photo that showed Kara's allergic reaction to everything I did or said to her—that it wasn't her fault, not really. This loathing of hers toward me, was all just part of her journey. I had to accept her as she was, I reminded myself. But that didn't stop her rejecting me from hurting.

Each photo I snapped, when Kara would turn from laughing and joking with Lizzy and her family, showed her shooting me a disgusting look, sending an arrow right through my chest. The developed snaps were proof of what I had to accept. Her slit-eyed scorn again sliced my wide-open heart to pieces. When would I learn?

My job now, as her nurturer, was to accept that I had no power over this Angel Girl's negativity toward me. I had to just watch it, and pray it would dissolve, in time.

So unfair, I groaned, the old hurt screaming in between my heroic repetitions of *So'ham, So'ham*. That fucking monkey-mind of mine hurled one more lump of its feces, right at Better-me's third eye.

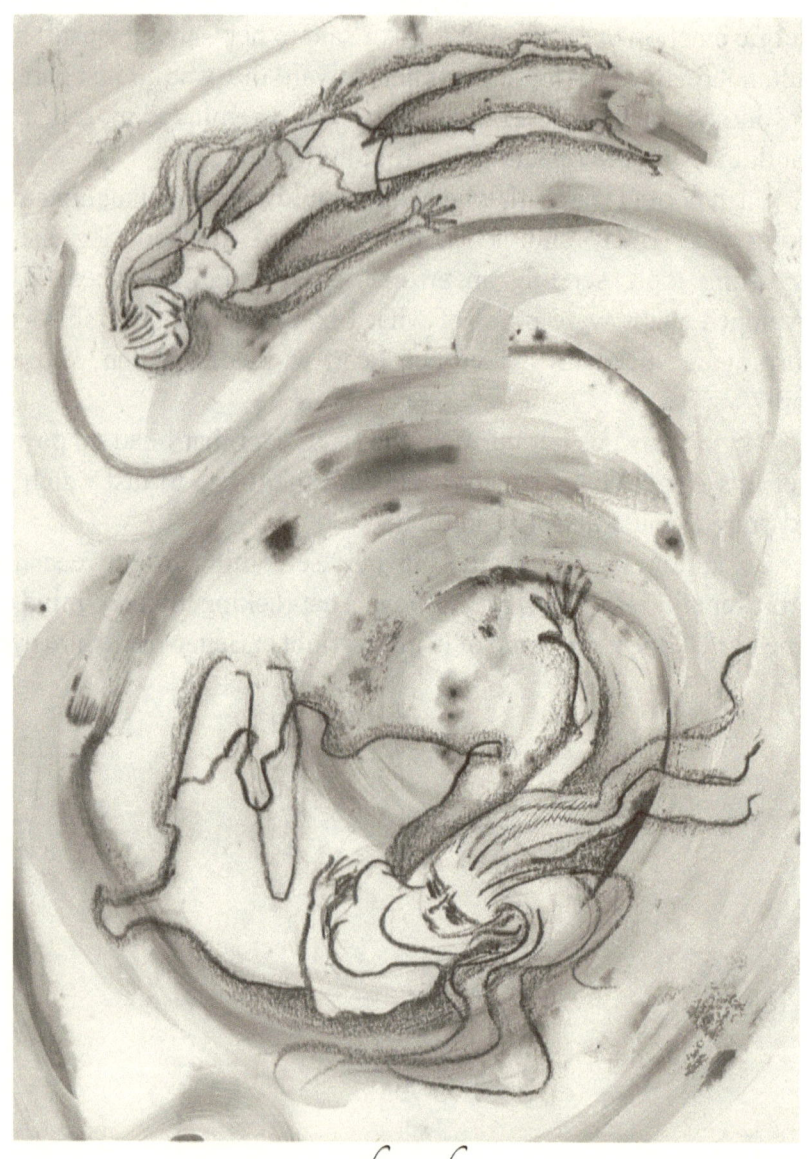
shipwreck

CHAPTER 23

shipwreck

Back in Lackland, I set out to create for Kara an arty memento of our time together. Secretly, I spent hours cutting out witty quotes from magazines, placing them alongside what few usable snaps there were of our trip, so many spoiled by Kara's tortoise-like, hunched-back shutdown. Painstakingly, I assembled the only photo album I'd ever made. "Kara's Girl-to-Woman Trip," I printed on its pink sparkly cover. This, I figured, would be a meaningful way to remember our shared experience of visiting earth-mama artist, a woman's-empowerment shaman, a world-class spiritual guide, and North America's most powerful energy vortex (tied with the Grand Canyon)—commemorating Kara's passage to adulthood.

The album made no allusion to our trip's darker moments. Piles of glossy rejected photos lay scattered around, from which I carefully chose the few with happy Kara in them. Each of the images I used, I made sure I wasn't in. I pasted the snapshots in nonsensical order, at wacky angles, adding sassy stickers and cool glittery materials, gluing some choice jazzy words cut from printed fonts, not in my handwriting. Among the hundred shots I'd developed in that pre-digital time, I used less than twenty, because that's all in which Kara wasn't scowling. On the last page of the album I included the one blurry shot I could find of me alongside my daughter—who stood not touching me, arms crossed over her chest, making a strained, half effort to smile at the camera held by Lizzy as we traveled over Niagara River in a gondola. I included it to prove I'd actually been there.

The secret album-making took me an entire week in between other chores. Presenting it to Kara I said, "We'll have a good laugh, looking at it together someday—maybe when you're a mom."

She took the album wordlessly from my hands, barely glancing at it. I shrugged my shoulders, chalked it up to teenage hormones and watched her turn and walk away.

Soon I would discover that Kara tore my time-consuming effort apart as soon as she got to her room, tossing its contents into her trashcan; not even bothering to hide this insulting act from me. Worse, she replaced the album's now-entirely empty plastic sheathes, with pictures of her own buds. My love offering, photos ripped to pieces, unwanted, in her room's trash bin, no effort to conceal her contempt.

"Why did you throw away something I made for you, with so much care?" I had to ask, struggling to understand. "Did you not know that would hurt me, terribly, Kara?"

She shrugged. "I don't know," she said, adding, "You don't have to rub my nose in it."

This is it, I thought. It's here. The day has come: my Kara-bottom.

I felt the wound of her words pierce me. I decided this had to be the last time. I couldn't afford another bout with my booze-dragon, he'd kill me for sure. There had to be no next time.

In my bedroom, I said it slowly, three different ways, as if to solemnly put a seal on it. My farewell to the memory of the gentle cheek-kissing Angel Girl who used to love me. She was lost to me—maybe not forever, but for right here and now, she was gone.

I vowed to put this hurt behind me, for Better-me's benefit. Silently I ordered myself to neither speak of, nor ever think about the too painful subject of Kara's rejecting me, ever again. Three times I whispered aloud, "Life has too many positives to let a few lousy negatives ruin things."

PART THREE

nearing port

CHAPTER 24

steady at the helm

Life would no longer be defined by any role I happened to be playing, I now determined.

Okay, I'm a female and I'm human, but other than those two factors, I wanted to be free of labels. Artist or seeker, my spirit would be free of restrictions to do what I needed to shake off any limitation I or anyone else stuck on me. All of them—I ordered gone! In particular, I needed to not think of myself as Angel Mom any longer. The kids were old enough, grounded enough, sort of, to not need me so much. Kara would soon be driving and out of the house most of the time. Jonny was already fully absorbed in his quest to be the best football kicker the world has ever known, was even more attached to his dad, his hero, and no longer needed me as he had before. My job now was to give myself permission to *just be*.

The Teacher had taught me that the best way to let go is by accepting *what is*. That's all I needed to do, to remember that. By remembering to accept myself, and others just as they are—this was the mother lode of truly being free. I did this by practicing, *remembering* to nurture Better-me. By accepting each new defect, I kept discovering about my own character (and they seemed to pop up from every upturned rock), I could only hope that one day I might be able to accept the rest of life exactly as it is.

In this peaceful core of mental detachment, I continued to learn about acceptance, and practiced continuously. Detachment became my newly revised, sanctified form of household yoga. Not letting the everyday, small stuff get stuck in my craw, I'd take a deep breath and press my third eye, firmly commanding Better-me: *Detach!*

Some days, I had to do this thousands of times, it seemed.

△

Pain creates the need for seeking shelter from the storms of life. Without emotional pain, detachment isn't possible. I learned how much effort detachment takes. I learned that it's an art, and like any other art form, like playing an instrument or speaking a new language, it takes time to perfect. I won't lie; learning to detach became a full-time obsession. I had to detach, you see, or else my dragon might reawaken; I knew this with all certainty.

The Teacher had said: Aum reigns over chaos.

With lots of practice, others' trials and torments as well as my own could no long throw me off the epicenter of the Better-me bliss I'd tasted, and was now addicted to. Best of all—when I operated from a detached state of mind, I was most useful to myself and others.

Floating down Rio Blisso on Aum's invisible, companion-rescue vessel—named *Detachment*—I imagined the process of detaching from my disturbed emotions as if floating in a safe, luxurious raft, a lifeboat of sorts, that's always tied closely to my family's cruising vessel. In this way, by hopping right into my life raft, caring for myself was always available when needed. No longer was I deeply, emotionally drawn in anymore, by either Will's, Kara's, Jonny's, or Phil's needs.

I was learning to think with a steady heart, not an emotion-fueled head.

My imaginary life raft was attached to, yet separate from, our action-packed, dramatically overloaded family boat that often seemed to be careening wildly out of control; always at odds with my efforts at trying to steer it through Rio Blisso's oncoming, ever-oncoming, strong cross currents.

Times like these, the drama-filled family crisis times, it was easier to turn the tiller over to Mr. Know-it-All Will, jump into my imaginary, tethered-to-our-sailboat life raft, and separate myself from the goings-on of family strife. This is how I practice detachment:

Press my third eye and envision myself hopping into my imaginary detachment-lifeboat, and easily glide away from the chaos of each new crisis. I swore to remain in this metaphoric, completely aware-of-reality, yet uber-unaffected-by, spiritually-safe emergency craft, to which I'd cling for dear life—at a safe psychic distance from every next drama.

In time, with practice, with each new crisis, this detachment ritual became easier.

The safe raft of detachment became my survival tool, even when the waters of Rio Blisso started to really heat up and churn in turmoil.

Running away was no longer an option, either from Lackland, a feral teen, or my hard-won measure of emotional serenity. Instead, I stayed close, but no longer reactive to the endless episodes of my family's drama, or the ongoing conflicts of an insane world all around me. Happily, I found I could stay in my heart-realm this way. I didn't need to yell *Rebellion!* get high, or run away ever again. Our blended family thrived on our main vessel with Aum at the helm while I stayed a safe and secure length apart, tied to them in my trailing life raft of easeful, loving, and more effective nurturing, thanks to cool and calm detachment. If I hadn't learned how to do this, using the Teacher's and Dr. C's guidance, quite possibly I probably would have lost my grip on sanity, as I'd done earlier in my marriage, and had nearly done at the end of Kara's and my trip.

By learning how to distance myself emotionally, but still be loving and kind and available to anyone in my family who asked for my assistance I chose not to become one of today's countless anti-anxiety, anti-depression or anti- whichever spectrum of whatsits disorder that script-users cover.

This new challenge of healthy detachment was teaching me how to open the door to my inner Light even further. I wasn't numbing or fighting pain, fleeing from my fright-or-flight monkey-mind, the amygdala part, deep within every human brain's primordial center that we share with other primates and our prehistoric ancestors. When that "old" section of our brain is allowed to be in control, it's definitely a bummer. That's when people are more fearful, reacting animal-like.

In my pre-spiritual, still-asleep life, Lesser-me was prone to follow that animalistic mentality. Before detaching became my best recourse to keeping serene and sane, my remedy to stress—once booze and drugs went bye-bye—was curling into a fetal position on the floor, preferably behind a locked door, so I could let the screams and inner terrors out without disturbing others. Or others knowing I was such a basket case. I never cried, but shivered and shook for as long as the know-I'm-dying fear took to pass. Before I learned to detach in my imaginary life raft, those old killer blues kept trying, however, sporadically, to take me down. I was desperate enough to know real contentment, and knew the dragon of Nameless Fear still frothed inside me, waiting patiently for me to let my guard down—so I kept practicing detachment.

Replacing the next arising bout of fear or resentment with a cool mental visualization of me floating in Bahamian-clear blue waters, relaxed and coolly detached in my solo raft, tethered closely, a heartbeat's length away from the family in the bigger craft, easy to manage, completely safe … until … in the spirit of faking-it-till-making-it, I started to realize that the most nurturing kind of love I could offer, required this spiritual safety-net—of being compassionately detached.

△

When he turned thirteen, I asked Jonny if he'd like to learn how to meditate. He answered half-heartedly, "Sure, why not?" Giving him a lesson on how to still his mind was my pleasure to gift him for that birthday. We walked to Grandpa's pasture next to our house, empty except for Mr. Bull and his grazing herd, all twenty-something bovine heads facing the same direction off in the distance. As we walked we reminisced about how we'd had to tie a pink plastic bag around Bruno the CBD's neck in this same pasture, to slow him down once, many years before. Angel Son and I settled down in the sweet-smelling tall grass. The sun warmed our faces as I taught him how to tap into his inner serenity, the energy of Oneness.

"Let's get comfortable first. Then, when you're ready, we'll close our eyes. Good. Let's breathe-in real long and real slow. And we'll breathe-out the same way. Now, keep taking in air deeply and then ... release it slowly. Let no other thoughts be in your mind, other than following your breath, in and out. Relax with your breathing. That's right, Jonny. Now, in your mind repeat this after me. Silently, softly say *So'* on the in-breath ... and *hăm* on the out-breath. This is an ancient tool to still the mind, a holy mantra. *So'hăm* is the mind-quieting technique my Teacher gave me. Let's sit now and watch our breath and repeat the mantra silently."

Jonny followed my instructions. He was very trusting. Totally chilled. After a few minutes I whispered, "You can open your eyes anytime now."

"Wow," he said, in his recently changed, lower register. "That was weird."

I laughed.

"Now I know why you're always mediating, teZ. That was awesome. I feel all still inside. Like, nothing bothers me. It's weird."

I laughed again. "Yes, but a good weird, right?"

Later, Will took him on his coming-of-age journey, along with a good pal and his son, who was exactly Jonny's age. They went on a ten-day fishing trip deep into Canada's wilderness. Riding into the backwoods on horseback, the two fathers-and-sons lived rough'n'tough in tents, cooked over a campfire, and threw back into the stream all the catch-and-release trout they couldn't eat.

Will showed Jonny more about how to enjoy surviving in Nature. The other father-son team was another story entirely, not at all experienced in the outdoors. To accommodate their greenhorn companions, Will hired a guide to handle the horses and lead the party far from any town, road, or grocery store. The guide also served as the group's cook, although everyone pitched in to help.

When Jonny returned home, I could tell there'd been a major shift within him.

He hugged me and laughed in his new deep voice, "I didn't see Sasquatch, teZ." He knew I'd ask about the hairy man-beast who'd fascinated both him and his father since boyhood.

"Ah well, maybe next time," I smiled.

They'd done something both fun and grown-up. Will modeled for his son a respectful stewardship for all things wild. On many earlier occasions, Will had shown Jonny how to be comfortable with who he is, to appreciate the joy of being who he is, and laugh at life, outside or inside. Because to Will and me too, a sense of humor is the best way to measure how close a person is to Spirit. Come to think of it, that's one of the main appeals I find about the Teacher.

△

In everyday life, not just on trips, Will showed Jonny how to follow his bliss. From budding filmmaker to suburban dad, Will was a change-maker. He'd created each new iteration of himself (and livelihood) by planting his positive thought-seeds, and good honest hard work, lessons every father ought to share with his children.

"Go where you feel God the most," I know Will told Jonny up in the Canadian wilderness, just like he always told both kids at home. "Be true to yourself and your life will unfold as it should."

△

I was getting pretty good at this keep-cool, float on the raft-thing. I was on my way to crowning myself the Queen of Detachment, having chosen, many times over, to not allow hurt in my heart from others, ever again. One thing became eminently clear to me during this period. Acceptance is the real name of forgiveness. Without acceptance—the kind with absolutely no strings, neither resentments nor expectations—detachment is impossible. I found that out the hard way.

Before the Teacher demonstrated how to embrace Aum, while I was learning to forgive Lesser-me for all the lowlife schemes I'd subjected Better-me to, I'd never been able to fully grasp the meaning of unconditional love. Before detachment's safety net, unless I was on some grand adventure—soaking under some warm tropical waterfall where no one could find me, merging with Nature's unspeakable awe—I really thought I'd never find happiness in ordinary life. Then the Teacher taught me the secret to real joy: I learned to let go of people, places and things that hurt me, by accepting them. And that process, however long it takes to heal the heart's hurt, is true forgiveness.

▲

With each passing year, our chances of ever leaving Lackland, had become increasingly unrealistic, especially after Phil's divorce. I had to accept I was in this dreaded place *for the duration*. Even if Phil hadn't needed us—which he did, but only in small, infrequent doses, thanks to his competent caretakers—the kids were much too involved with their teenage friends for us to yank them away during this crucial time of life. We couldn't add more setbacks, which the newness of a move would be, to alter their steady embrace of emotional independence and security.

No matter. I was dedicated to Phil. Often, when I spelled the caretaker by sitting with him, out of the blue the old man I was so fond of would say in a moment of mental clarity, "I get a lot of pleasure seeing the lights on, down there at your house, teZa."

But no longer did we have discussions, about dreams or anything else. Phil's mind wandered the restless plains of a dimension unknown to any but him. I'd sit comfortably next to his lounge chair, and smile, listening as he'd sing one more of the silly racy ditties from his youth. Without saying a word, he'd break-out in a completely new melody, his crackling, ripped, and paper-thin voice warbling unsteadily, verse after verse of funny and complicated stories of a simpler, bygone era. His songs made me, and anyone else lucky enough to hear them, stop and wonder at the stunning capacity of a lifetime's worth of memories. His face unmoved, Phil sung without interruption with quiet, peaceful, emotionless recall, as if each of the unceasing songs were directly linked to an inner chamber of his fun-time memory bank. Phil's croaky baritone fascinated all who heard him. He'd never sung before, ever! Not in all the years I'd visited, back when Claire was alive, and certainly not during his time with gloomy Dolores. Each song was completely different, his repertoire as vast as the wrinkles on Phil's face, his unmoving features never betraying any feeling as he sang …

> *On a lovely day in early May,*
> *Betty Sue and I did pay*
> *A visit to the old … brick … church*
> *But before the Preacher did it*
> *Before we did it … I raised my glass to say …*

A dozen complicated, precisely recited verses later, not realizing I was leaning up closely right next to him to hear better, Phil's half-there sound abruptly stopped. He opened his squeezed-tight eyes and reverted once more to silently, steadily gazing at the crackling fire in the hearth before him.

▲

I continued driving back and forth to Sarasota, transforming neglected properties into rentals, so we'd have enough funds when it came time for us to leave Lackland. While Will took his now-completed film to as many festivals as it won entry, my traveling away from home during the week gave me the physical distance, along with my raft's emotional detachment, to keep seeing things more clearly.

This is how I came to realize that Kara had inadvertently, and quite preposterously, become the next important teacher I needed in life.

Ironic, I thought, how those things that bring us the biggest headaches and heart punches, also bring us our most essential lessons.

As soon as I let go of holding onto any expectations—about Kara ever grooving with me, about myself as an artist-writer with important work to share, about being a useful, nurturing sort of person—things got surprisingly easier just as our family began to navigate the increasingly turbulent, trembling-with-expectation waters right ahead of our boat.

CHAPTER 25

oh, starry night

We visited Phil as often as we could. These days, he slouched instead of sat in his overstuffed La-Z-Boy, drifting in and out of a muddled yet peaceful state. Sometimes he'd give up speaking mid-syllable. He appeared lost in his own memories, too distracted by them to share with anyone. Had he Alzheimer's or common elderly dementia? It didn't matter. With every visit, Will and I noticed Phil weakening, mentally and physically.

Although his frame was melting away, spiritually Phil remained a giant, a living icon. Sometimes he was lucid enough so I could share about a dream I'd had. But no more questions came from him. Nothing like before when we'd plunge into the depths of the subconscious, exchanging insights. Now, I sat patiently close by his side on a stool, sharing just for the sake of sharing, a dream or a thought, my intermittent burst of words never answered, neither of us needing or wanting anything, both of us staring in silence for long periods at the flickering flames.

Summer and winter, Phil's fireplace constantly crackled. Outside between two tall pines, a cord of firewood was stacked and curing. We made sure there was enough wood on hand for Phil to always be mesmerized by a fire—from the moment he finished breakfast, to when he retired at night. Even though the house was temperature controlled in all seasons, Phil's pleasure was having a three-log fire going, no matter what.

When I asked, "How's it going, Phil," he gave the same lame response: "Well, I'm still in the ring."

We'd both chuckle. I looked at my friend's papery-wrinkled face, his watery eyes whose fading blue still sparkled, reflecting the hard-earned easeful rest that was now his. Sometimes Phil would burst forth with another ditty without changing his sunken pose, as if his body were a mushroom that was slowly deteriorating right before me, where he sat in the lounge chair. With no emotion but without faltering on a single word, he sang:

Oh I grabbed a girl
and gave her a whirl
and took her for
a ride on the bay, hey!

The tune went on for at least ten stanzas, each one a marvel of Phil's rekindled-fire of long-ago memory. He must have learned all these songs before marrying Claire and settling down, perhaps at college drinking parties, we figured. Phil just shrugged when asked. His frequent visitors were amazed he could remember so many and such varied songs, surprisingly complex verses from three-quarters of a century ago, so effortlessly—yet not recall what he'd had for breakfast minutes before.

With a bony hand covering his eyes, Phil sang another stanza, his body slumped in the sweet surrender of euphoria.

Yes I took her hand
and gave it a squeeze
And she looked to me
as the gentlest breeze, hey!

He was reliving his generation's tradition of belting out a verse for each white-mustached slurp of the next round of beer getting slugged back. Gathering from the impressive amount of songs Phil knew, he must have been quite a frosty mug enthusiast in his day. Hearing his crackling, wobbly warble made me smile as I sat close to him, pleasantly amused by the unhesitant, but unlively meting-out of each new song. When he finished, he went quiet, sinking further into his easy chair, bygone dreams floating in his head, weighing him down like an anchor. The old man no longer had to sleep to be present in his dream state.

Will was the first to notice the mark when it appeared in the middle of his father's forehead.

"Dad, you've got a third eye popping out there."

"No kidding," Phil said, touching the spot between his eyebrows to ascertain if something had changed overnight.

Indeed, the old man's forehead had sprouted a distinguishable mark, an orb. It might have been a liver spot but it was in the same exact place, slightly above and between the brows that East Indians mark with red, black, or white dots of powder, sometimes with sparkly glue-on decorations. Religious Catholics get marked in the same place on Ash Wednesday, to remember their commitment to walk with Jesus to his crucifixion, I know because I'd been a properly brought-up Roman Catholic. This newly pronounced third eye of Phil's, a deep bluish-umber in hue, shone like a far-off planet. With each passing day, it glowed more noticeably. Once, I came into Phil's darkened meditation room, I saw his third eye radiate a greenish hue, remarkably different than any skin spot I'd ever seen, as if emerald crystals were glowing internally from this spot. Phil's forehead glowed with that eerie greenish light out in the daylight by the fireside, whenever his disassociated voice burst out with another of his insouciantly, rambunctious songs:

Old Joe came down from the heights of the mountain
To get a better glimpse of the sea, his dear sweet sea
Oh yea Oh gee, Oh give us a cheer and a beer for Old Joe ...

No longer did Phil ask for even a thimble full of wine as he did during those years with the socialite. Soon we'd find out how Phil got suckered into that unlikely pairing.

A few years after the divorce the paper announced that Dolores had died. Not long afterward she came to visit our family via her own words, written in a forgotten, left-behind diary. The spiral-bound notebook fell from a long-forgotten carton of Dolores' belongings that Helmet-head must have left behind, placed deep within a dark, unused closet after the court-ordered hasty departure. I happened to come across it while searching for something I needed in a storage area shared by everyone in our three-generational family.

I suppose I could have, maybe should have, shut the book without reading someone else's private thoughts. But I didn't. I knew Dolores was dearly departed, so I didn't think it would hurt to read some of her flowery cursive. Some might call finding the diary a coincidence, this book that fell out of its opened carton, onto the cobwebby floor for me to discover. Yes, I could have packed it back in the disintegrating, ripped carton, or made a phone call to return the whole box to her children; but you'll see why I didn't.

After reading only a few words from that one entry the fallen diary had serendipitously opened to, I knew it was fate that had let me see this. Instantly, the head-banging puzzle was solved, of how Phil could have been so bamboozled by the person our entire clan now referred to as "that floozy." These are the words I read in Dolores' own handwriting:

"I told Phil today," she wrote, "I insist we need to marry before I let him continue with this Kundalingus thing he says will help me, something he wants to awaken, that he wants to do with me."

"Poor Dad," Will shook his head and sighed after I right away showed him the incriminating diary entry. "Dolores obviously mistook Dad's intentions, and thought he meant gross-out geriatric cunnilingus, when all he meant—I know my father better than this hogwash she's written here—Dad *really* meant to help her have a *Kundalini* awakening, to awaken her nonexistent spirituality. But we'll never know the truth now, will we? His mind's too far gone. And I'd never ask him, even if he were totally with it. She showed off those tits of hers and he got suckered in, that's what happened. Knowing him, he wanted to help by teaching her the Jesus-focused A.R.E. meditation he and Mom did together. Period. He'd never have fallen for her if he'd gone for a spiritual match instead of that come-hither business that was all Dolores had in her bag of tricks."

Will shook his head, holding the diary in his hands. We read a few other entries that spoke of Dolores' lifelong depression, the nightmares that had haunted her since childhood, and, prior to marrying Phil, her terrible anxiety over money.

"How ironic, teZ," Will said, "Dad, practically the smartest guy in the world, here at his end game—too foolish for his own good. I guess this is how he got suckered in by Dolores. He got duped by her pretty face and that big set of boobs she showed off every chance she got. Geez, where have I heard this before? Sounds like me getting suckered by every woman who came before you!" Will laughed at himself.

I shook my head, knowing my man was probably right.

Now we understood how Phil, always trying to help someone find their spiritual center, as his Swendenborgian mother had taught him, got trapped and caught in a foolhardy marriage. Dolores' not understanding, mixing up two BIG words, Kundalini and Kunda-lingis, that sound so similar—another great paradox. This diary was proof of the undoing of Phil's pre-Dolores, peaceful utopia. His real mistake was to have chosen a showy socialite—splashier and glibber than deep or thoughtful—over any of the many dear old friends he had, whom he cherished in Lackland or at the Edgar Cayce group. He could have chosen a woman with more spiritual substance. Like his angel Claire, who'd been a knockout mix of both glamorous and spiritual.

Will shook his head and said, "Dad just didn't figure his karma could attract a contentious woman like Dolores. Mom was always cooperative and curious about everything."

Another entry in Dolores's diary Will read aloud clarified even more, excruciating as it was to hear:

"Phil knows," Dolores wrote, "I'm not going to let him do anything with me till we get married next week. He keeps saying he wants to arouse my Kundalingis, but how's that going to cure my nightmares like he says? What does sex have to do with it, anyway? I'm way too old for that stuff, so he's going to have no bedding with me. But Phil keeps saying I'm going to be happier when my Kundalingis is awakened. Good heavens, he's so wrong! All I need is for him to pay my bills."

Will stopped reading and shook his head. "Shit!"

"Oh my God, that's so pathetic," I moaned, looking over his shoulder. "He married her to help her spiritually, and she thought all he wanted was sex, which she didn't plan on giving him even after marrying, by her own account. Poor Phil."

"That's about it," Will said with a long face. "Let's not mention this diary to him, or anybody, ever."

My gentle giant always asking me to behave, hmmm.

I tried to picture Phil trying to explain to his new hottie about the completely human yearning for understanding the Divine, the Kundalini awakening, the sacred *energy* all of us have that sooner or later gets activated. Cayce's legacy foundation, the A.R.E., speaks of the Kundalini energy, the Divine in each of us. In Christianity, it was depicted in early sacred art as a flame or halo around a person's head. In Eastern symbology it's shown as a coiled serpent lying in repose at the base of the spine, waiting to "be aroused" by either reaching adolescence, natural curiosity, or a pivotal event such as the death of a loved one, or some other trauma dished out by life's serendipity.

To Will and me it was obvious: Phil only had pure, good intentions. He'd only wanted to help his friend Dolores out of her aforementioned nightmares and lifelong emotional turmoil that had driven her to drink. It was a bad stupid cosmic joke on a good honest man. But we figured his karma needed this last kick he got, however painful it was for everyone concerned. Will and I somehow managed to laugh at it now, reading how Dolores had insisted they get married before she let "Phil arouse my Kundalingis."

Whatever transpired between these two—there'd been no sign of their ever being anything beyond platonic companions—but we'll never know. Separate bedrooms from day one had been their arrangement, discovered only when Sally stayed overnight to investigate, at the very end of their loveless marriage. Besides going to parties and boozing, there'd been no outwardly shared affections between them. With Dolores dead now, her diary spoke the only truth we'll ever know, moronic as it was.

Will told me to burn the diary, which I swiftly did.

△

All of us, interconnected, by what? Seven degrees of separation, isn't that how it goes? I'd say it's more like half a degree. Look how Will came into my life, just when I made my sober want-list. Then Kara, born the exact year, the exact month, in fact, when I met my Teacher, right after embracing Better-me.

Yes, everything is inexplicably, irrefutably connected.

In my birth family, my father's alcohol-fueled bad behavior catapulted me into searching, maybe more than the average person might, for a semblance of sanity in my disjointed world of having been abused. From my early teens, I'd been band-aiding mini-freak-outs with my own mood-altering addictions, then scrambling to have breakthroughs instead of repeating my old pattern of breakdowns. My biggest desire in life, like Dolores' had been, was to be free of those haunting nightmares that never left me alone, that only drugs or alcohol numbed—until my own Kundalini was awakened by the Teacher. Desperation forced me to start on my journey, seeking my own truth. Away from suburbia, away from my father's boozy transgressions.

Amazing, and yes, it is Grace, all of it. Pain serves us when we let it lead us to our Truth. I found mine, my connection with Oneness, introduced and established via the Teacher's vigilant instructions; while Phil, Claire, Will, my mom's and dad's people, and millions of others like them, find theirs through the guidance of religion.

We need to find our own way as much as we need to accept others' paths to what life is all about. One God: many paths.

Some say we choose the family we're born into. I don't know. But why not? Why not anything? All Great Teachers say, "Things are not what they seem to be." Certainly, my Teacher said this many times, urging her students to experience the subtleties of life, and be open to all possibilities. "Make it relevant," the Teacher said about Aum. "Test it."

After many tests, I now expect things to be no other way than … *It is.*

Instead of seeking, I am content with *Being*. And this makes whatever I do—whether arting, adventuring, detaching, nurturing, having fun or learning, feeling the next *aha!* moment or creating a next delicious healthy meal—so much more meaningful.

It seems to me that after seeing Phil's divinely orchestrated, late in life kick-in-the-ass, I understand better why we all have to get knocked down, even the best of us. Whether we view the challenges of life as evil or constructive opportunities, things happen as they must. We never know why we're experiencing what we do, if we ever do, until much later. Yet with time, things gradually begin to make sense. Even so-called bad things come together, inevitably, like a giant jigsaw puzzle. It's as if disparate pieces of chaos are drawn together magnetically, to finally make sense, show some kind of meaning in the end, without us having to lift a finger or figure anything out, when we've learned to accept *what is*. When we give situations time to sort themselves out.

Whenever I couldn't accept the "hand of cards I'd been dealt"—as I used to when I played run-away or deny-it with drugs and alcohol—I stayed miserable.

If I can continue to accept each new situation—yet choose to make as many positive changes as I can, within each new moment—I'm successful at being who and what *I am*.

△

During my next session with Dr. C she asked, "So, how're you doing, distancing yourself from the bio-mom, Debby? Especially since she's become so sick, and the kids are super worried about her all the time?" Unbelievably, Debby had recently begun drinking again.

"Oh, I'm pretty good at this boundary stuff now," I answered.

"Do you have a certain method, queenie?" Dr. C sarcastically asked, never letting me live it down after I'd proclaimed myself, in a past session, to be the Queen of Detachment.

"Years ago," I said, "my pal Jane taught me how to pray for the object of my resentment—whether it's Debby, pornographers or polluters, sexists or racists. Whatever or whomever bugs me, I silently plea, *Help! Help me to accept*, and insert a *proper noun* there. I find beseeching Aum releases my mind that'd been bound-up, or obsessed by whatever. Of course, I have to repeat this mini-prayer as often as it takes. But I keep it up, and I've learned it works. I find peace again, eventually. Having a firm boundary by which I can separate from the object of my pain is my aim. Even if it takes days, weeks, or months, as it did once, with a soul-close girlfriend. It took two years' worth of praying to accept her being a jerk to Will and me. I'm over being sucked in by others' bad behavior."

"Sounds like you're protecting your heart pretty well these days."

"I'm learning how, Carolyn, more and more."

She smiled, saying, "The kids' destiny with their birth mom, is theirs. You've done your duty: showing them other options in life."

"Thanks. It helps knowing Kara's off to college next year, and Jonny, he's next."

Then Dr. C surprised me. "Have you ever wondered," she asked slowly, "about what role Debby has played in *your* life, now that you're Miss Detached instead of always reacting?"

There was no hesitation in my reply. "Funny you've asked, 'cause I've recently figured out how Debby and I are really more similar than different."

"I'm all ears," the doc said.

"Well ... you know how, in private only, Will and I call Debby the BM. I realized just the other day, that could also be how I call my higher Self, Better-me, which I've told you about before. Only Debby's version is a big, stinky BM and my Better-me is, well, just the opposite from what I mean when I call her *that*. In Debby's mind though, she must think me an even bigger shit, a real pompous ass, probably. So we're both BMs to each other, both the stinky and the pleasing varieties."

"Hmm ... point well made," Dr. C nodded and smiled. "Everyone lives from their own truth, certainly. This analytical, everything's-connected business puts your inquisitive, fill-in-the-dots mind at ease."

"I guess it makes me feel freer," I said, "focusing on similarities between things rather than differences. It thrills me to see and understand how everything is unequivocally interconnected, instead of just wishing it were so. I don't know why, it just makes me feel satisfied with things. I've finally figured out there's hardly any difference at all, between any of us. From the worst of us to the very best human.

"Some of us have opposite beliefs, sure, but we're still equally part of the One. What's the difference between being in Love, in the Light, and someone stuck in fear, in the darkness of controlling judgment? We're equally believers, aren't we? We just believe opposite sides of the pole. Seeing this, I want to strive to be in the middle, at the axis, the core of that see-sawing pole. Like Buddhists do.

"So yeah," I continued, "I can call myself a BM too, just the same as Will and I call Debby. My Better-Me is different, but equal to Debby's BM, she being the stinking doodoo who always tries to throw a wrench in our family dynamics. Boy, did that knock me over when I finally got that, how all of us are sons and daughters of God. Good or bad, we're family."

"You're losing me here. Please expand," Dr. C said, as she had so often in our private talks.

"I see Life, the big picture, I mean—how everything's part of the whole—using the famous allegory I prefer to explain it with: *The Waterfall of Life*. It's a visual metaphor, a common motif that I use in my art work, Carolyn, the Cosmic Waterfall. I use it to explain how two disparate things, or people, like Debby and me, are the same. I do that by seeing us—and everything in existence, virtually—as separate molecules of water existing together in life's unfathomable, cosmic flow of energy, a Waterfall. With uncountable molecules within it, we're each a corpuscle in the body of God, performing our individual functions and living out our lives, intertwined, like cells of blood in one big body are also."

A hum of pleasure came from Dr. C. "Interesting image. You artists!"

This dear heart, who graciously shared her professional and motherly advice, Dr. C—who'd guided and honed my abilities to be a caregiver since before marrying, so many years before—looked right at me and asked, "So Debby doesn't bum you out anymore?"

I took a deep breath. "Sure, I admit it'd be nice not to be hated. Just like it'd be nice if my own mom thought I was capable; or my dad hadn't been such a drunk and done what he did to so many, not just me. I accept both my parents, as un-nurturing as they were to my young, un-spiritualized self-esteem. But that's the hand I was dealt. So yeah, I can accept Debby being the BM, just like I've come to accept I'm a BM of another ilk; and my mom's a pain in the butt; and Kara's a teenage vampire."

I paused. Dr. C sat patiently, waiting.

"I know I can only change myself," I continued. "My job is to keep playing the hand I've got, and stay in the game. These days I'm more glad than mad about Debby. And I'm trying to be grateful how her mini-me daughter keeps pushing me to the brink. She's my new spiritual master, did I tell you? For sure, learning to be Better-Me is as much my destiny as Debby's being the kind of BM she is. I see that now. I'm getting pretty good at this Queen of Detachment business."

Laughing out loud, Dr. C said, "Queenie, BM, Angel Mom—so you're saying all these are interchangeable now?" Her head bobbed and eyes twinkled. "How many different names can a girl have, anyway?"

oh, starry night

CHAPTER 26

boy overboard!

One Sunday afternoon I was quietly writing in the teZ Mahal when the phone rang. My concentration was instantly broken by Will's urgent voice: "Come right away, Jonny's at the hospital! He broke his leg playing pickup football at a friend's house. It sounds bad."

Without shutting down the computer or turning off lights, I ran out the door, hopped on my bike and took the orchard shortcut instead of Grandpa's long driveway. When we got to the hospital, I found seventeen-year-old Jonny, wretchedly groaning, stretched out writhing on a gurney, was stuck out in the hallway. Three ambulances had arrived just behind Jonny's, one of them with a DOA and the others holding people near death from a multi-car wreck on the interstate. Other than a quick once-over by an ER doctor, our son wasn't able to receive any immediate medical attention. Will rushed up to the first doctor he saw sprinting by.

"Look," Will said, perfectly rational and reasonable in a low thrum, "we can drive our son over to the next hospital half an hour away."

"No need," the doctor hastily replied. "His is an everyday, normal tib-fib break. It's not even compound, the skin's not ruptured. We'll get to him right away, don't worry. Your son's in no danger. Please sir, just be patient."

Will and I stood next to Jonny's gurney, watching helplessly as he winced, twisted, and yelped, muffling the screams I could feel inside him. He couldn't speak a word. Jonny was given nothing for pain, and wouldn't be, the nurses informed us, until he'd been assessed. Wait was all we could do. And pray.

Frantically, Will paced the hall while I lightly stroked Jonny's arm, both of us growing more worried by the minute. Green-clad ER technicians, some blood-spattered, raced between several rooms filled with crash. victims. Will grabbed the white sleeve of the same doctor he'd spoken to earlier.

His stature and brashness did not intimidate the slight man as Will's voice boomed, "What about Jonny, here? What's going on with our son? He's in agony, look at him!"

"Try not to worry, sir," the doctor urged in a calm practiced tone, barely glancing Jonny's way. "I told you before your son is perfectly all right. His fracture will soon be set. His injury is no problem. We have people dying here from auto crash."

"He's in pain!" Will's voice raised decibels.

"We will look after your son. Please, be patient," the doctor said, rushing away.

Another twenty minutes crept by. Jonny put on a brave face, but could not hold back the tears. His face distorted in distress, his upper torso twisting in efforts to control pain that must have been unbearable. My heart was breaking, Will's too. We couldn't take it any longer.

"We're driving him to that other hospital right now," my determined man said, jumping up.

At that exact moment a green-coated person, new to us, came rushing up to the gurney and told Jonny he was going to be wheeled into emergency surgery. Several attendants pushed Jonny's bed through the swinging doors where we hoped our son would get relief. For the previous three-quarters of an hour we'd had to just watch him suffer. Will and I stayed in the waiting room, silently praying for Jonny's injury to be a "normal, easy-to-fix break," as the first doctor described. In the middle of this nightmare, lost in the surreal standstill juncture of time and this medical reality, I sent out a thought-seed on Jonny's behalf—*Help our son!*—I silently kept shouting to the Universe, to anyone or anything that could hear my urgent plea.

▲

Four hours later, when we finally got to see Jonny in the ICU, he was heavily sedated. His expression at last relaxed from the ghastly pain-mask he'd worn before. The same ER doctor to whom Will first talked came into the room. I asked him about the towering mound of bandages surrounding Jonny's leg.

"Your son is a brave boy," the man said.

"Yes, we know that," Will stated. "Tell us about those bandages around his leg. That doesn't look like any cast I've ever seen."

"Your son's leg isn't set yet. The good news is, it's a clean fracture, just like we thought. Both bones snapped with no splintering or tearing of skin. But I'm afraid there is a problem."

I stopped breathing while the physician, the hospital's best orthopedic specialist we'd discover later, explained. His mechanical voice resounding in my brain, his unwelcome words hammering my skull. He told us that Jonny had a rare complication, an abnormal build-up of blood pressure in one of the injured leg's fascia. An infection in a compartment of tissue that includes muscles, ligaments, tendons. He told us how *compartment syndrome* could happen at any time, but so rarely does, with all types of trauma to the body.

What he didn't tell us, and what we'd soon find out, was that Jonny's fracture, having been left unattended for so long, especially without having been iced-down, was a significant factor to the rare occurrence, his occurrence, of the condition.

Hearing "compartment syndrome" Will immediately recognized Jonny's as the same freak condition that had happened to a college football buddy of his. Will instantly knew, as fully as I knew nothing about how this drastic turn would forever change our son's life.

When Jonny awoke several hours later, we were there. He asked about his leg and we told him the truth. He looked scared and I'm sure he would have wept again had we not been with him. We repeated to him that same stupid, useless word, "Sorry," that the ER white-coat could only offer us as consolation.

The same arrogant doctor, who soon stopped saying sorry and started chastising Will, now took to shouting, "Stop second-guessing me, you're not doctor!" whenever Will asked intelligent questions that the orthopedic surgeon found annoyingly detailed. Whether in fear of being sued, or suffering from the proverbial God-complex physicians are often accused of having, he'd been on the defensive with Will from the moment they met.

We mentioned none of this to Jonny right away, assuring him that the doctors were doing everything they could to make his leg right.

The truth is, just a few short years earlier, most individuals who suffered this unfortunate complication brought on with many types of bodily injury, from bruises to snake bite, had to have the affected limb amputated; compartment syndrome still comes with that grim possibility. Like a short-wave radio set to Aum's great Power, I non-stop sent thought-seeds out that this wouldn't be Jonny's case. Will and I were still worried about the doctor's pomposity, that original unconcerned approach of his.

We immediately consulted by phone with a nationally known specialist. Then Will and I decided to keep Jonny where he was. He was receiving all the care he needed, we were informed by the expert. For the next week, our son passed in and out of a morphine stupor. Underneath a foot-high tower of frequently-changed sterile wraps, the calf fascia of his injured leg was splayed out like a gauze-encased filleted fish. Several times daily the grotesque wound was freshly flushed with antibacterial fluids. This painful procedure was repeated until the internal pressure of Jonny's lower limb gradually returned to normal. Only then, more than a week after the accident, could his double fracture be set, when all danger of infection had passed. During the leg's set, his calf needed a graft, which was taken from his hip, to replace the large area of skin Jonny had lost due to morbidity, the death of his injured calf's tissue.

All living cells within that specific fascia of Jonny's leg that'd been infected—had died. Including the major tendon that controlled the bending of his ankle and kicking of his foot, the right foot that his life's football dream relied on. In one drastic turn, Jonny's kicking pigskin again seemed dead as well now, because there was no tendon remaining for his foot to get into the proper position to kick with.

When he healed, his wound looked like it was an angry landmine he'd stepped on, as spine-nervy warlike for others to view as it was for Jonny to live through.

As he lay in his hospital bed, too blitzed on narcotics to realize the full impact of this catastrophe, Will and I attempted to cheer our son up, although we too were crying on the inside. We knew what lay ahead: the hard job of his, and ours, of accepting what life's rotten roulette wheel of hardships had dealt our precious boy.

I sat with him. Will sat with him. And when I wasn't there, Debby came and sat alongside her son's bed too. After three weeks Jonny was discharged. A hospital bed was set up in the biggest room of our small house, the TV den, where he could hold court with his friends. This was the only time we allowed Debby in our home, to visit her son, but only in that one room that was next to the back door.

After another couple of weeks, Jonny returned to school, first in a wheelchair, then on crutches. We hired tutors to help him get through the months of schoolwork he'd missed. By the time his sophomore class broke for the summer, Jonny would be walking on his own, tall and proud and, as long as he wore shoes, without a limp. He was up to date with his college-prep trajectory. After months of nerve-regeneration healing, excruciatingly painful, Jonny decided on his own, after discussions with Will and me presenting the pros and cons, to not give up his football aspirations.

In the future, after many years had passed, he finally shared with us how despairingly low he felt during this time. I have a lot more sympathy now for the frequency of teenage suicide, and commend our son for not giving in to his own inner demons, right then, when he faced his own personal darkness. I can't help but believe our family's prayerfulness helped all of us through this family tragedy. He kept his depression hidden from us, sharing only his determination to make a comeback. By the beginning of his senior year, after a year of nights and days at rehabbing his leg, doing nonstop spine-sharpening nerve-exercises at PT and at home, Jonny achieved the impossible: he was back on his team. He wasn't the big star he'd once been, but now … just one of many skilled kickers.

We applauded Jonny's major accomplishment he'd set and reached, all by himself.

From being his team's kicking ace to mostly sitting on the bench, he'd lost his hero status, he sadly told me in private one day, putting on his brave face as we sat closely in his room, doing another round of the body-wrenching, nerve-reviving exercises. In the year following the accident, his foot and ankle would require three reconstructive surgeries, and several more in years to come, traveling to other states to have all of these performed by specialists.

Despite his handicap, Jonny achieved the impossible. He proved to himself he could be a halfway decent kicker, even though he knew he'd never be the force-to-reckon-with he was before. I understood why he went for this seemingly impossible personal-best only after he explained. Jonny confessed to me as we did those nervy exercises together, in between his winces and howls: "I'm a nobody now, teZ! I'm just a plain normal guy. There's nothing special about me anymore. It sucks."

His fragile ego had taken as mean a blow as his leg had.

△

From the day his leg snapped in two, Jonny never stopped trying to reclaim his specialness. Attempting to offer him encouragement, I reminded him of the importance of everyone's having a Plan B.

"You'd make a great environmentalist, Jonny. You love Nature and wild animals. There's an alternative route, in case it doesn't work out with the kicking thing."

"It's true, I do love the woods," Jonny admitted, "even more than playing ball."

I smiled. "Life is about following signs that Great Spirit puts out for us, like crumbs on a trail, in order to find the right path our lives are destined to take. Sometimes the plan we envision for ourselves doesn't turn out to be our real destiny. We have to pay attention to our gut to really know what life has in store for us, where we're supposed to go, when to make changes."

I stopped speaking. It dawned on me, sitting there with my Angel Son, that I'd never received wisdom like this from either of my parents. Humbled by being able to share with Jonny so intimately, as we always did, I smiled, and continued.

"Instead of thinking life is cruel, we can choose to believe it's always exciting, and exactly what our soul needs, no matter what happens. There's no telling what's going to happen next, right? Life is a Mystery, Jonny. But even when supposed *bad things* happen, it's part of the journey. Real life is way crazier and unpredictable than the weirdest fiction ever imagined. So-called bad things, accidents like yours for instance, they're part of God's plan too, as well as what we call the *good things*. This Mystery we call life always turns out, in the end, for the best. We learn as we go. Look at the world around us—we human beings are pretty new on the planet. We're just learning what it is, to be human. Although, true, we've done a pretty lousy job of it so far, with all the wars, the killings, and trashing the environment like we've done. But we humans, we're just babies in terms of our past, present, and what's in store for our future. Right here, today, we're a biological speck, a cockroach smear on Earth's overall continuum of evolution, compared to the millions of years our planet's been around.

"The way I see it, Jonny, we're the new guys on Earth. And our job as aware, awakened, and now becoming spiritualized humans, is to follow the energy, the signs—using inspiration from God, our highly evolved intellects, and always, always! our free will—to make as wise a choice as we can in each circumstance we meet. Even though, sure, we may suffer. But our pain always teaches us something. Trust me, I know. It'll all add up to make sense, sooner or later. Trust me on this. As your Angel Mom who loves you, I'm excited for you, Jonny. And I'm just as excited about my life, and Dad's, Kara's, and Grandpa's."

Jonny and I talked a lot during this time, as we sat together every day in his bedroom doing the hair-raising nerve-rejuvenation exercises he had to do. From his hospital bed, then the rented one in the den, and later, as we sat in a tight huddle for endless hours, doing the painful repetitions I helped him with, we spoke as we tried to awaken deadened foot nerves by touching his unresponsive foot's bare sole with feathers, tin foil, crunched up paper, all different textures meant to awaken different nerve fibers, helping to heal, day by day, what nerve connections had been broken, one by one. This quiet time we had together allowed me to glimpse just how deep our son's thinking went. Jonny was a profound wonderer, not a worrier-warrior like my clown Will was. I talked gently to keep Jonny from drowning in the well of hurt I knew he was stuck in. Never once did Jonny let me or anyone, see him shed a tear. But I felt his depression, as deeply as I felt the cries of Mother Earth, wounded and weary, in desperate need of those who could restore her to balance and health

I made up my mind. My job with Jonny, as it always had been, was to cheer him up. Even more now than I had to, when he was the sad little fellow upset over losing his White Goddess mama. The same deeply caring knee-high fellow who went after the baby gator with his father's spear when Bruno was attacked.

I told my suffering son, "Be true to your own self. Put your trust in Great Spirit. And seriously, think about having a Plan B … just in case. The world doesn't need another overpaid football player, sweetie, but we sure need all the open-hearted, woods- water- and creature-loving Earth protectors we can get."

I was sitting next to Grandpa Phil, being mesmerized right along with him, staring at the flames roaring in his fireplace. The old man turned to me with misty-eyes and spoke suddenly the longest string of words in years.

"Jonny's accident is the worst thing that's ever happened to anybody in our family."

No ditties were sung that day. Long silences followed short questions as I recounted to Phil the saga of his grandson's slow recovery; how he was in a hospital bed right then, in the middle of our family room; how he wasn't quite off the stiff pain meds yet; how he was so groggy he mostly slept; and when awake he was in nerve-pain hell.

"Poor little fella," Phil moaned. "He sure doesn't deserve that."

Groans erupted involuntarily from Phil's shrunken body, betraying his own misery. Sitting right alongside him so I needn't raise my voice, I started to reach over to lightly touch his quivering, gnarly blue-veined hand, to comfort my old friend. But Phil didn't like that sappy stuff, so I pulled back. He wasn't a touchy-feely kind of guy. Will said his dad never told any of his kids that he loved them, ever. Not once. Yet somehow, everyone knew, wordlessly, that Phil loved all in his tribe, equally and deeply.

Claire and Phil never said anything critical or nasty about anybody, even when someone deserved it. They kept their opinions to themselves, or to each other. Silence was their fiercest form of judgment. Silence was not only Phil's response to anger, but unfortunately, also the only way he had of saying "I love you."

I saw his emotions clearly now, for the first time since his mind had sunk below the surface of everyday consciousness. Out of the corner of my eye, not wanting to embarrass him, I saw that Phil was quietly weeping. Not wishing to disturb such a private man, I kept silent, and did not intrude in any way in his rare display of emotion. His tears showed how he was completely overwhelmed by deep sadness. I'd never seen Phil crack open like this, not during the worst pain he'd suffered, from either Dolores' verbal abuse or losing his private angel, Claire.

Phil reached for his ever-present, white ironed handkerchief he always kept in the jacket pocket of the heavy tweed suit he wore every day, winter or summer. Quietly, he dabbed his eyes with the hankie and put it right back in his pocket. I saw, but didn't have the heart to tell him, that what Phil thought was his handkerchief—was actually a worn-out, wrinkled one-dollar bill.

I flash-remembered. His daughter Sally had told the caretaker to "… make sure there's always a bill in Daddy's pocket, so he feels he has some buying power left. He needs to know he's always got a buck on hand, in case he wants to buy something."

Phil's tears continued to slide down his craggy parchment cheeks. Over and again he reached into his pocket and brought out the damp dollar bill to dab his eyes, oblivious to the fact that it wasn't the square of fine linen he'd always relied on.

boy overboard!

CHAPTER 27

the waterfall

Just when it felt as if the turbulence of Rio Blisso's hardship-rapids were abating—its currents suddenly tripled in intensity. Popping up dead ahead of us came a rock, a dangerous eddy, a sudden drop—a sheer precipice or submerged, unseen boulders—as ever more tempestuous cross-rips kept a-coming at us. Sometimes, we'd have a warning and Will's or my steering could avert the oncoming catastrophe.

Too often, though—by the time we sensed the rush of another gut-clenching challenge coming straight at us—it was too late. Times like this, when we were being inexorably swept toward impending doom, or rather, feeling like it—when neither Will nor I could hardly steer our family's resistant vessel, and sometimes, when the water's force sucked us into another tornado-like swirl—we'd lose all control of our vessel. There was no turning back at times like these, reaching this point. We had to weather the storm, fasten our safety lines, and bravely take whatever next frenzy that life was dishing out to us.

As we drew nearer to another waterfall's jagged edge of the horizon—*imaginary* waterfalls I'm speaking of, friends, just as Rio Blisso is a *made-up* river—I'd first tell our real-life crew to batten down the hatches, then to hang on. It's all we could do.

A waterfall can be thought of as a vital, monumental energy core made from water's voluminous immensity of motion. At the same time, each of its individual H_2O molecules—whether measured by a single drop, a cupful, bucketful, or a handful drawn from the waterfall itself, the powerful rush of converging rivers being the waterfall's energy Source—each portion contains the same explicit identity and composition that comprises the waterfall's entirety. Each separate cell, or molecule of water, therefore, contains the same power within itself as its Source. Just because a handful or a spoonful of water has been removed from a waterfall, doesn't mean that the tiniest amount, a drop even, is any different—in potential—from its more colossal, more powerful energy Source.

Each of us—we individual humans in this cosmic Waterfall analogy—contains the same spiritual potential as the Source from which we originated. The "water" of our beingness is the continuum of life itself, from which we originated and into which we'll dissolve again someday.

And isn't this a perfect explanation for The Mystery, this Waterfall of Existence, knowing that we humans are comprised mostly of water in our chemical composition?

I remember when the Teacher explained to us: "The microcosm is the same as the macrocosm. Every individual person contains the same unlimited power within, as the very Source of life—consciousness itself."

This is why my personal Waterfall, an iconic, moving, illuminated archetype standing for nothing less than the totality of Oneness itself—the indescribable-ness of Love, of Aum—comforts me in times of stress. Maybe it's my artist's need to reinvent old ideas, but however it's explained, I relate to this union of my smallness with the overwhelming bigness of an imagined, cosmic Waterfall.

To my hungry sensibilities, the Waterfall image is a satisfying fairytale, scary yet thrilling, magical in the extreme, into which I can plunge instead of popping Prozac, sipping wine, smoking a J or seeking some other reality shift as others may choose to do when facing life's stressors. The idea of this Waterfall's, and my own *unlimited* potential power fascinates me. My comfort food might be chocolate, yes; but my go-to thought-seed is to visualize a safe and

The Waterfall

secure traversing of any size waterfall as the ultimate challenge—physical, mental, or spiritual—which regularly crosses my path.

This phenomenon I'm painting for you is the vivid picture I create in my mind's eye, of how all in existence fits within one mystical, infinity-representing Waterfall. We're all part of the immeasurable power of this Waterfall of Life. Yet—just as a handful of water is taken from, say, a stream, river, or ocean, not just waterfalls—each of us humans are, similarly, as separate (in our individual bodies), yet interdependent (within the human blended family) as water molecules are in a bucketful: we human-molecules, we separate beings in this immense Waterfall of Life.

In essence, in composition, and energetically: we are no different from our Source. This amazing realization happens—instantaneously for me—when I mentally jump right into this fantastic Waterfall whose overwhelming-ness offers me such comfort and understanding.

It takes being a sucker for a spiritual adventure to want to jump in with me. Ready?

Every human being is like a seed; I fondly call us *human beans*. We've already seen how we have the same power within ourselves as the all-powerful energy Source of the cosmos, from which we originated; just as an acorn has the same power within it, to sprout up and grow to be the giant oak tree from which it fell.

The Waterfall portrays this potential Force within us, the egoless state of pure consciousness. That thought-free state—called pure universal Consciousness—is imbibed only in the state of meditation. That's why everyone who wants to experience the One, whether Buddhists, mystical Christians, Hindus, Quakers, Taoists, yogis of all sorts—just as my Teacher and all great spiritual masters do—urge their students to meditate. The best description of God, to my artist's mind, is the image of the cosmic Waterfall that's depicted in Suzuki Roshi's "Zen Mind, Beginner's Mind." If one can do this, understand the Waterfall, a person achieves awareness of the state of ultimate Oneness ... that has no second.

Each person has their share of being barraged by mundane mini-waterfalls: circumstances of ordinary life that constantly try to beat us down. I gradually learned to courageously face each new waterfall crisis that hit me, thanks to listening to my teachers. It sounds so obvious, but some of us forget that going-through—not denying or magnifying—life experiences, especially fearful ones, is the key to embracing the Sacred in everyday life. Today, I can easily recognize the Divine everywhere and in everything, after having trained Better-me to go with the flow. But first, I had to learn to let the power of each new waterfall-kind-of hardship guide me to wherever it would lead me. When I resisted—ahh, this was when I could count on the disastrous happening.

Each large or small waterfall I ran into expanded my consciousness (enough to benefit from an inevitable fall from the waterfall's dangerous precipice) because each "falling experience" altered something within the balance of my life. With each successful surviving of the next waterfall, I gradually learned that I'm not as powerless as I once thought I was.

The Teacher keeps saying to us: "When you students learn to be the masters of your own lives by embracing your divine consciousness, then I can go to the beach because I don't have to work this job anymore!"

When I remember that life is pure consciousness, that it's about choosing Better-me opportunities and, say "No" to Lesser-me's random chaos—I can relax.

This, of course, is a lot harder to do than it sounds.

Nonetheless, through trial and error, following my heart instead of my head, I trained myself to accept the current of the flowing rivers I found myself on: to *go with the flow*. Before, I used to imagine I was a leaf floating over the next, and the next waterfall, terrified, holding my breath, and I was anything but relaxed. Listening to the guidance that's available to us all, I'm able to travel comfortably in our family's trusty boat (or tethered to it on my lifeboat of detachment). I get to enjoy the ride, even the hard bits.

Nonetheless I'm always on the lookout for the next oncoming waterfall, that's ready to appear, often without warning. That way, I can brace myself. And the roller-coaster ride down the Falls isn't so jarring.

Being stranded in Lackland too long was getting to me. Other women there thought me too unconventional to sustain lasting friendships, or maybe I was too fussy. Other than with family, managing our house rentals, writing, or doing yoga, I spent most of my time alone. I was a nut cracking in half, my insides squished by no outlets for the strains of unfulfilled promises and life's responsibilities. There were only so many *So'ham, So'ham*s a person can do, right? I no longer felt like I was such a great Angel Mom. My art-making was on permanent hiatus since my hand injury. I knew something had to give in the physical realm.

Sensing the next approaching waterfall long before I smelled the sharpness of its ozone-rich air, I felt the pace of our boat's journey quicken, I saw eddies of upcoming turmoil swirling about on the syncopated-rhythm, no-longer-smooth-running surface of Rio Blisso every which way I looked. I knew something serious lay ahead. Suddenly, I was keenly aware of a new imbalance inside me. Something drastic needed to break the whirlpool of unease I felt stuck in; I was neither here nor anywhere.

Fortunately, Better-me, was fairly well trained by now and usually on duty. When Lesser-me's voice got whiney, out of hand, I could usually shut 'er down with the mind-steadying repetition of *So'hăm, So'hăm* and frequent sweaty sessions of kick-ass yoga. I tried to keep a wagonload of detachment handy, to get through each day. I tried to remember.

Through all this struggle, I knew there was no way we could leave Lackland. Phil needed us.

Yet each day brought real potential for our boat to flip over in the next waterfall's riptides and whirlpools. And with each new watery hurdle over the abyss of angst, I managed to quickly recover from being bruised, because of my long standing mind-massaging routine.

Then—another waterfall challenge appeared. A big PUSH—and over the rocky ledge I'd fly! At the bottom of the powerful force I'd somehow surface, gulping air as I bobbed among hellishly fierce froth and crushing rocks, whipping out more breath, mantra, detachment—steadying my mind with whatever spiritual tool I found afloat in the flotsam around me.

For each narrowly escaped or fully materialized catastrophe, I repeated this routine endlessly, it seemed—whether the waterfalls could be detected ahead of time or not. I knew there was always going to be a next, and the next after that, plunge into crisis.

△

The time had come. I didn't realize it, but I was approaching the worst skull-crusher, the badass mother of all Weird and Wonderful Waterfalls.

Ahead of our boat's prow was the much shorter distance to our final destination than what our family had already traveled since embarking on this mad caper of ours, when Will and I committed matrimony. With every crisis we vowed to never give up.

As if I could, I looked out over the expanse of Rio Blisso's bends and forks that lay ahead as we approached what I suspected to be the last leg of our journey. I remembered the recurring dream of flying I used to have as a kid. This, I thought—seeing the river shiny and snaky, the unknown lurking ahead, hidden-from-sight on the silvery water-path—is better than flying. This is the where the real thrill of life is, going with the flow, not fleeing from it. Not needing to control any of It. The surprising gift of ease I got by letting go—even from Kara's loathing, or Jonny's life-altering accident—allowing myself to float with the hurts as well as being uplifted by life's many delights, finding out where Rio Blisso was leading us … this is the magic of our journey, I thought.

Right then, I made a decision.

"From now on," I said aloud, to the river, the sky, the wind, to the benevolent sun and invisible stars above, "I swear to always focus on the Light, and not give any energy to the Dark, within me or in any other. Sure, I'll give a casual nod of recognition to evil, you have to!—but then, after accepting its necessity, I'll do everything in my power to make it stay way *over there*, out of my energy field. But if it creeps too close, I'm clinging to the simple truth: The Light always overcomes the Darkness. I know this as well as I know both our kids will be healthy and wholly healed, if they choose to be. When all of our demons have shown each of us what we need to learn from them."

Better-me had become Rio Blisso's own Lighthouse. I felt illuminated from within, being released from the essence of Darkness. I wondered if anyone noticed me glowing.

Zen Love: The True Journey of a Blended Family

the waterfall

CHAPTER 28

ready the anchor

I focus on the early morning traffic as I drive to Sarasota, watching the sun's blazing disk pierce the indigo darkness of Florida's flat horizon.

Rio Blisso keeps pushing us in the right direction, I trust now. Each of its many waterfalls provides each one of us, every day, with exactly what we need to be fulfilled, each experience tailored for our own life's special purpose.

I will keep trying, keep hoping, keep positive. The world needs to be nurtured now, as our kids had before. Ahead, the horizon mirrors layers of dawn's crimson, pink, and orange glowing streaks. Rush hour traffic thickens. My work lies just ahead. My healing hands lightly grip the steering wheel and I'm grateful they no longer hurt. I'll never give up, I affirm silently. Love heals all.

"I remember the day," Grandpa began at our family Sunday gathering the evening before, "when we saw ... Bruno getting hit ... by that baby gator ... out in the pond." His ninety-nine-year-old face winces, his knobby index finger gesturing out the window toward the back pasture's glistening pond. Phil was in his green recliner with arthritic Bruno fast asleep at his feet, his all-gray muzzle resting on the tips of the old man's well-worn but newly polished oxfords.

Phil said this as if seeing the long-ago scene enacted right before him, a haunting, moment-by-moment, slowly re-played, stealthy reptilian attack only he could see.

"All that blood was so gross, Grandpa," Kara declared. "I remember how sick it made me feel to see it."

"Yeah, that was really upsetting for us all to witness," Will said. "It still is. It feels like it happened yesterday, when Bruno almost bought the farm."

"But Grandpa," Jonny softly interjected, after a moment's silence, "you weren't there. And Dad, you weren't there, and Kara wasn't either," he insisted. "It was just me and teZ that saw Bruno nearly get killed by that baby gator. Come on, what is this, group hypnosis? We're reading about that now in history class, what Hitler did to the German people."

All three of them were, of course, missing parties to Bruno's close shave, yet they protested and kept claiming, as they had on other occasions before this day, that they'd *really* been there. Yet truth is truth: it was only Jonny and myself, he and I kept saying, who'd witnessed the attack. Over the years Bruno had become a constant companion to Phil, now that the kids were too busy to bother with our dog. To the rest of the family, however, our CBD having come so close to almost being killed, had somehow made them feel they'd witnessed it themselves—Kara, Will, and Grandpa—but it was real only in their imaginations. Perhaps it made them feel closer to Bruno, believing they'd seen his near-demise for themselves. Several times before, when I noticed father and daughter, along with Phil, all speak as if they'd personally seen Bruno's death-defying attack, they spoke as if all three of them had been standing there, together, during the whole grisly affair that, in reality, was only witnessed by Jonny and me. But the three of them never believed me before when I tried saying they were wrong.

So now I clear my throat. "Jonny's right. I've tried telling you before, Kara and Will, that neither of you, Grandpa either, were there that day. It was just Jonny and me. Our family has talked about how awful that day was so many times, and you all love Bruno so much, that all three of you have obviously mixed up what really happened with what your mind insists did. Sorry, but none of you were there."

Will jumped in. "You keep saying that, but it's sure dang hard to believe I wasn't there," he said suspiciously, as if a Vegas-style magic trick were being played on him. "I distinctly remember *being there*."

"Me too, Dad!" Kara insisted.

"Must be the group-hypnosis effect we studied about Hitler," Jonny repeated, as emphatic as a quiet but deep thinker can be, just like his taciturn Grandpa.

"Well," Phil said slowly. "I don't know … I prefer to believe … I was there. Poor little fella."

Grandpa reached down to the floor and scratched Bruno's upturned furry head. The CBD arched his neck up higher with pleasant grunts, glorying in the old man's touch.

Rio Blisso's rushing waters flowed on, casting memories that bobbed around the buoys on the kaleidoscope-patterned, circling oily surface of our passing boat. Phil fished out what events pleased him most, and discarded the rest. He let each selection caress him like a treasured breeze on a hot Florida day, offering its distraction from any current unease. I was happy for him, to take such joy from his remembrances. His was a perpetual state of bliss now.

As for the other three, on our walk home that night, Will spoke of what a nice visit we'd had with Kara on her winter holiday from her western-state college. Jonny and I spoke again of making sure that she and his dad both knew real from not-real.

Will and I always laughed at how similarly we felt, awarding ourselves an A+ for relationship stick-to-it-iveness, for not ever giving up.

We went giddy portraying ourselves as a matching pair of worn-out old comfortable shoes that fit so well together, finally, after years—no, eons—of having searched for the other one, and then more years of working to appreciate each other's humanness. No one had ever satisfied our quirky neurotic ways, the way each of us did to the other. Whenever we talked about this peculiar feeling we both had, of our two lonely souls having united, and grown into one completely comfortable pair, we'd snuggle closer, feeling like a set of two soft leather shoes, like Phil's shiny oxfords, a right and a left neatly matched, equally joined after looking everywhere—in every other human face practically—until we'd found our missing piece reflected back in one another's eyes.

▲

Jonny was in his last year of high school, between more reconstructive surgeries for his ankle to function properly. He worked hard on Grandpa's football field of a lawn, determined to make it as a decent kicker on the team. As for Phil—whenever we could, Will and I joined in his half-here, half-there twilight times, reminiscing with him as he fished out of his memory-stream more wonders, more drinking ditties.

Phil recalled the bull that had escaped soon after Will and I married. On that day Phil and I were alone, walking along the edge of his pasture, enjoying getting to know each other. All of a sudden, a young black bull jumped over the three-tiered post and wire fence, landing right in front of us! Impulsively I approached the boisterous beast, not so much from bravery but because I needed to protect this fragile old man who had such a kind and gentle soul, whom I'd already become uncommonly fond of, and would have taken a bullet for, if truth be told.

"Watch out," Phil said in his droll New England monotone. "He'll butt you hard, teZa, if you aren't careful."

Just as Phil said this, the damn punk bovine charged me. Propelled by my protective guardian mode, I met the animal's cowhide head with a double whammy punch right in the middle of its startled onyx eyes. Dazed as much as I, the bull shook his head, then instantly hopped right back over the fence, astounding my father-in-law and me, and the rest of the bull's herd standing attentively placid, observing this daredevil act of the rogue renegade.

From the very moment we met, I'd loved Phil. I knew I wanted to marry his son when I heard Phil's cornball greeting to classy, cool Claire's entrance, "I must be in heaven, I thought I saw an angel." Phil never objected to anything about me, neither my purposeful unstylishness, my weird-to-Westerners mystical bent, or my penchant for bare feet. He told Will he considered those guileless attributes assets, along with my hard-working artist persona and Third World subsistence mentality. "Self-sufficiency credentials," he'd chuckled, "for successful partnering with my half-redneck son." When Will told me his dad said that, it made me laugh out loud.

Unlike my own mother—who'd tried to talk Will out of marrying me, reporting to him, "She has absolutely no experience with children"—Phil never doubted my mothering skills. The blended family that Will and I were a-brewing, I was told later, "was a good idea," father had assured son. "Your match with teZa will bring Kara and Jonny great new possibilities," he'd said.

In private, Phil told Will that he saw only advantages of my being so different, so refreshing from the working stiffs of Debby's clan, and the silver-spoon previous generations of his and Claire's families. He held an appreciation for the forging of our blended foursome, from Will's and my disparate backgrounds to our different expressions of faith, cultural influences, and political leanings, or lack thereof in my case. Will related how Phil, ever optimistic, had viewed the fresh bloodline that Will had created with his Debby, as "a most useful evolutionary device," a father's delicate way of condoning his son's odd choice, back when Phil could still carry on a conversation. He'd said, "Maybe our family needed a little back to basics—a fresh, healthy infusion of hardy common-man stock—instead of all the high-brow intellectuals we've cultivated for so many generations."

My man and I shared some good laughs over how Kara and Jonny, his cross-pollinated fruits, were in our eyes physically hardier and, therefore, better suited in many ways, for the complexities of today's toxic-world challenges. They could be called *New and Improved*, sturdier versions of a family's many generations of over-protected stock. We agreed that with Debby's throwback DNA, our kids were stronger and more adaptable, *hybrid vigors*, I called them, borrowing a term from my botanical studies. Like Phil, I too was interested by the biological implications of a blended family. I liked the idea of the surprising possibilities of an ever-improved, blended humanity: a truly evolved, superior species of humankind—and I saw it starting right there, in my husband's half-breed offshoots. Kara and Jonny were of the same race as the rest of Will's family, but in every other aspect, besides the color of their skin, they were different.

So many people and nations in the world today, are letting go of previously held rigid classes of all sorts. Economic, racial, religious, sexual, cultural barriers are quickly dissolving. I see this universal tendency heralding an exciting, innovative future for the human family—through interbreeding, and mixing-up of previously separated divisions of classes—the quintessential act of acceptance by humans.

Having had to surmount the early trauma of such sad childhoods, and continually being subjected to Debby's anachronistic Lesser-me tendencies—Will and I always believed Kara and Jonny had far better odds for achieving happiness than most of today's millennials and generation Z kids, those largely material-craving, hyper screen-addicts who clamor for more, more, and more. We comforted ourselves—especially when Will or I worried about Kara's negative influence, or he regretted having messed up his gene pool, about his having chosen Debby. We talked about, and believed that our kids are innately better equipped to survive in this incredibly challenging time we live in. "They'll need the strength provided by Debby's more basic survivalist instincts," I reassured my man when he doubted himself, "to face life's constant waterfalls of crisis."

I grew to appreciate, instead of question as I had at first, why Will had indulged his own base instincts, being attracted to Debby, back when he chose her as his children's mother over other women with at least a parallel pedigree to his own. I never told Will how confused I'd been, doubting his sanity even, in the beginning, that he'd brought dangerous Debby into his family's otherwise superior lineage. As soon as I saw she was uncooperative, and acted down-right nasty to me, that's when I never let her into our safe and secure home base, to protect the love of our family's marrow. That was my initial, reactive thinking, which took me time to get over. As I opened my mind, I began to see other possibilities that I could never have foreseen had I not been a member of our uniquely blended foursome.

In the end, I accepted Will's mating desires as his being true to Nature's call. I could see how Debby's genetic donation to her kids provided a fresh shot of basic survival skills, immense physical strength, and immune systems like twin Fort Knoxes, which would certainly come in handy in today's ever-in-flux, challenging, environmentally-toxic world. I was happy the kids inherited Will's intellectual and spiritual prowess, rather than Debby's lacks in those areas. Added to his family's many generations of outstanding mental proficiency, the social and educational leadership from Claire's parentage thrown into the drive, the thirst to know Spirit intimately that came from Phil's political and industrial stallions' line, we often mused that Kara and Jonny's blue-collar heritage from Debby's side, the same collars worn by my own family, made them better equipped for life's travails. We sensed both kids would thrive just fine in this spiraling out-of-control, trans-everything tango taking place in our modern world.

▲

When Jonny joined Kara as a college student, Will and I took off cross-country to celebrate our empty nest. Each evening we pulled up to the next spectacular wilderness campsite as we made our way westward. Biking trails, cooking simple meals on campfires, we rested and rejuvenated in each other's companionship, released at last from nonstop kid-raising. Happy to be a pair of comfy old shoes huddled in our tent, under tall aromatic pines, peaceful meadows, alongside bucolic streams.

In front of our roomy tent every night, Will whipped out and laid down a miniature red carpet, a long piece of bright vermillion felt he'd brought along. Then he bowed like an attentive doorman, awaiting my entrance. "To honor you," he said with a sly grin, sweeping an arm out in a grand gesture usually saved for royalty. "For having sacrificed so much to help raise my kids all these years." Our first night camping, he would have carried me down the red carpet (if I'd let him), over the threshold, into the tent, and every night afterwards of our belated (by fifteen years), kids-free honeymoon.

Both of us were exhilarated by our newfound freedom—at last! Our jobs well done, the kids were nearing voting-age, arrived at the threshold of adulthood, safe in their college dorms, preparing for careers of their choosing. Even though we were still paying the bills, both kids were healthy and independent self-discoverers. Jonny was deep in his conservation and wildlife biology studies, intent on protecting the environment and its critters. And Kara, lordy lord! apparently tiring of being the drama-queen she-wolf, had chosen a serious dual major of art and medicine, of all things.

A month after starting our long-planned-for western getaway, we received a phone call. "Daddy's life is coming to a close," Will's sister Sally said. "I'll call when he needs you home."

Will and I had been riding our bikes around South Dakota's Wounded Knee, close to the Lakota Indian Reservation. We were inspired by the desert landscape, as foreign to us salty-beach and freshwater-springs Floridians as if we'd landed on a sci-fi set. After putting away his cell phone, Will and I rode off to explore a rocky outcrop. Leaning my bike against a wall of stone, I wandered off by myself, while Will knelt to investigate a small animal's hole in the sand, of a prairie dog, or maybe a tortoise. After striding a few paces across the desert's crusty surface, I came to a group of big rocks, arranged as if a prehistoric melting glacier had deposited them there from far away, in an isolated cluster. Circling around one of the head-high boulders I was startled to come upon a jaw-dropping sight: lying supine, totally silent, was a gray-tinged, straggly pelted, thick-horned behemoth, surprisingly relaxed right before me—a living, breathing Great Mammoth, a bull bison.

I stopped moving. Instantly I saw he was alone, as I was. Such an ancient creature, peacefully basking in a patch of waning sunlight. The old bull glanced in my direction—I stopped breathing—but he paid no heed to me whatsoever. Still holding my breath in anticipation, I crept another few steps closer, into his secluded sanctuary of rocks. Perhaps he was blind, or somehow sensed I was safe. Quietly I concealed myself, and then peeped out to see from behind my solid wall of high rock, not wishing to disturb the wild beast, but fascinated to be so close to such an imposingly magnificent, colossal being.

First his twitching ears, then his massive head slowly moved toward my direction. He'd caught my scent. The buffalo gazed right at me. Slowly, he blinked, unperturbed. The old bison looked as if he could read my thoughts. I froze, softened my breathing, and directly met his gaze. Then he raised his boulder-sized head a few inches and closed his eyes, as if to better catch and relish the last of the sun's lingering ray of warmth. With his nose lifted high, he followed the sunset's call. His wildness, his wise-ness tolerated my presence. His body so still, mine frozen in awe, I saw his chest push-out beneath him with each breath, his sides expand. His one ear rotated alertly toward my direction, zeroing-in on me, signaling his keen awareness of my presence. He accepted me. I hardly dared breathe. There was nothing to fear. The beast lay there quietly, trustingly, his eyelids serenely closed. My head stayed out from behind my rock. As if in a spell, I felt blessed, deeply touched, honored by this intimate moment. Impressively muscled under his grizzled, tattered coat, the old bull rested in absolute peace, content with himself, in complete harmony with his surroundings—not bothered by the strange human spying on him.

I felt him, his nose high, aimed heavenly, celebrating the retreat of the bright solar disk in the sky as it neared its disappearance. I wondered if this was a daily ritual of repose the old goliath performed, and for how many preparatory days had he done this, before this one? Suddenly I thought of our soon-departing patriarch—Phil back home. I wondered, Did he know this was going to be, or maybe tomorrow, or the next day—his own last twilight? I wondered if the decrepit old bull was getting as close to drawing his last breath as we'd just heard from Sally that Phil was, back in Florida.

I couldn't help but think of their similarities, this solitary, magnificent beast—no doubt a revered old alpha male from his mountain-size and his coat's scarred battle wounds—and our own family's chief, our tribal elder. The news had been that Phil was failing fast. I wondered, as I continued gazing at the huge, oddly contented wild animal, seeing it in such a calm state, if Phil too, might then be savoring—in the same accepting manner—these last moments of that day's ending. Had Phil felt the gentle touch of that day's diminishing sun, which had already set hours earlier back east? Could this buffalo before me be a hairy harbinger of Phil's time now arrived? I wondered. Yes, our family's old bull was soon to leave us. There was no mistaking that. Uncannily, I sensed the ancient one before me might never get up from his chosen spot. That he was, indeed, Phil's animal totem, my surrogate father's spirit proxy.

Two days later we were in Kalispell. Will and I received Sally's next, urgent call, the one we'd been expecting. "Daddy," she whispered, "is nearing his end." He was asking for his son and me. Will flew out right away because only one seat was available from that part of Montana. I followed later, having to drive hours to the Seattle airport in the dark night on an icy highway. I knew he'd wait for me as I caught the next plane. I felt him calling me. Phil had asked for both of us, Sally said. He knew exactly what he wanted at his deathbed's farewell party: his four grown children and me, the "outlaw" as another irreverent spouse, an in-law, called himself.

I was the last to arrive. Going straight upstairs to his bedroom, when Phil heard me softly greet him he sat right up in bed, as agile as a trapeze artist in his prime. He saw who it was and exclaimed softly, "Oh, it's you. You're here." Then he fell backwards. Within an hour he lapsed into the veiled shadows of his last sunset—no longer here, but forever there. Home.

△

Phil's passing-over wasn't the time-stopping euphoric event I'd been fortunate to share with my own dad on his last journey, back to the beyond. My dad had also been a spiritual giant—in the few years he'd let me know him as a sober man, that decade before his death.

Will and his three siblings and I formed a circle around our patriarch's lifeless form, joined hands, and said the Lord's Prayer.

We quietly communed with our own thoughts, hovering around Phil's stillness. Then everyone left the room, all but Sally and myself. She'd asked me to join her in the same intimate ritual I'd performed with my mother at my father's passing, before Will and I ever met. Sally and I proceeded, mostly in silence, to gently bathe her father's worn-out, limp doll-like man-body. Then, daughter delicately shaved father's hollow cheeks, dressing him in his favorite, invisibly patched old wool suit. She placed Phil's soft and malleable, waxy hands around his frayed Bible, its gold leaf holiness and our silent prayers preparing our beloved father for cremation.

Later, when we were alone, I turned to Will, this man who'd inherited his father's pure and noble heart, who emulated his capacity to love, nurture, and unconditionally care for others, and asked, "Why do you suppose Phil wanted me here, along with your siblings?"

There was no hesitation in my man's reply. "Because he loves you, teZ."

My heart pushed against my expanding ribs. I floated, overjoyed to be included in Phil's inner circle, among his own children—by having made each and every choice that had drawn all five of us to be there, together—at that exact moment.

One small thought-seed leading to another Better-me choice, followed by yet another.

The Mystery, this journey of ours.

The ballooning warmth, the expanding of my chest—I remembered how it started. The moment I recognized that tingly, throbbing, warm feeling beginning deep within my guts, the day I let Better-me feel the knocking, pulling, yell-of-recognition arising from the sound of Will's voice on the phone, that long-ago spring equinox day.

port compassion

CHAPTER 29

port compassion

Finally, it was time for us—Will and teZa—to have our long-awaited twosome, all alone. Our family was functioning at a peaceful level now. Within our circle, for the moment, all was well.

I was free of resentments because I'd burned them all away with prayer. Old enemies, fears, insecurities, no longer slayed or paralyzed me on a regular basis. I was practiced at giving no space in my Light-filled mind to worry over Kara, her crazy mom, or any other kind of terrorists, or anyone who tried to burn acid holes in my laughing heart. Politics, money woes—I'd trained myself not to focus on any of them. Why bother? Worries are always with us. The trick for me, was not to take them too seriously. I'd train my awareness to go around or under or over them, not *into* life's painful realities. Things always get sorted out, just like the minutiae of throwing a large party always seem to.

Instead of obligations holding us back any longer, Will and I made a long-awaited decision: It was time to relocate our family's central headquarters. Nothing held us to Lackland anymore. From separate colleges, busy with their exciting now-adult lives, the kids cheered when we announced our move to a seaside town everyone loves.

Aside from Will, my best pal, an integral part of who I am, everything was now about me and my work as writer and artist. I felt like a kid gone wild in a candy store, a bee flitting freely in a nectar-infused riot of flowers.

So many gardens to grow, planting real- and thought-seeds, cultivating them with great intention and care. But first, we took a long-dreamed-about vacation in Costa Rica.

"The world is the garden of my heart," I declared as Will and I rounded a bend in the mountain road we were traveling, on our way to a famous land formation, an astounding display of Nature's whimsical use of earth for Her own delight. I said this as we viewed for the first time the sandy contours of *Playa Ballena*, a whale's tail-shaped beach far below us, where mountain-sized humpbacks happen to, synchronistically, serendipitously, come each year from thousands of miles distant, to frolic and mate. This unique spot on earth amazed us, realizing the magical pull the earth has for all its creatures.

The Baru, an indigenous tribe in Costa Rica, think the globe-wandering giant animals, the whales, are naturally attracted to this coastal protrusion that echoes their own shape. From our vantage point, high in the overlooking mountain directly in front of Whale's Tail Beach, Will and I could see the distant half-mile-wide, T-shaped sandbar. Its long narrow peninsula is attached to the mainland but only visible at low tide, which was happening just then. Its unmistakably distinct shape is sheltered from sight at high tide, being only discernible as an exact rendition of a colossal whale's tail formed by the beach's shifting sands, from the nearby heights of jungle-clad hillsides.

Later, after we'd driven the switchback road down to Uvita, Will grabbed my waist and pulled me close as we walked the oddly cetacean-shaped sandbar. Its distinct contours, the only ones like it in the world, startle anyone who sees them, but not while walking it. At sea level, a person thinks: This is an ordinary, plain beach I'm seeing. But as I walked with Will, I was thinking something different, how extraordinary it was after having glimpsed the beach's remarkable, bio-mimicking shape from the nearby heights just twenty minutes earlier.

How ironic, I mused, that we need to get so far away—as high as we can, expanded and elevated from our ordinary, limited sight and thinking—to comprehend with our mind's eye what's really going on below, beneath, not on the surface of things. Do we really know what's going on in mundane everyday life? I believe not, unless we expand our thinking, just like Will and I clearly viewed the whale's tail from up higher on the mountaintop, but here, walking it—it appeared as a long stretch of pebbly sand sticking out into the Pacific, with some big rocks at its end.

Things are not what they appear to be, I sublimely remembered the Teacher's wisdom that gently guided me to this simple truth, which explains so much.

I turned to my love and said, "I feel reborn, Will. Just like how you described to me your long-ago religious awakening when you realized Jesus is your inner guru. Now that the kids are happy and grown, I feel baptized in a gator pond of my own, like how you explained you felt, during your dousing surrender ritual."

I laughed and twirled in place and kicked up more sand, shouting, "I christen this renewed freedom of mine that I feel so strongly in my big heart now—I call it Port Compassion!"

Amused as ever, Will shook his head and watched me dance before him. I felt loony with the kind of effervescent joy one has after a treacherous journey's end. Survivor's glee, call it.

"Finally, I get it!" I hallelujah'd to the sky above and the man always by my side. "Port Compassion is where I feel best—loving everyone as I love Aum. Holy jubilation! I feel re-me'd! I claim this place, right here, inside me, as my heart's homeport. Now I know that compassion is the highest, the safest and the happiest state. I hope every human alive gets to feel this connection between heaven and earth I have in my heart right now."

△

We returned to the States, packed up and moved from suburbia to the small coastal community I'm writing from, a dozen years beyond my man's originally promised five.

△

We are everywhere, lovers of life, the positive thinkers, the non-judgers of others. *The Army of Love* is real. We are an interconnected phalanx of what all Great Beings say is the essence, the true human condition: we are individual embodiments, corpuscles of God; different notes of Aum's holy sound. Divinity is to be found within each and every human heart. And it doesn't matter what one calls *It* or by whichever means this spiritual revelation arrives. The only thing that matters is that this awareness resides in our big heart, in Port Compassion.

In our search for our own truth, we humans endure conflict and tragedies, human made or from Nature. The two conflicting forces, good and bad, Dark and Light, are forever providing naturally occurring transformative energy for our world, including the entirety of our species, the whole of humanity, as much as within each and every individual seeker.

Just as Earth has thus far survived the abuse dished out by Mother Nature, including meteoric cataclysms, floods and other upheavals, we human children residing on Earth's surface have similar, naturally destructive tendencies. I could only admit this after raising our own children, who had their bouts of fears, violence, disrespect and abuse. The point is: just as we humans keep surviving and evolving, becoming better with each new waterfall's pounding of our individual life, so too, our entire species of humankind, homo sapiens, is evolving. Our collective consciousness is ever expanding.

Today's gripping frights of terrorism and climate change are forcing us—the human species as one big blended family—to grow up, fast! So far we have managed to survive because conflict and adversity are intrinsic parts of Nature, and we bravely face them the same as we do challenging human experiences. It's helpful to remember during conflicting times that our species is only in its still maturing, teeny-bopper stage, in terms of our existence upon millions-of-years-old Earth. We have barely begun to evolve. Great things await humanity in future generations. I know this in my gut.

Just as Kara and Jonny *did* grow up to be whole and healed, emotionally mature adults, so too will we, the cumulative human blended family, grow wiser, and spiritually evolve to the Better-Us our species is right now roaring full-speed toward. Humanity's teenage-like errors, committed by the human race of yesteryear and today, with our sadly lacking but *normal*-for-teens screw ups, a mishmash level of comprehension—will continue to saliently ever reach upward as we evolve, en masse. Until we eventually achieve unimaginable heights of accomplishment in all areas, including a higher level of human compassion. This is already happening to a large degree in the consciousness revolution taking place around the world.

Nothing will stop humanity from continuing to transform. My dream is this:

Our combined species, made up of blended and varied races-cultures-creeds ... one heart opening at a time ... as our entire race evolves into a transformed version of humanity, becoming, one by one ... *Homo spiritus* ... a magnificent flowering of humans, at last bursting from our tightly-wound bud stage.

△

We humans, busy with our conflicts, scurrying around solving dilemmas, have been evolving for hundreds of thousands of years, maybe way longer than the recently added *Homo naledi* to our hominid family tree. Only now, already beyond the initial wave of our global awakening, for the first time in recorded history, we are endeavoring to venture high enough, deep enough, intrigued by the summit of spiritual exploration. We're beginning to glimpse the bigger picture from a step away, a step up. From a heightened consciousness. Just as anyone can plainly view the Costa Rican beach is shaped like a phenomenal whale's tail attached to the mainland, but only when viewed from the nearby jungle cliffs, *can we get it*. In the same way, we can get what joy being alive really is.

Countless people continue to send out positive thought-seeds for our future, rather than allow ourselves, our civilization to be bogged down by trivial human drama. Expanded awareness has already been glimpsed, and reported on by an unimaginable number of folks' personal experiences. Just check out #PositiveThought on social media. Enlightenment is our species' lifeboat, sure to carry us through any tumultuous shock wave of yesterday, today, or tomorrow. Filled with Light—en-Lightened—folks do not despair, neither do they forecast doom for our species or our world. They know that new solutions arise every new day, just like the sun does.

The Truth is simple: we are interconnected with all in existence, energetically.

What we do to one, we do to all.

Keep positive thoughts in your mind, and all is well.

We're all headed for the same destination—Port Compassion.

△

My Lithuanian-immigrant grandfather was the only one of his fellow U.S. Army bunkhouse mates, during World War I, who was spared and didn't die, one night during the 1918 influenza pandemic. He had sense enough to protect himself from the sickness he felt entering his body as he got ready for bed. Like many times before this, he made and ate the home remedy for illness used by generations in his family, which he'd brought with him to America when he'd recently emigrated. The rest of my grandfather's platoon, the story goes, were found lifeless the next morning. Every single man had died of the Spanish flu in his sleep. My grandfather survived, but only because he remembered to eat a simple bread-and-onion sandwich, a regular preventative his peasant mother, my grandmother Antonina, taught him, as the natural-healing farm boy he'd been raised to be.

He knew onions and garlic had *a kind of super power within them*. My Grandpa was indeed lucky because the onion's *invisible but powerful* antibiotic properties negated the fast-spreading flu that he sensed as it entered him when he was undressing that night. The deadly pandemic, one of the worse in human history, would go on to kill what some estimate at fifty million people globally, a huge proportion of the world's population.

Each person can equally protect themselves from the spread of any injustice and horror by ingesting similarly strong spiritual food. Just as all diseases run their course, terrorism, the environmental crisis, the mistrust and perceived-evil of government agendas will as well, after they've done their job of infecting, affecting, and altering our planet's development—pushing us humans to evolve, to improve, to change.

Surviving that deadly flu led my grandfather to be the best New Jersey tomato farmer he could be, and also led to my mother, and then me having been born. Everything happens for a reason. Without catastrophes, we would never have challenges; without challenges, there is no growth. Just look at a stage play where everything is wonderfully peaceful, wholesome, non-conflictual. That's call: *No drama, no play at all!*

Life is, as one yogic sage puts it, *The Play of Consciousness.*

By planting positive thought-seeds of unconditional Love, threats either get eradicated or dissolve on their own from no attention. A thought-seed is the healing *invisible* power that compassionate Love evokes.

Seeking healing to our fears—the biggest one, of course, being death and total annihilation—has been the human story since our cave relatives began looking up at the sky and wondering, What's it all about?

Love is the weapon of mass illumination. Love is the answer to all of Life's woes, as well as her triumphs.

△

As a family person, observing the metamorphosis of both our challenged kids, has brought Will and me *Infinite Joy*. Jonny, turning the loss of his childhood kicker-dream into a career as a committed conservationist, today manages a team of biologists, overseeing thousands of protected acres of tenuous wilderness, guarding the ecology and its critters. He's now as passionate as I am about helping our global environment be more balanced. And Kara, as a divorced young mother, she has come to know the purpose of experiencing life's hard knocks for herself.

Everything we do in life adds up. In the long run, there's not a single thing we put our effort into that doesn't count.

Where humankind is at right now, collectively, is exactly the place where I once saw our half-baked kids (and all other teens). Right in the middle of physically, mentally, and spiritually maturing. Right now, we humans are committing the requisite myriad foibles and follies of every adolescent's in-between stage. So, what are we learning from our collective mistakes, dear human?

Our global family, way more astounding and awesome than a handful of bewilderingly awful villians, is fast becoming spiritualized. Scientists venture to say the worldwide blending we're in right now, will completely transform our species in less than a hundred years. A new, improved Blended Humanity awaits us, people who are variations of shades of brown, indistinguishable in skin color and other archaic separators. If we look at Homo sapiens' progress on that goofy evolutionary graph we've all seen, from the all-fours monkey-man to a walking-upright GQ-guy—and compare it to the goof-ups of a typical teen, a half-formed adolescent who fluctuates between complete confusion and total invincibility, the kind found in every family, blended or not—I see today's worldwide family of humanity on a similarly upward, positive track as our challenged kids took. In our little family and in many other I know, young adults prove to be more aware and awake than their 'rents were at that age.

I for one do not believe that the many troubles our world faces today are anything but a Perfect Storm, a do-or-die impetus for us to continue evolving, as we're doing right now. Okay, we're evolving faster and at a more widespread pace than at any other time in human history, thanks to the internet. The spiritualization of humankind is already happening. Our world, our family of awakening souls, is already well on its way to becoming transformed, one opened heart at a time. We are now midstream, becoming spiritualized humans.

If we didn't have such imminent, deadly planetary threats as we do today, our need for enlightenment wouldn't be so urgent. But the need *is urgent*. And the good news is—we've already reached the tipping point of humankind's awakening, from our being slaves to fear and keeping separate, to being forced to accept *what is*. For us in the Army of Love, Love is *what is*. It's a numbers game, how shifts in consciousness occur. Look around you. Notice all the Light-filled souls at every street corner, checking out your groceries, delivering your mail and your babies.

Love is the weapon of mass illumination. Remember this, and take comfort.

▲

Port Compassion is the Big Heart of our humanity. Port Compassion is the ever-expanding possibilities of our joined-existence, the homeport of everyone's Better-me. Instead of being Politically Correct, *live freely* in the real P.C.—Port Compassion. Its fortifications annihilate Lesser-me's addictive, destructive tendencies. This is not heresy or a magical incantation, my friends. I'm merely acknowledging the spiritualization of our blended human family already in progress.

▲

I'm sure you get it, that Better-me is joy and Lesser-me is pain. This is why people say that getting spiritual is *an inside job*. One can reside in P.C. and have joy, for instance, even while on death row or living as an impoverished street-sweeper. Who's to say what each of our roles are to be … a martyr, or an agent of tidal waves of change? Which one of our children, I wonder, will find the secret of making fuel from air, or water? Which will discover the cure for cancer?

The Big Heart of compassion is within all of us. Really, who cares what it's called, this mysterious force, Life's essence. The important thing is to recognize, and remember, that Love connects us all. This measurable, yet tiniest energetic force that's within all known matter, that's been given the best, most prescient nametag of all by physicists of all people—the *God Particle*—is as real as you and me.

▲

Pain prods us along. Pain *makes us*, forces us to change—as I was compelled to get out of the dis-ease of being addicted-to-discontent that once plagued me. My spiritual wanderings began in my early years, the result of some freaky inborn alienation from my roots, hailing from the typical dysfunctional American family I was born into.

Feelings are *signs*, like dreams are. They come from our soul's mischievous topsy-turvy trickster sense of humor. It's how Spirit sends out urgent calls for assistance. Recurring bad feelings (or dreams) mean: change something! Feeling bad about myself before Better-me, I was left with the only choice I had—to rise above my pain or settle for a miserable existence.

All of us know someone who's chosen to rise above life's adversities, shake off the leaded weight of a lousy job or spouse, or a defeatist attitude; lose a hundred pounds. Each of us gets many opportunities to climb above our own life's sand-covered, obscured-by-tide beach, so we can clearly see the true shape of how wondrously magical this world of ours really is. We all have a magical Whale's Tail beach to discover, if we can get high enough above it to see clearly.

about the author

Finding the sacred in the ordinary is the theme of teZa Lord's life and work. A student of consciousness-exploration of all types, Lord's work chronicles how she survived an irrepressibly wild youth, to paint for us her true experiences, using mystical brushstrokes and uplifting words. Her mission—as an artist who writes, and a public-speaking spiritual activist—is to clearly communicate how to achieve a more fulfilling, balanced, and holistic way of living.

Focusing on expanded awareness that is available to anyone who wishes to know inner peace, even if the outer world is terrifying and toxic, Lord's work continues to explore the evolution of human awareness and interconnectedness with all beings: past, present, and future.

Her other books are: a full-color art manifesto, *We Are ONE*; a nonfiction allegory using yoga and meditation in a true empowerment story: *In the 'I': Easing Through Life Storms.* Another nonfiction narrative is *Hybrid Vigor: A True Reveal of Love*, about how animals inspire us to be better humans.

Listen to her calming *MindStillers* on SoundCloud and get *Army of Love* info-updates at teZaLord.com. Look for the *ZLORD Podcast* on iTunes and everywhere. Join @tezalord on Insta, Twitter, FB, write dearteZa@gmail.com.

teZa's motto is: *Love is the weapon of mass illumination.* She sends love and respect to each and every one of you!

www.ingramcontent.com/pod-product-compliance
Lightning Source LLC
Chambersburg PA
CBHW022220090526
44585CB00013BB/480